TO JEAN

WHO SHARES MY DREAM

ACKNOWLEDGEMENTS

My grateful thanks to all the people who attended my seminars and courses and, by participation or contribution, helped perfect the Intertec® "List More, Sell More." system.

My special thanks to Trina Bresser whose attention to detail made my task much easier.

CONTENTS

CONTENTS

FOREWORD

Many people in the sales field today settle for less than their real potential because it is easier than striving to achieve the higher ground. Mediocrity is a way of life.

The author is not one who has settled for mediocrity in any aspect of his life, be it personal ambition, family, hobbies or even his faith.

Among the myriad of real estate speakers, motivators and sales trainers who have appeared over the years, only one has grasped the challenge, researched the problem and produced the solution for success - mastering the language a professional must use.

This book is hard hitting and easy reading; yet, it has the effervescence and fun characteristic of Jerry Bresser. It projects his message and techniques in language that works.

Jerry Bresser is a man who knows who he is, why he is here and where he is going. I am delighted to recommend this book; it just may make you a million.

Richard P. Robarts, B.A., S.I.R., C.P.A.
President, Robarts and Company, Ltd. Realtor

INTRODUCTION

As I write this introduction, I am flying from Michigan to California. The engines of my plane pull me westward at 200 miles an hour, a little more than three miles every minute.

I have been carried smoothly for two hours above cities and farmlands, lakes and rivers, flatlands and hills. It is an absolutely clear day with almost unlimited visibility. I can easily see 80 miles in every direction, and I am filled with the immensity, the vastness, of our land . . . and our opportunity.

I am alone at 4500 feet above the small town of Prairie du Chien, Illinois, which is located on the east bank of the Mississippi. The river stretches across my path to the left and right, cutting across the countryside with great sweeping curves.

Looking down on Prairie du Chien, the streets all form neat, orderly rows. Cars and trucks stop and go in response to traffic lights I cannot see.

I can even see people moving about. It occurs to me that at least one of them must be a real estate salesperson, and I wonder how he views this world.

Does he see a small town with just a few homes and not much turnover, or does he see a land of unlimited opportunity? I wish he could be up here with me today.

As I look about and reflect on the sheer wonder of it all, I am inspired by the truth that the greatest gift God ever gave, anywhere, at any time, is the gift of humanity. Our humanity comes complete with a mind greater in power than the most advanced computer. We can use our minds to read and write, to communicate and reason, to paint a picture or fly a plane. We can use our minds to learn a thousand things and use that

INTRODUCTION

knowledge to determine and control our destiny here on earth.

Today, as I chase the sun across a flawless sky, I can look to the horizon in every direction, and all I see is opportunity. Unlimited opportunity. I am both awed and humbled by it.

There is so much opportunity, so much of everything, that the truth of something I recently read hit home with unprecedented impact. "You were born to win," the words had said. "God didn't create any failures. We can only fail ourselves."

It's true, isn't it? We are only limited by our own lack of determination to develop the true potential through a professional career in real estate brokerage.

The ideas and methods described in the chapters to come have worked for thousands of people, and they will work for you. My research and experience has proven to me beyond the shadow of a doubt, that there are truly no limits to what we can achieve - except those limits we impose upon ourselves by failing to develop our true abilities and potential.

PREFACE

HOW TO GET THE MOST FROM THIS BOOK

The listing and selling techniques described in this book are the result of more than seven years research conducted from coast to coast in both the United States and Canada. Not only were the techniques used successfully by the individuals who shared them with me, they have also been used successfully by the thousands of salespeople who have attended my seminars and courses. From the reports of hundreds of people in hundreds of situations, I can say without reservation that you can use these techniques to earn an extra $200 a year, an extra $2,000 a year, or an extra $20,000 a year. How much you profit from this book will ultimately be controlled by your own image of yourself.

We are not the victims of circumstances - we are the architects of our lives. If we take total responsibility for ourselves, we can create the life that we really want.

From 1969 to 1974 I shared these techniques with over 20,000 salespeople through a one day seminar we called "The Advanced Listing Seminar." One survey I did showed that, on the average, individual salespeople who attended the seminar were increasing their income by approximately $2,500 while individuals in the same firms who had not taken the seminar were only increasing their incomes by an average of slightly less than $1,000.

We found that the more techniques an individual memorized and the more accurately he memorized them, the more that individual would earn. We also found that most people didn't know how to memorize well. So in 1975 I began conducting a five day course in which 80% of the time was spent in memorizing and practicing language techniques. Three years later, a survey showed that individuals who had taken the five day course had increased their incomes by an average of $11,000. Individuals who had taken the one day seminar were still increasing their incomes by an average $2,500, but individuals who had not attended either course had only increased their incomes by about $1,000. Again, I found that the more techniques a person memorized, and the more accurately he memorized them, the more that person would earn.

One question continued to bother me. Why did some people memorize more material than others? Why did some people earn an extra $2,000 and others an extra $20,000?

At one point, I was doing a series of courses for one particular firm. The owner and her sales managers, all graduates of the course, were convinced that the course could teach people how to earn $50,000 or more a year. We decided to set a specific goal for the next group. To be conservative, we told everyone that we were going to teach him or her how to earn $30,000.

At the end of the five days everyone said he or she would like to make $30,000 the next year, but not all felt they would be able to earn that much. One man thought the course was overrated, that the techniques were not good enough to produce $30,000. He felt that most people, himself included, would be able to earn maybe $12,000 as a result of the course. About two-thirds of the class thought they would be able to make between $15,000 and $25,000. Only one-third felt they could actually earn $30,000 using the techniques. And one person said that I had underestimated the value of the techniques, that I didn't realize how good the system was and that a person using the techniques consistently could easily make $50,000.

If you have studied psychology, or even discussed it just a little, I'm sure you can guess the results. The first man made just under $12,000. Two-thirds made between $15,000 and $25,000. One-third averaged $30,000, give or take $2,000. And the person who thought that a person should be able to make $50,000 actually made a little over $80,000.

Same course. Same ideas. Same instructor. Same time span. Same commission plan. Same opportunity. Same common goal. Why do some people do better than others? Different perspectives. Different self-images.

To get the full, exciting benefits from this book, you must first accept the truth that there are no limits to what you can personally achieve except the limits that you impose upon yourself. These techniques work! They have worked for thousands of people for over fifteen years and if you learn them, they will work for you.

You should also realize that these techniques were selected because they are basically universal. In my seven-year research I collected over 2,000 techniques. I kept these two hundred because they work in big cities and little towns, buyers markets and sellers markets. They work for experienced people and for beginners. And they work when presented to sophisticated professionals living in mansions or to ordinary folks living in average homes.

As you proceed through the book, you will notice that certain chapters are stories about successful people in a specific listing or selling situation and that the next chapter or two goes into a greater depth in analyzing the techniques presented in the story chapter. I chose this format to help you understand the full power and effectiveness of the techniques being presented.

I think you will find it helpful if you read a story chapter, then study the following explanatory chapter or chapters, memorizing the individual techniques as outlined. Then re-read the story chapter to develop a feeling for the flow of things.

If you make every effort to learn these techniques and procedures so well that they literally become a part of you, you will build your self-esteem, your confidence and your ability to operate calmly under pressure.

When you learn certain skills really well, you gain freedom from uncertainty and embarrassment, You also gain acceptance as a knowledgeable professional.

If you will accept total responsibility for yourself and the perfection of the skills needed to be a true professional, then you can create the life that you really, truly want. At that point in time, there will be no limit to how much you can achieve and earn.

YOU CAN ALSO LEARN THE JERRY BRESSER
"LIST MORE, SELL MORE." SYSTEM FROM:

VIDEO — The 16 session, 10 1/2 hour video tape series offers an economical way for a company to provide complete training in listing skills. Leaders guide and sales aids included. VHS and Bata.

AUDIO — The complete sound track from the 16 session video series is available in an audio cassette tape program for "Listen & Learn" training.

SEMINARS — Jerry Bresser can be scheduled for private or Board sponsored half or full day seminars.

COURSES — Accelerated, advanced instruction in the 4 day "Intertec Listing Course" and the two day "Intertec Selling Course" is the ultimate training for the serious professional.

For information contact

BRESSER PUBLICATIONS
P.O. Box 8666
Detroit, Michigan 48224
(313) 881-7755

CHAPTER 1

COULD A MILLION DOLLARS
BE SLIPPING THROUGH
YOUR FINGERS?

For 20 years Sam Brown averaged $20,000 to $30,000 a year listing and selling real estate. Yet all that time Sam was just a tiny bit away from having the skill to earn $75,000 to $100,000 every year.

It cost him a million dollars!

Couldn't the same thing happen to you?

Sam missed his million . . . because $25,000 wasn't really a bad income . . . because no one in Sam's family had ever made big money before . . . because Sam never really thought seriously about the possibility that *he* could earn $75,000 or more . . . because everyone told Sam that he was one heck of a good salesman and why did *he* need more sales training?

If you miss your million, it will probably be for the same reasons.

Actually, Sam's story is pretty typical. Most people are happy to settle for an above average income and the respect that goes with doing a bit better than most. Sam and his family were never unhappy with the things they could afford on his earnings.

1

COULD A MILLION DOLLARS BE SLIPPING THROUGH YOUR FINGERS?

But a million dollars *did* slip through Sam's fingers. And Sam was just a little irked when he found out how close he had been all those years, and how easily and casually he had been talked out of the one situation that finally made the difference.

You see, one thing Sam never told anyone, not even his wife, was his secret dream to own a beautiful sailing schooner about, say, 50 feet long. Many nights in the summer he would lie on the grass at the top of the hill overlooking his cottage on the lake, watching the moonrise and dreaming about *his* yatch slicing through moonbeams on the Mediterranean while he took a winter vacation retracing the voyages of Homer. Then with a wry smile and a reminder to grow up, to quit kidding himself and accept reality, he would stroll down to the lake to make sure the boys had tied up his 18 foot day-sailer properly, just in case the wind shifted.

Sam's transition came one January when John, a young agent from another firm, called with an offer on one of Sam's listings.

"It better be a good offer," said Sam. "The seller says he won't even look at anything less than a full price offer and I think he's one guy that means it."

"Why don't you call and set up the appointment before I tell you how much the offer is," responded John. "Then if he asks, you can truthfully tell him you don't know."

"Also," continued John, "why not ask him to come down to your office. It's not far and there will be less distractions. I'll come by half an hour early so we can discuss things first."

When John arrived at Sam's office, the first thing he asked was, "Sam, do you have a current market analysis on this home?"

"No," replied Sam, "I've worked this area twenty years. I know how much almost every house is worth."

"I'm sure you do," said John. "Still, if we had a few figures in writing, maybe your client would feel better. How about three recent sales, three current, well priced listings, and three expired listings, O.K.?"

With Sam's years of experience it took only a few minutes to assemble the information, which John quickly entered on his Market Analysis Form.

"Colored paper for a market analysis?" asked Sam, as he watched John enter the figures on a blue form.

"Selling the price is an important part of the sale," said John. "I figure it's worth an extra penny or two per deal."

"Can't argue with that," responded Sam, and his memory flashed back about five years to a time when he had thought about a two color Market Analysis being a good idea. He had given up the idea when another agent said, "Color shmolor! All that counts are the prices. You can give 'em figures on the back of a shopping bag. Don't waste the money."

Finished with the market analysis, Sam and John relaxed with a cup of coffee, waiting for Mr. and Mrs. Fax to arrive.

"I've noticed your name on the MLS sheets quite a bit this year," said Sam. "You must have hit a million."

"Just short of three," smiled John, "and I would have made it except that one closing was delayed just at the end of the year."

"Three million!" thought Sam. "Why, he's just a kid! Three million! How in the world could a kid do three million?"

Just then the Faxes walked in.

"This had better be a full price offer," said Mr. Fax. "I'm not

COULD A MILLION DOLLARS BE SLIPPING THROUGH YOUR FINGERS?

giving my house away."

Sam started to respond, but his mind was still awhirl. "Three million! He's just a kid. Still. . .maybe he's got something I can learn. I'll let him do the talking for awhile."

Actually, John had already taken charge.

"Well folks," said John happily, after introducing himself, "we have a sale! Your home is sold!" And laying down the offer in front of the Faxes he said, "It's to Mr. and Mrs. Edwards. . .from Cleveland. . .for $66,500."

"Sixty-six five!" exploded Fax. "Are you kidding? Don't you know how much my house is worth?"

"Mr. Fax," responded John softly, "What *I* think your house is worth has absolutely no merit whatsoever. The *only* thing that counts is. . .what are people *willing* to pay. . .for *this* kind of home. . .in *this* area. . .at *this* time. Isn't that right?"

"Well, yeah," said Fax, softening a bit under the logic. "But I think my house is worth every cent of the $72,000 I'm asking. I'm asking $72,000 and I want $72,000, so don't try to talk me down."

"O.K., now what?" thought Sam.

John leaned forward, his face relaxed but serious, and looking Fax straight in the eyes, said softly, "Mr. Fax, Sam and I are not here to pressure you into making a bad decision, but we would like to give you enough information to make a good decision. Is that fair?"

"Sure, sure," said Fax, softening a bit more.

"Mr. Fax," continued John, "in addition to price, is there any

4

other reason you would hesitate to accept this offer?"

"No," said Fax, after looking over the other sections of the offer. "No, the price is my only objection. I'm just not giving my house away."

"Mr. Fax," continued John, "here's a current market analysis that Sam and I prepared just a while ago. Here's your home at the top. . .and I think you will agree that all of these homes in the area are similar to yours. Do you agree?"

"Yes, they seem similar," responded Fax.

"O.K.," said John, "now, here are similar homes recently sold. These tell us what people are willing to pay. . .for this type of home. . .in this area. . .at this time: $66,600, $66,900 and $67,000. Here are similar homes currently for sale. These tell us what we are competing against. The buyers for your home are also inspecting these homes: $67,500, $68,500 and $69,000. And here are some expired listings. These are similar homes that were unsold in 90 days or more. Mr. Fax, these tell us what people are *not* willing to pay. . .for this kind of home. . .in this area. . .at this time: $69,700, $71,300 and $72,000."

"Mr. Fax, based on this current market analysis, this appears to be a reasonable offer, don't you agree?"

"Reasonable isn't good enough," retorted Fax. "I set my price. I want my price. Find someone who will pay it. I'm rejecting this offer."

"Counter-offer!" The words clanged in Sam's head like a fire alarm. "Gotta say something to get him to counter-offer." But before Sam could formulate a thought, John was talking again. .

"Mr. Fax, as I remember, your home came on the market about

eight weeks ago, isn't that right?"

"Yes."

"Mr. Fax, it has taken us eight weeks to find a family that wants
your home. . .and qualifies to buy your home. If we lose them it
could take another eight weeks to find another family that
wants your home and qualifies to buy your home. . ."

"O.K. I'll counter at. . ."

"Mr. Fax," John cut in, "may I make another comment?" Fax
nodded curtly.

"Folks," said John, trying to include Mrs. Fax, who had not yet
had a chance to comment, "folks, if you do *not* accept this
offer, you will have just become real estate speculators. May
I explain?"

Sam closed his eyes in agony. "You've blown it kid," he said to
himself. "You had that hardhead ready to counter, and now
you're going to blow it trying to go all the way."

"Mr. and Mrs. Fax," continued John, not really waiting for an
answer to his last question, "right now. . .your home is sold! Mr.
and Mrs. Edwards have just agreed to buy your home for
$66,500. If you accept their offer, your home is sold! It's done.
Finished! But. . .if you do not accept their offer, you are, in
effect, buying the house back from the Edwards for $66,500 and
putting it back on the market. . .hoping to make a profit. And
based on recent sales. . .that would be a profit of $100 to $500.
May I ask. . .as real estate speculators. . .would you do that?"

Fax picked up the offer and began to study it in the deliberate
way of a man buying time.

The silence that followed reminded Sam of two gamblers waiting each other out, weighing the odds. The word odds caused Sam to think about Fax's alternatives: "Accept the offer-ten to one against, he's taken too positive a stand; reject the offer-no, he's already agreed to counter. So, he has to counter, but unless I miss my bet, he'll say he wants to think about it until tomorrow morning."

Sam couldn't help smiling when Fax said, "We'll think about it and let you know in the morning."

"In addition to thinking about it," responded John quickly, "is there any other reason you would hesitate to accept this offer?"

"No."

"Mrs. Fax, may I ask you a question?" John asked, softly.

"Why, yes," she replied.

"Mrs. Fax, if. . .it was your decision. . .if for some reason Mr. Fax was not available. . .based on the information I have given you. . .would you accept this offer?"

"Yes," she replied softly. "Yes, I would. It seems to be a reasonable offer. If that's what other homes are selling for, I think it's fair."

"Mr. Fax?" John's gaze turned back to Fax.

"Well, as long as my wife is willing to accept $66,500, I suppose it's O.K. with me."

Later, after the Faxes had left, Sam said admiringly, "John-boy, you sure have the gift of the gab. If I could think that fast and say the right things like that, why I bet I could make an extra

COULD A MILLION DOLLARS BE SLIPPING THROUGH YOUR FINGERS?

million dollars in the next 10 years."

"It's no gift," replied John. "I learned every word. As a matter of fact, everything I said was memorized."

"No way," blurted Sam. "There's no way you can use a canned pitch for negotiationg. No way."

"Sure," said John with a grin. "I memorized about 25 techniques. Then I just use the ones that I need. It's really flexible."

"I can't believe you didn't ad-lib the whole thing," said Sam.

"Not a word," replied John. "Other than hello and their name, I don't think I ad-libbed one single word. I can even tell you the names of the techniques I used."

"Your techniques have names?" asked Sam.

"Sure," said John. "As soon as I introduced myself I used a technique called 'We Have A Sale.' Fax rejected the offer and said not to try to talk him down. I responded with the 'Depressure' step and then the 'Isolate the Objection' step. Next I used the 'Reasonable Offer' technique which included the market analysis we worked up.

"When Fax rejected the market analysis, I used the 'Time and Urgency' step. You know, 'It has taken us eight weeks to find a family, etc.' Then, when I thought he was going to counter offer, I gave him the 'Real Estate Speculator' technique. That's all there was to it."

"I'm saying this as a compliment," said Sam, after a few minutes thought, "but I don't think I'd like to have you sell me anything. I think you could manipulate me right out of my socks."

8

"Oh no," said John. "No manipulation. Professional selling is doing something *for* people, not *to* people. No. . .the way I see it, my job is to give the clients enough information to make a decision. Their job is to make the decision. After all, it's their house.

"That's all that happened today. I gave the Faxes the kind of information that would help them make a good decision. It was a good offer. The market analysis bore that out."

That evening, as Sam sat by the fire in his family room, recalling the events of the day, he remembered a sales meeting from his first year of selling. An old, successful broker, now dead, had said to a group of young agents, "Boys, there's a price tag on everything. There's a price for doing something. And there's a price for doing nothing. Eventually, doing nothing will cost you a lot more than doing something. The hardest price to pay is investing time and money developing sales skills. Why? I don't know. Maybe because it's so intangible. But, if you invest time and money in yourself. . .if you attend the best sales training courses available. . .and then. . .if you develop a powerful, planned presentaiton and memorize every word so well you can say it at three in the morning coming out of a dead sleep, you will make an extra million dollars in your lifetime."

"No way," responded one agent strongly. "There's no way you can use a canned pitch for negotiating. No way."

"That's just about word for word what I said to John today," thought Sam ruefully to himself. "It looks like there's even a canned pitch for failure."

He thought for awhile about how easily he had been talked out of what now appeared to be the long lost key to success. When the embers began to dim in the fireplace, Sam set his jaw, made a decision and went to bed.

For the next month, Sam was a flying tiger. He spent more than

9

COULD A MILLION DOLLARS BE SLIPPING THROUGH YOUR FINGERS?

$1,000 in air fare and hotel bills and almost another $1,000 on books and sales courses. If there was any promise of good language techniques, he bought it or attended it.

Extracting the best techniques, he stayed up till two and three in the mornings, memorizing and polishing until he began to have instant, word perfect recall of each technique.

Then abruptly, he returned to work and began to apply what he had learned. By July he had posted an $18,000 gross month. In August he broke $20,000 for the first time in his career. September brought another $20,000.

In October, he took a day off to attend an in-the-water sailboat show. And that night a dream became a goal. Sam tacked onto his family room wall a four-color poster of a 50 foot schooner. . . slicing through golden beams of moonlight reflecting off the sea.

CHAPTER 2

PRESENTING OFFERS
AND NEGOTIATING

Sam got the boat.

People with purpose. . .and ability. . .almost always reach their goals.

Isn't it time for you to think seriously about the possibility of your earning $75,000 or more each year?

Are you ready to pay the price for doing something? Or are you content to pay the price for doing nothing? Are you ready to become a tiger?

You can decide to become a flying tiger or a walking tiger, but a tiger you must be. The object of your hunt will be language techniques. Pursue them relentlessly. Ferret them out of books, courses and other salespeople. But remember you will need at least one hundred techniques in total. Or examine this book carefully. You may find everything you need between its covers, because this book contains almost 200 techniques - the result of a seven year, coast-to-coast research program. However, when you come across a technique outside this book that appeals to you, commit that technique to writing. Write and rewrite it. Every word counts. If you can communicate an idea in twenty words instead of thirty. . .choose twenty. If you can do it in four words instead of six, choose four. Eliminate vague words. Use strong, positive, exciting words.

Try to give each technique a name or label such as I have done for the techniques in this book. The titles, like song titles, will help you memorize and recall specific ideas.

Next, memorize. Memorize and master every technique, until you can wake up at three in the morning from a dead sleep and give them word for word. Style and power will come *after* you have developed instant, word perfect recall.

Finally, apply constantly what you have learned, and in your lifetime you, too, will probably earn an extra million dollars. Why not?

Now, let's take a close look at the techniques John used to present the offer to Mr. and Mrs. Fax.

First, notice the procedure that John used. He called Sam's office for an appointment to present the offer, and he asked Sam to have the sellers come to Sam's office where there were fewer distractions. While there will be many times this cannot be done, there will be many times it can. But it certainly won't happen if you don't ask. Psychologically, there are a number of benefits to conducting business in the office, not the least of which is the elimination of distractions: T.V., crying babies, fighting teenagers, unexpected guests, and barking dogs are only a few of a thousand possibilities. More importantly, selling a house and making the decisions regarding price and terms is business. Important business. And the home is not a business place. The bottom line is that sellers will usually place more importance on an offer if they come to your office to review it. Finally, if you need additional comparative data to reinforce your reasons for accepting the offer, you will have immediate access to the information.

In terms of procedure, note too, that John arranged to come to Sam's office a half an hour early in order to review the offer with Sam. Consider the benefits of this approach. If Sam had been an inexperienced salesperson who did not know the market or how to use a comparative market analysis, or if he proved to be an individual whose ego would have been threatened by an offer lower than the asking price, John would have needed that time to sell the offer first to Sam, the listing agent, before selling it to the sellers. I have used the word "sell" purposely because although we usually say "present" the offer, we are, in fact, selling it.

Additionally, I have talked to a great number of professional salespeople who make a practice of preparing their own comparative market analysis when presenting an offer on someone else's listing. That way, if the listing agent does not have one, the pro has the necessary information. In our story, Sam had all the figures in his head, so John just used them to complete the comparative market analysis.

Note too, John's attention to detail. The selling price is an important part of the sale; it's worth the extra few cents to have a very professional looking comparative market analysis.

Continuing with the procedure, note that John was prepared to take complete control of presenting the offer. In many parts of the country the practice is simply to let the listing agent present the offer. But a lot of pros question that procedure.

"If I invest twenty or thirty hours with my buyers educating them on the realities of the current market, and assist them in arriving at a decision to look at houses they can afford, and finally find them a house they really like, and then get them over the hurdle of actually making an offer and signing it and writing out a substantial deposit check why should I allow my time investment to go down the tubes because the listing agent is new or untrained, or uninformed or unprofessional?" One top salesman says, "When it's my listing, I present the offer. When it's someone else's listing, I'm prepared to present the offer. And I usually do just that unless the listing agent proves to be well informed, professional and determined to sell the offer.

One of the most important things that most professional salespeople do is to create a flow of events that helps them maintain control of the situation. But control of what or of whom? If professional selling is doing something *for* people, not *to* people, how do we maintain control without controlling people? Look at it this way. My job, as a professional salesperson, is to give you enough information to make a good decision. I can create a flow of events that will keep me in control of the information giving, without controlling you as to the decision making. I control information giving. You control decision making. And that way, you will not feel threatened, because you are in complete control of making the decision. Let's see how that worked for John.

John creates a flow of events by using a special four step procedure. His first step is "Initial Introduction of the Offer" in which he states, "Well folks, we have a sale! Your home is sold!" Then he shows them the offer.

Observe John's choice of words. "We have a sale" is a lot better than "we have an offer." It might be argued that we don't have a sale unless the sellers accept. True. But we do have a sale, if they do. And since, as we will see, there is valid data to support the logic of accepting the offer, it is most correct to take the position that we have a sale. Based on 15 years of experience, I would suggest that if an offer were five percent or more *below* the average of recent sales, determined by a well prepared comparative market analysis, you may be better off saying "we have an offer." But if the offer is close to the average

14

of recent sales, I would recommend saying "we have a sale."

Let's continue. John then laid the offer down in front of Mr. and Mrs. Fax, the sellers, Mr. Fax exploded, which is just about the worst thing he could have done. John knew that when he laid the offer down in front of him. John also knew that Fax could have reacted differently. Fax could have accepted immediately, grumbling only that he was hoping to get more. He could have accepted slowly, first making a long speech about the inequities of life, how people nowadays don't appreciate the value of special homes like his and so forth. He could have asked John, in a somewhat pleading tone of voice, if there wasn't some chance the buyers would increase the offer. In Fax's case, that change of character wasn't too likely, but there are thousands of cases where belligerent, outspoken people completely change character when confronted with an actual offer. Additionally, Fax could have immediately countered at the offer, either close to the offer or closer to his asking price. In any event, it really doesn't make much difference how Fax answered. Except for complete acceptance of the offer, none of the other possible answers would have prevented John from responding with his second step in the procedure, which keeps him in control of the situation: "Depressure."

John is typical of many professional salespeople who have a good understanding of human nature. Most people don't like to make decisions. Many people feel pressured by the fact that they have to make one. Most people especially don't like to change a decision. They look upon salespeople who try to modify their thinking as "pressuring" them. John understands this. So the second step in his procedure for presenting offers is to "Depressure" by saying, "I'm not here to pressure you into making a bad decision. I would like to give you enough information so you can make a good decision. Is that fair?"

PRESENTING OFFERS AND NEGOTIATING

It would be most difficult for anyone to feel that that is not a fair proposition.

If you reread the story, you will note that Fax, by exploding and rejecting the offer, challenged John's knowledge of the value of the house. John's response to what he thinks the house is worth is a great technique, but not critical to his four step procedure. I recommend you learn it as it will come in handy in many situations, particularly when pricing a listing.

Onward! Having softened the seller's angry response with the "Depressure" step, John then moves to his third step, which again maintains his professional control: "Isolate the Objection." "In addition to the price, is there any other reason you would hesitate to accept this offer?"

This is a short, but most powerful technique. First it sets aside the major objection for the moment which allows John to review all other terms and conditions. Secondly, and this is the most important, the wording does not acknowledge rejection of the offer, only hesitation in acceptance. When a person says "no" to the question, he is actually saying, "No, if it weren't for the price, I wouldn't hesitate in accepting the offer."

The "Isolation" step, incidentally, can be used in any situation where people offer an objection: listing, selling, whatever. (Try it on your kids. "In addition to procrastinating, is there any other reason you would hesitate to clean up your room?")

Having isolated the objection and obtained approval on all other aspects of the offer, John now moves to the fourth step of his procedure: "Help the Sellers Think and Decide."

This fourth step in John's procedure contains four individual techniques, which also provide a flow of events that keeps John in control. First, John used what he calls his "Reasonable Offer" technique. He starts by presenting the comparative market analysis that he and Sam prepared in the half hour before the sellers arrived. After presenting all the data, he concludes with, "Mr. Fax, based on this current market analysis, this appears to be a reasonable offer. Don't you agree?"

There are a number of important points to discuss here. First, although Sam had all the data in his head, it would have been hard to keep Fax's attention while verbally covering eight different, yet comparable homes. Also, there's a strong possibility that Sam would not have thought of all eight under the pressure of the moment.

Additionally, Fax would have been more likely to challenge information verbally given. Comparative market data does have a lot more credibility in writing.

Second, John carefully explained the significance of each set of figures; he did not assume that Fax would truly understand the importance of each group of figures. What similar homes recently sold for tells what people are *willing* to pay for this kind of home, in this area, at this time. Information about similar homes that are currently for sale tells us what we are competing against. The buyers for your home are also inspecting these homes. Expired listings are similar homes that were unsold for 90 days or more. These tell us what people are *not* willing to pay for this kind of home, in this area, at this time. Notice how attention is drawn to current buyers. John showed prices they are paying, those they are considering, and those they are not paying. It is very hard for most people to completely ignore the reality of the situation.

Third, notice how John does not express his personal opinion about these figures. He did not say "I think this is a reasonable offer." In fact, he does not even say it is a reasonable offer. What he does say is, "Based on this current market analysis, this appears to be a reasonable offer. Don't you agree?"

PRESENTING OFFERS AND NEGOTIATING

Experience has proven at this point most people will agree the offer is reasonable and that most people will then either accept the offer or counter at a figure only slightly above the offer. Fax could have accepted or countered, but he didn't. He did not disagree that the offer was reasonable, he chose to ignore the reality of the situation by saying that reasonable wasn't good enough, that he had picked his price and that he wanted his price. That's very much like the fellow who once said, "My mind is made up. Don't confuse me with the facts." Because he was prepared with a system, John simply moved to the second technique in this step, which he calls "Time and Urgency."

"Mr. Fax, as I remember, your home came on the market about eight weeks ago, isn't that right?" Fax agrees. John continues, "It has taken us eight weeks to find a family that wants your home. . . and qualifies to buy your home. If we lose them it could take another eight weeks to find another family that wants your home and qualifies to buy your home."

Consider the impact this has to have on a seller's mind. On the average, people tend to make plans for closing and moving about 90 days after signing a listing. Eight weeks has used up two-thirds of their time. Another eight weeks will usually put them behind schedule. Since they will have to move before the home is sold, any delay can result in a great deal of cost, inconvenience and problems.

Experience has proven that most sellers, when confronted with this logic, will accept the offer or counter-offer at a reasonable price.

Obviously, this technique is unusable in the very early stages of the listing period. I can't imagine anyone obtaining a positive effect when saying, "Mr. Seller, it has taken me a day and a half to find a buyer for your home. If we lose him, it could take another day and a half. . ." The seller would most likely say, "Big deal. Go to it. Earn your commission."

18

As a rule of thumb, it appears that the "Time and Urgency" technique becomes effective at the mid-point between the signing of the listing and the seller's deadline for moving and becomes stronger and stronger as the deadline draws nearer and nearer.

In John's case, the "Time and Urgency" technique caused Fax to make a counter offer, but because of his abrasive nature, John didn't want Fax to express a price, so he interrupted Fax in mid-sentence by asking, "May I make another comment?" Fax gave permission, and John presented one of the most effective and powerful techniques ever devised for presenting offers: "Real Estate Speculator."

"Mr. and Mrs. Seller, right now your home is sold. Mr. and Mrs. Buyer have just agreed to buy your home for $—. If you accept their offer, your home is sold. It's done. It's finished. But. . .if you do *not* accept their offer, you are, in effect, buying the house *back* from the buyers for $— and putting it back on the market, hoping to make a profit of $— to $—. May I ask, as real estate speculators, would you do that?"

This is an emotionally charged technique. Most people do not like to make decisions where risk is involved. You are reversing their view of themselves from sellers who want the most for their house, to thoughtful investors who want to make a profit.

Consider, step by step, the power and effectiveness of this technique. Ever since they signed the listing agreement, the sellers have had one primary goal: get the home sold. And your first statement is, "Right now your home is sold." Next, you identify people. Mr. and Mrs. Edwards, Mr. and Mrs. Jackson, Ralph Timmons, Cathy Andrews are real people. A "buyer" just does not compare. Next, you are pointing out that the buyers have made a buying decision, not that they want to know if the sellers will accept an offer. "Mr. and Mrs. Smith have agreed to buy your home for $—" is much stronger than "Mr. and Mrs.

Smith want to know if you will accept an offer of $ –.." The Smiths have made a firm decision. They have agreed to buy. They have backed up that decision with a deposit and a signed purchase agreement.

The next part says, "If you accept their offer, your home is sold. It's done! It's finished!" Again, a power packed point. Once the sellers sign a listing agreement, and especially when they make additional firm commitments, they develop a great sense of urgency to get this home sold. To get it over with. To get it finished. Say that part out loud and feel the sense of finality, of completion. "If you accept their offer your home is sold. It's done. It's finished."

Now you take away that feeling of completion when you add: "But. . .(the three periods indicate a pause to let the thought sink in) if you do *not* accept their offer. . .you are, in effect, buying the house *back* from Mr. and Mrs. Smith. . .and putting it *back* on the market. . .hoping to make a profit." Notice the insecurity of the word hoping. And now you compare this offer to the prices of other similar homes that have recently sold. Subtract the differences and show a potential profit of $100, $500, maybe $800. Then add the final question, "May I ask, as real estate speculators, would you do that?" Very few sellers will say yes.

Obviously, this is another case where the conditions have to be correct. If the offer was fifteen or twenty percent below current market and you are showing a potential $10,000 profit on a $70,000 home, the sellers would be most willing to "buy it back" to make that kind of profit over the next thirty or sixty days.

Finally, John's system includes a technique called "Silent Partner."

When Fax had no other personal reasons to delay his accepting the offer, he fell back on the most common device two people can have for delaying a decision, "We'll talk it over and let you know." And once again, John was prepared.

First, he isolated the objection: "In addition to thinking it over, is there any other reason you would hesitate to accept the offer?" "No." The isolation question is critically important at this point for three reasons. First, it is vital to find out if the person who says, "We want to think it over," has any other objections. If he says, "no", you have generally eliminated the possibility of any other objection coming up later. Second, it would be rude to simply ignore that person and begin asking the other person if he or she would say "yes". And third, the other person, Mrs. Fax in this case, would normally be reluctant to answer for herself if she thought her husband still had an objection other than thinking it over. At this point the silent partner sees that the dominant partner has no further objections and will feel freer to express his or her own feelings or thoughts.

Therefore, when John, after isolating Mr. Fax's objection, turned to Mrs. Fax and asked, "If it was your decision. . .if for some reason Mr. Fax was not available. . .based on the information I have given you. . .would you accept the offer?" she felt comfortable saying "yes".

And now that Mrs. Fax expressed that she would, indeed, accept the offer, there was nothing for Mr. Fax to talk about. So when John turned back to him and simply asked, "Mr. Fax?" there was little else for him to do but agree. All of the evidence had been presented. The offer was reasonable. The market was not brisk. It had taken eight weeks to find a family who wanted the home. It could take another eight weeks to find other buyers. That would put Fax behind schedule and result in extra cost, problems and inconvenience. The offer was signed. There was a substantial deposit. The house was sold if he accepted. Mrs. Fax was ready to accept. She felt it was a reasonable offer.

And if he said "no", or countered, he was actually buying the house back. And the potential profit, based on recent sales of

21

similar homes was really only $600 to $1,000. It would not be too intelligent to pay $66,000 for a house hoping to make $600 to $1,000.

Some years ago, Ben Feldman, considered by many to be the top life insurance salesman in the United States for over thirty years, said, "When selling becomes a procedure, it ceases to be a problem." John's procedure proves the validity of that statement. A tough situation is effectively handled by a competent salesperson using a logical procedure.

Here, in summary, is an outline of John's procedure.

1. Initial Presentation of the Offer
2. Depressure
3. Isolate the Objection
4. Help the Sellers Think and Decide
   A. Reasonable Offer
   B. Time and Urgency
   C. Real Estate Speculator
   D. Silent Partner

To gain the maximum benefit from these powerful techniques, it is recommended that you memorize each one individually and then practice them in a role-playing situation with a partner. The individual techniques are listed below for ease of study.

**INITIAL
INTRODUCTION
OF OFFER**

1. "Well, we have a sale! We have sold your home! May I review the offer with you?"

2. "Mr. and Mrs. (seller), I have an offer to purchase from Mr. and Mrs. (buyer). May I review it with you?"

NOTE: Some experienced sales-people believe it is best to start with conditions and come to pricing and terms second. Other experienced salespeople believe it's best to present the price first and the conditions second.

Personally, I doubt that one approach is actually better than the other, but obviously one method will work better for you. A little experimentation should quickly tell you which way to go.

ISOLATE

"In addition to (price - method of finance, etc.) is there any other reason you would hesitate to accept this offer?"

DEPRESSURE

"Mr. and Mrs. (seller), I am not here to pressure you into making a bad decision, but I would like to give you enough information to make a good decision, is that fair?"

RELATE OFFER TO COMPARATIVE MARKET ANALYSIS

"Here's a Comparative Market Analysis that I/we prepared before coming out today." Present CMA.

"According to this information, this appears to be a very reasonable offer, don't you agree?"

23

TIME AND DIFFICULTY

"It has taken _____ days to find a family who _want_ to buy your home, and _qualify_ to buy your home. If we lose them, it could take another _____ days to find _another_ family who wants your home and qualifies to buy your home. Let's not lose these buyers."

REAL ESTATE SPECULATOR

"Mr. and Mrs. (seller), if you do not accept this offer, you will have just become real estate speculators. May I explain?"

"Right now your home is sold. Mr. and Mrs. (buyer) have just agreed to buy your home for $_____. If you accept their offer, your home is sold. It's done. It's finished! But, if you do not accept their offer, you are, in effect, buying the house back from Mr. and Mrs. (buyer) for $ (amount of offer) and putting it back on the market, hoping to make a profit. And based on recent sales, that would be a profit of $_____ to $_____. May I ask, as real estate speculators, would you do that?"

**SILENT
PARTNER**

Isolate objection of first person to speak, then to silent party, **"Mr. (Mrs.), may I ask you a question?"** Obtain agreement, then, **"If it were your decision...if (other party) wasn't here...if (other party) wanted you to make the decision by yourself...based on the information I have given you, would you accept the offer?"**

NOTE: If second party says yes, turn back to the first party and ask them again. Usually, all you need to do is say their name with a question mark. **"Mr. Fax?"**

25

CHAPTER 3

PROFESSIONAL SELLING:
IT'S NOT JUST A LOT OF JAZZ

Alex Walker is a part-time real estate agent with a full-time job as a waiter. He had hoped to earn enough in real estate to go into it full-time, but after two years he still had not secured enough listings or made enough sales to make the leap. Then, one Saturday morning at the restaurant, while preparing the tables for a special party, Alex watched his boss, Pete, audition some musicians and learned what professional selling is all about.

Pete Groble owns a very fine restaurant featuring gourmet seafood. The atmosphere is elegant and relaxed. The food is renowned. To augment the pleasant environment, Pete bought a Steinway grand piano and made room for it just to the side of of a beautiful fireplace with a hand-carved oak mantle imported from an old hotel in Stuttgart.

To keep the atmosphere simple, elegant, subdued and conversationally pleasant, Pete advertised for a pianist who could play semi-classical, light opera, Broadway show tunes,

PROFESSIONAL SELLING:
IT'S NOT JUST A LOT OF JAZZ

Strauss waltzes, favorites from yesteryear and generally pleasant dinner music.

Ed, Carolyn, Fred, Alice and Phil all heard about the job, all were "in between engagements" and needed work and all, except Phil, made appointments to audition.

For his audition, Ed showed up on time, asked Pete what he would like to hear and in a most relaxed manner proceeded to demonstrate his skills. Mechanically, he was flawless. His range of memorized music included every category that Pete had specified. Pete was impressed, in fact, very impressed, and told Ed so, but he also told Ed he had several more auditions and would call him later.

For her audition, Carolyn also showed up on time, but unlike Ed, she was a touch nervous. Just a touch, mind you. It was not very noticable. But it did show. Pete asked her to play something. She responded by asking if he had anything special he would like to hear. He said, "No, whatever you like." She fumbled for a piece of sheet music from her briefcase and began to play. She played rigidly at first, but after a few moments began to relax and soon had Pete swaying to the easy rhythm of her music.

"She's a little inexperienced," thought Pete to himself, "but people will like that kind of style. It will touch them, reach inside them and make them feel good." Pete was impressed, in fact, very impressed, and he told Carolyn so, but he also told her he had several other auditions and would let her know. Carolyn pointed out that one key on the piano was a little out of tune and would need adjusting. Pete thanked her for her comment.

For his audition, Fred showed up half an hour early, just as Carolyn was leaving. He said he wasn't sure whether Pete had said on the hour or half past, but "better early than late, right?" Pete hesitated for a moment. He had carefully scheduled the audition times so he could do a few other things between appointments. Fred's showing up early threw his plans off. He felt a bit of pressure, and he didn't like pressure.

"Why don't you warm up for a few minutes while I make a phone call," he told Fred. "I'll be about ten minutes."

Fred settled himself at the piano, wiggled his fingers to relax them and plunged into the keys with a great New Orleans jazz beat. Rhythm followed rhythm, piece followed piece, as his fingers flew from one end of the keyboard to the other. Suddenly, 15 minutes later, in the middle one very fast, very loud piece, he became aware of Pete standing in the doorway of the kitchen. He stopped and said, "Ya got a bad key here. It oughta be fixed, but it don't really bother me much. Well, do you wanna hear some more?"

"No thanks," said Pete. "I've heard enough. I'll let you know."

When Fred left, Pete came over to Alex and said, "Alex, I want to think out loud. Just listen for a minute. The last guy - Fred he's out - no class, and he's not on our wave length. So, it's between Ed and Carolyn. Ed certainly had more poise and experience. He probably knows a lot more music. Carolyn played with more feeling, but was up-tight. She'd probably get over that soon enough, so I shouldn't hold that against her. Man vs. Woman; the audience doesn't care. Tight decision - good. I always like to make a decision between two good choices."

He paused, thinking deeply, then expelled his breath with a touch of frustration. "Do you have a coin?" he asked Alex. Alex offered a quarter. Pete flipped it into the air. "Heads it's Carolyn, tails it's Ed," he said as the coin spun in the air. He caught it, slapped it over the back of his other hand and said, "Tails - Ed it is."

PROFESSIONAL SELLING:
IT'S NOT JUST A LOT OF JAZZ

"Don't you have another audition still coming?" asked Alex.

"Oh yes. Blast. I don't need it. I wonder if I can still cancel out." He dialed the number Alice had given him, listened to the phone ring eight times and said, "Too late. She's on her way."

Half an hour later Alice entered. Pete glanced at his watch in the manner of a person who is behind schedule and impatient to get on to something else. With a wave of his hand, he gestured Alice to the piano and said, "Play a couple of tunes."

"Mr. Groble," said Alice, "may I ask you a few questions before I play?"

"Sure, sure," he said impatiently. "What do you want to know?"

"May I ask why you want the kind of music you stated in your ad?"

"Well, look around," he said with impatience. "I've put a lot of money into this place to make it rich and elegant. I want to attract the kind of cultured people who will appreciate the atmosphere and pay the price I have to charge to provide the quality of the food. I want music to add to - not detract from - the atmosphere."

"Great," said Alice. "May I ask just one more question?" And without waiting for an answer, she asked, "Do you want someone who can respond to the various moods of your customers?"

"What do you mean?" asked Pete.

"Well," said Alice. "Some nights your customers might tend to be mostly older folks - maybe in their seventies. On those nights I'd probably play something like this. . ." and turning, she began

30

to play a series of waltzes that were popular fifty to sixty years ago.

"On another evening," she said while she played, you might have a large number of people who are in their fifties, and for them I'd play music like this. . ." and abruptly she shifted from waltzes to a medley of show tunes from thirty years ago.

"I'd also watch the hands and the heads of people, and if I see someone who starts keeping rhythm with his fingers or by swaying his head, I might play something like this. . ."and now she played a few Scott Joplin numbers, including the theme from "The Sting."

When she finished, she turned and said, "Mr. Groble, most people develop their taste for music in their late teens and early twenties, so people in their seventies will like music that was popular fifty years ago, and people in their fifties will like the music that was popular thirty years ago. Everybody likes to hear a song he felt good about as a youngster.

"In addition to that, some nights, when it's rainy and the barometer is falling, people tend to feel melancholy, so I play melancholy music. On other nights, when it has been a glorious sunshiny day, I play bright, exciting music.

"And one more thing," she said. "I even watch the boss, and on an evening when things aren't going too well and he looks troubled, I play something like this. . ." and turning back to the keyboard she played a song titled "Love Walked In."

When she finished, Pete asked, "How did you know that is my favorite song?"

"I called the cook this morning and asked him."

"Lady, you've got the job. What's your name?"

31

PROFESSIONAL SELLING:
IT'S NOT JUST A LOT OF JAZZ

"Alice - Alice Dian."

"Welcome aboard, Alice. You can start tonight."

"Thank you. By the way, some of your customers will have a good ear for music. There's one key that is off just a little and might bother them. Would you mind if I had someone tune it?"

That afternoon Alex sat in his car outside the real estate office where he worked part-time, mulling over the events of the morning. Suddenly he saw it. Music and selling were almost identical. Pete's objective was to create referrals and repeat business through the atmosphere created as much by music as by food and decor. He needed a musician who could create that atomsphere and this morning four people had auditioned for the job.

Ed and Carolyn were both very good but not outstanding, while Fred was completely unprepared to deliver what his prospect wanted. But Alice - she would bring in so much business there would be a constant waiting list. She knew how to pinpoint what the prospect wanted, even made him aware of a few things he wasn't even aware he wanted.

Then, thinking about real estate, particularly listings, it occur- red to him that every time he made a listing presentation he was auditioning for the job. The seller would give the listing - the job - to the salesperson who could demonstrate the greatest skill in making sure the house would sell. . .quickly. . .and for the most money.

Then another thought hit him. The musician's responsibility is to make *sure* people enjoy themselves so they will recommend the restaurant to others and will come back themselves. It is the obligation of the musician to make sure the people enjoy themselves, just as it is the obligation of the salesperson to make sure the listing sells. In accepting the listing, the salesperson accepts that responsibility. The selling of the home becomes an obligation.

"Now," thought Alex, "what do *I* need to know to make sure a home I list will sell, regardless of the market, regardless of the competition? There must be a lot more to selling a house - making absolutely sure it sells - than putting a sign on the lawn, advertising in the paper and maybe holding an open house."

For the next thirty days, every chance he had, Alex analyzed the problem. He found that the average buyer looks at twelve homes before making a decision. That meant his listings would compete, in the minds of the buyers, against eleven other homes. He realized that the buyers would select the home that appealed most to them. He also realized that the selection would be based both on price and showability.

His thinking was reinforced when several experienced real estate people confirmed that a home which showed exceptionally well almost always sold faster - and for more money - than an average home. The key to assuring that his listings would sell quickly, he decided, would lie in convincing the sellers of the importance of preparing the home for sale, as well as in selecting a good initial market price - neither too high nor too low.

He also discovered that most homes are sold co-operatively through the multi-listing service. To sell a home once, he reasoned, it would actually have to be sold twice. First, he would have to sell it to the salespeople so they, in turn, would sell it to their buyers; all the more reason to make the effort to prepare the home for sale and select the best asking price.

PROFESSIONAL SELLING:
IT'S NOT JUST A LOT OF JAZZ

EPILOGUE

Alex quit his job at the restaurant and soon became a top real estate agent. Within six months he was leading his company in listings and in the percentage of homes sold. In fact, except for a few early mistakes, he seldom had a listing expire and seldom took more than sixty days to sell a home. By the end of his first full year, he had made sixty-three presentations, secured fifty-eight listings and had fifty-one sales - four still active, three expired.

His system was very simple. He made sure each listing was prepared for showing, priced right and sold to all the top salespeople in his area. He looked on each appointment as a chance to audition, so he memorized a presentation to explain his method of merchandising to a prospect. Because he was prepared - and confident - he almost always won the audition.

And speaking of auditions, remember Phil? He also heard about the auditon. He needed work and was a very skilled pianist. In fact, he was better than he thought he was. But Phil didn't make an appointment with Pete, because he heard that Fred was going and figured he didn't have a chance against him. He defeated himself by measuring his chances against a person who failed to get the job. Tragic, isn't it?

How about you? How do you see selling? As a skill? As a profession? Or just a lot of jazz? Do you have the skill to win your "auditions" eighty percent, ninety percent of the time? Do you have the skill to make sure your listings sell - in spite of the market - in spite of the competition? Can you make sixty-three presentations, get fifty-eight listings and make sure at least fifty-five sell? Would you like to be able to do that? What do you need to know to make it happen? What are you willing to do to make it happen?

34

The opportunity of a lifetime lasts only for the lifetime of the opportunity. Will you be ready?

CHAPTER 4

PROFESSIONAL
SELLING
ANALYZED

If you were to ask one hundred people to define selling, you would obviously get a lot of different responses, but the most common response would be "getting people to buy your product or service."

"Getting" people to buy, however, sounds like something we are doing *to* people. Since most of us don't like the idea of having someone do something *to* us, we really don't like the idea of doing something *to* them. The end result is that most sales people do not do a good job of actually helping the prospect make a decision.

My philosophy is that professional selling is not something we do *to* people, it is something we do *for* people. My job is to give prospects enough information to make a decision; their job is to make the decision. Many top producers apparently feel the same way, based on what I've heard them say when they demonstrate their selling skills.

When I first began to sell, I was told to "control the interview." Well, that felt very much like doing something *to* the prospect, so in the beginning I didn't do that very well. But once I

37

understood that my job was to give information and the prospect's job was to make the decision, then I became very comfortable controlling the interview. I decided that it was my job to control the part about giving information and to let them control the decision making part.

Alice Dian did that very well in the preceding chapter. When Pete impatiently told her to "play a couple of tunes," Alice did not know that he had already made a decision or why he was impatient. But she did understand that her job was to give Pete enough information to make a good decision.

She also understood that in order to give the right information, she had to know what he was trying to accomplish. So Alice took control of the interview by asking qualifying questions. Why did Pete write the ad the way he did? Why did he want the kind of music he specified? When she had the answers she was in a better position to explain and demonstrate her professional ability. And as she explained and demonstrated, Pete began to understand that he was seeing a real professional in action.

Finally, Alice did not have to "close" the sale. Pete "closed" himself. Why? Because Alice gave him enough information to make a decision. Since the information clearly demonstrated that she knew her business and that she was indeed a professional, the decision was in her favor.

There is an old saying that "a good presentation eliminates objections and makes closing automatic." I think the previous chapter demonstrates that very well. Pete started out with an unreceptive attitude based on the fact that he had already made a decision. Alice made a good presentation which eliminated the objection and let Pete close himself, automatically.

Now, let's apply this to selling real estate.

When sellers decide to sell privately in order to save the

commission that normally goes to real estate sales people and firms, our job is to give them enough information to realize the odds are against them and that, statistically, they will net more by listing with a professional real estate agent and paying a commission, than by selling the house themselves.

A home owner is transferred to another town and must sell. He believes he should talk to three or four salespeople and then list with the one who showed the most enthusiasm about the highest asking price. Our job is to give him enough information to understand that listing with the highest bidder is not the best way and that overpricing can cause a loss of time and ultimately a loss of money.

As you progress through this book, you will see, time and time again, that a successful sale was made because the sales person gave the prospect enough information to make a decision and then let the prospect make the decision. This does not mean that sales people do not "close" the sale by asking for the listing or asking the seller to accept the offer. It does mean that in each case, the sales person was careful to give his prospects the kind of information that would make them feel comfortable about making a good decision.

If you can give your prospects and clients the kind of information that makes them feel comfortable in making a decision that is beneficial to them, then you have done something *for* them, not *to* them.

That's what professional selling is all about.

CHAPTER 5

EVERY
WORD
COUNTS

Two priests were among the 1000 killed in a train wreck. Arriving at the Pearly Gates, they found St. Peter and his assistant, Charlie, flustered by the rush. Addressing the two priests, St. Peter said, "Look you guys, we can't handle all these people at once. Since you are men of the cloth, I can give you a special deal. You can sit on the bench over there and wait your turn like the rest of the folks, or I can let you go back to Earth for two weeks, off the record, as anything you like."

"Terrific!", said the first priest. "My life-long dream was to spend time in the Rocky Mountains in Colorado just enjoying the natural beauty, but I never got there. I'd like to go back as an eagle so I can soar over the mountains and really enjoy the majesty of those peaks and valleys."

"Done," said St. Peter, and the priest disappeared. "Now," he said to the second priest, "how about you?"

"Off the record, eh? Well, considering what I had to give up to become a priest, I'd like to go back as a stud."

41

EVERY WORD COUNTS

"Done!" said St. Peter, and the second priest disappeared.

Two weeks later, just about sundown, Charlie was about to go to dinner when St. Peter said, "Not yet, Charlie. I just remembered, we have two priests down on earth and their two weeks are up today. You have to go get them before we quit for the day. Now, finding the first one won't be hard. He's an eagle flying over the Rocky Mountains in Colorado. Finding the second guy will be a bit tougher. He's somewhere in Wisconsin on a snow tire."

Every word counts.

One of the reasons that the listing and selling techniques presented in this book have proven to be so effective is that the individual words used in each have been chosen with great care. Most of the techniques are the product of careful scrutiny and years of actual use, often by people who got into the habit of carefully analyzing the effect of the words they used.

Time has proven, again and again, that people who choose their words carefully are more effective than those who don't. Yet the challenge that we face is the feeling that selling should be natural, therefore, we should all ad-lib, free-wheel, put things in our own words, be "ourselves."

When I first began to sell, my manager, Henry, said there was nothing to selling - just go out and be yourself. I asked him how to get started.

"Just introduce yourself," he said.

"What do I say next?" I asked.

"Don't worry," was his reply, "it will come to you."

It didn't come.

I asked Henry what he said to get started, to make certain points and to overcome objections. I suggested that maybe I could just memorize what he said. Since it worked for him, it would work for me. "No," he said, "put the ideas in your own words so you develop your own style. You have to be yourself. Don't copy others."

I tried it. My own words were a disaster. Nobody bought.

There was a fellow in our company making about $400 a month. Four hundred dollars a month wasn't much money, but when you are starving, anyone who makes anything looks like a genius. I asked Frank what he said, wrote it down, memorized it and pretty soon I was making $400 a month.

Funny thing happened, though. Try as I might, I couldn't get past $400 a month. Then I heard about a guy in Cleveland making $700 a month. I went down there, learned what he said, memorized it, and pretty soon I was making $700 a month. But as time passed, I found myself stuck at $700.

Later I discovered why. Frank's words were worth $400 a month. That's why he was earning $400. The guy in Cleveland had words worth $700 a month, that's why he was at $700.

Then I met a very experienced and highly successful salesman who asked me a most challenging question. "Which self do you wish to be? Today's $10,000 self, or tomorrow's $100,000 self?"

When I said $100,000, he said, "Then why are you seeking advice from $10,000 people? Find the top earners, learn what they say and learn it exactly the way they say it. Every word counts. When you learn it perfectly, you will be yourself."

EVERY WORD COUNTS

This book is the result of finding the top producers in listings and sales and writing down what they said.

As you read and study this book, you will often find yourself wanting to rephrase a technique. No problem. There are often many ways to express an idea. But some ways are better than others. So here's an idea that may help. Don't just wing it. When you feel tempted or compelled to put things in your own words, just write down what you want to say. Then compare what you have written, to what was presented. If yours is better, by all means use it. But if the way it's written in the book is better, don't let well-meaning people talk you out of memorizing what is here.

Let me give you a specific example. One of the techniques you will find in this book begins this way: "There are eight good reasons why you will benefit by having me represent you to sell your home." When people are told to put that in their own words, about 80% say, "There are several reasons why you could benefit by letting me sell your home for you." They have made three changes that have made the statement less effective. "Eight reasons" sounds like you have a lot more to offer than "several reasons." "Will benefit" sounds like you are a lot more sure of yourself than "could benefit". "By having me represent you to sell" is more correct and less threatening than "by letting me sell for you." Correctly speaking, we may sell the buyer on an offer, but the owner sells the house when he or she accepts the offer. More important, however, "By having me represent you" keeps the final decision in the hands of the owner, while, "by letting me sell it for you" takes the decision making, and the control, away from the owner and is therefore more threatening.

These may seem like small things at times, but keep in mind that one stroke, out of 275 strokes, can make the difference between winning a golf tournament or coming in second. The financial difference can be $50,000. In golf, every stroke counts. In selling, every word counts. And the financial difference can also be $50,000 a year for ten years.

Every word counts!

CHAPTER 6

EIGHT BALL IN THE SIDE POCKET IS WORTH A LISTING EVERY TIME

Sam Brown sat in a window seat watching the snow covered land silently disappear under the leading edge of the left wing of the airplane. A year had passed since his encounter with John, the young salesman who had first exposed him to the idea of memorized language and specific procedures. During the year he had mastered all of John's techniques, traveled extensively and attended many seminars and courses. He had gathered a great number of good techniques from professional speakers, books and cassette tapes, and, as a result, he had tripled his income. Still, he was not satisfied in total.

More money, more listings, more sales, more local acclaim were not his objection. He was delighted with his current income which was, in fact, considerably more than he had expected. He had not set a goal to beat anyone else's records. He had not set a goal to win any awards or recognition.

His original goal, a year ago, was to become good enough to buy his fifty foot sailboat - or yacht, as the dealer insisted on calling it. Well, he'd earned enough for a good down payment and was ready now to place an order for spring delivery. His current

EIGHT BALL IN THE SIDE POCKET
IS WORTH A LISTING EVERY TIME

earnings would easily satisfy the insurance, the maintenance, the payments and the rest of his living expenses. No, money and fame were not the reasons for his trip today.

Sam's goal was very simple. He had become challenged by the idea of becoming the very best Sam Brown he could possibly be. He wanted to become better for the sake of being better, for the satisfaction he felt as he acquired new skills and in doing his job more effectively.

And now, Sam was on his way to meet Lauri Lee McKier, a real estate lady who, by reputation, had made one hundred appointments and listed one hundred homes in the last 18 months. One hundred listings from one hundred appointments! In 18 months! The idea was exciting. High volume and a perfect score!

Sam had tracked Lauri Lee down by phone, and verified that she had indeed accomplished what rumor said and asked her if she would be willing to share her key to success with him if he came to see her. She agreed, and Sam had booked a flight the very next day.

In Lauri Lee's car, heading towards her office, Lauri Lee said, "Sam, you asked me for the key to my success. Well, my key is this: an eight ball in the side pocket is worth a listing every time."

"Pardon me?" said Sam, "I think I missed something there."

"An eight ball in the side pocket is worth a listing every time," she repeated, with a big grin on her face.

"I thought that's what I heard you say," responded Sam. "What does an eight ball in the side pocket have to do with getting a listing?"

"Did you ever skip school to play pool, Sam?" asked Lauri Lee.

"No," he responded, "I skipped school and I played pool, but never on the same day. But what does pool have to do with getting listings?"

"Did you ever watch a champion pool player in action, Sam?"

"Sure, a couple of times. But what. . .?"

"Do you know why a pro can run the table? Do you know the key to expert pool playing?" Lauri Lee persisted.

"No, I never noticed. But what does pool have to do with getting good listings?"

"Patience, Sam, patience," said Lauri Lee. "Let me show you the key to expert pool playing, and then you will understand the key to my success in turning appointments into listings." And saying that, she pulled up and parked in front of the East Side Family Billiard Hall.

"My dad was a professional billiard player," explained Lauri Lee, as they went inside and racked up the balls on a table. "We always had a table at home and Dad had me playing since I was three. Go ahead and break."

Sam stroked the cue ball as hard as his unpracticed arm would allow and smiled as the triangle of balls exploded over the table and a striped ball fell into a corner pocket.

"Good break," said Lauri Lee. "Keep going."

Sam had one easy shot and sunk another ball but then found his next shot to be long and difficult. He missed. Lauri Lee picked up a cue stick, chalked it, and in the easy manner of a pro, proceeded to sink ball after ball until the table was clear.

"What did you notice?" she asked Sam.

"You never had even one hard shot," he responded. "The cue ball was always in the right place for an easy sink."

"Exactly!" exclaimed Lauri Lee. "That's the key. It's not just sinking the ball. It's making sure that the cue ball stops in a position to make the next shot easy. And that's my key to effective selling. It's not just asking a question or making a point. It's doing it in such a way that you always get the kind of answers that lead toward eliminating objections, solving problems and getting good listings. Come on. I've made an appointment so I can show you the whole system."

"A few years ago," said Lauri Lee, as they drove towards a nearby residential area, "I began making a list of all the questions I was asking people to find out if they were serious about selling, and why they were selling, and when they had to sell by and all that. I was trying to see if there was a pattern that could help me be more consistent because I had noticed that when I asked certain questions first, I'd get better, more positive responses to other questions.

Then one night, when my dad was showing off on the pool table to some old war buddies, I suddenly saw the whole picture. Within two weeks I had worked out the pattern I now use."

"You are going to tell me what your dad did that gave you the clue, aren't you?" asked Sam.

"Sure," said Lauri Lee. "In fact, I want to because I think it will help you understand how important my sequence is. Here's what happened. Dad had just racked the balls on the table when he said to his buddies, 'When I break, the 15 ball will fall in the end pocket. Then I'll sink all the striped balls in reverse numerical order. Then I'll sink all the solid balls in order starting with the one ball and I'll sink the eight ball in the left side pocket.' Well, they all laughed and one of his friends bet him ten dollars he couldn't do it. It was a bad bet. Dad was very good and he did it just the way he said he would. Then someone bet him twenty dollars he couldn't do it again. That was a bad bet, too. It was while he was doing it the second time that the light came on. His goal was to sink the eight ball in the side pocket as his final shot. He could almost always sink the 15 ball on the break because of where he placed it when he racked the balls. And then, because of his fantastic control of the cue ball, he could almost always have it stop so his next shot was easy. In fact, I can still hear him say, 'Control the cue ball, m'dear, and you control the world'."

"Well, I suddenly understood what I had to do. I made a list of everything I wanted to say or ask when I was on a listing appointment. Then I started at the end and worked backwards. All I did was figure out what I could say or do that would make it easy to go from one point to the next. When I had it worked out, it was so simple I couldn't believe it. And once I began to use the system, I hardly missed. If the prospects were serious about selling, I'd get the listing. And at the right price. And with the right terms."

At that point they arrived at the prospect's home. A professionally done sign reading "For Sale By Owner - No Agents" was centered on the front lawn. "The people with the 'No Agents,' signs are the easiest ones to get," said Lauri Lee, anticipating Sam's question. "All I do is call and say, 'I see your ad says 'No Agents,' but if I could find a buyer that would pay a decent price, would you accept the offer through me?' and they usually say yes. Then I ask them if they are absolutely serious about selling, and I really stress the word 'absolutely'. If they say yes, I make an appointment to see the house so I can tell poten-

tial buyers about it. Now, let's go get the listing, and afterwards
I'll explain my system."

Inside the house, after introductions were completed, Lauri Lee
asked the sellers, Jodi and Walter Dyer, if they had a few
minutes to answer a couple of questions before they walked
through the home. Mrs. Dyer responded by saying, "We aren't
listing, you know. But we will accept a reasonable offer, just like
we told you on the phone."

"Bad break," thought Sam.

"No problem," said Lauri Lee, "but may I ask, why are you
selling?"

"Oh, Mr. Dyer has just retired and we are moving to Florida,"
responded Mrs. Dyer

"Oh, great! Where in Florida?" asked Lauri Lee.

"Boca Grande," responded Mrs. Dyer. "That's on the west coast
not too far from Ft. Myers. It's very nice there. We like it."

"Terrific! And when do you have to be there?"

"We don't have to be there any particular time," injected Mr.
Dyer. "We'll go when this house gets sold."

"Ouch!" thought Sam. "Kind of low motivation."

"Yes, but when would you *like* to be there, Mr. Dyer?" responded Lauri Lee.

"He'd like to be there in time for the tarpon tournament," said
Mrs. Dyer with a smile. "Tell the truth Walt."

"When does the tournament start, Mr Dyer?" asked Lauri Lee.

"Ninety-seven days." he responded.

"Oh-ho!" thought Sam. "Ninety-seven days, eh? More motivation than meets the eye."

"Are you going to be buying a home or condominium in Boca Grande?" asked Lauri Lee.

"We already bought a small home there. We take possession in just under ninety days. Walt wants to be settled-in two weeks before the tournament starts. That's why we have to sell this house. But I've noticed that a fair number of homes in this area have sold recently, so I shouldn't think we'll have too much trouble. Anyway, Walt and I have decided that we want to have one last Christmas and New Years in this home. It's been our home for twenty-seven years, you know. That's a long time. And we've put so much into it. Why, we just put new carpeting in all the bedrooms just last year. We think it's one of the nicest homes in this neighborhood. I just don't see why we will have any trouble selling it. We should get a quick sale, don't you think, Walt?"

Lauri Lee waited until Mr. Dyer said he didn't think they'd have any trouble selling and that's why they really didn't need a broker, but as they said before, they would accept an offer if it was reasonable. Then she leaned forward a bit and now looking quite concerned, asked, "What happens if this home is not sold in ninety days, what will you do?"

"Oh, it will sell," said Mrs. Dyer.

"We'll stay until it does sell," said Mr. Dyer.

"But what happens if you have to close on your new home before this one is sold?" asked Lauri Lee. "What are you going to do?"

EIGHT BALL IN THE SIDE POCKET
IS WORTH A LISTING EVERY TIME

"We'll just get some interim financing and close down there. No problem," said Mr. Dyer.

"What do you think it would cost you in total if you had to close on your new home thirty or sixty days before you closed this one?" persisted Lauri Lee gently, but firmly. The tone of her voice and the look on her face were ones of concern, not demand.

"Oh, this home will sell quick enough so we won't have to do that. Won't it, Walt?" responded Mrs. Dyer.

"I hadn't given it much thought," said Mr. Dyer, "but whatever it is, we can live with it."

"Well," injected Mrs. Dyer, "the cost would be the interest on the interim financing, and we'd have to keep this home heated and we'd have insurance on both places, and. . .and taxes on both places. . .and don't we have to come back to close up here? Why, I bet that all would cost a thousand dollars!"

"Thank you, Mrs. Dyer," thought Sam.

"Mr. Dyer, Mrs. Dyer, would it be in your best interest to have this home sold *and* closed in the next ninety days?" asked Lauri Lee.

"Yes!" they both said at once.

"Since it normally takes about thirty days from the time someone agrees to buy your home until the time you get the money, we should have this home sold in sixty days so you can have the money in ninety days, isn't that right?"

"Yes!" they both said again.

"One other thing," said Lauri Lee, "what happens if the only way you can get a sale here at this time is by land contract, that means that you would be holding the mortgage, what will you do?"

"I already anticipated that probability," said Mr. Dyer. "That's why we bought the house in Florida on land contract."

"Mr. Dyer," asked Lauri Lee, "if you felt that you could get the most money, the quickest sale and the fewest problems, by giving me an exclusive listing today, would you do so?"

"Of course," he said. "But what can you do for me that I can't do myself. Most real estate companies just put a sign on the lawn and maybe stick an ad in the paper and sit back and wait. I've done that much myself."

For the next five minutes, Lauri Lee explained the problems and challenges of getting homes sold in the current market and outlined her solutions to those problems and challenges. She presented all of her facts with confidence and quiet enthusiasm. Then she asked, "Mr. Dyer, Mrs. Dyer, what kind of sales-person do you want to have representing you to sell your home. . .someone who understands the problems and his solutions. . .or someone who just puts a sign on the lawn, an ad in the paper and waits for buyers to come?"

"Someone who knows how to get the home sold," responded Mr. Dyer. Mrs. Dyer nodded her agreement.

"I've got a great idea!" said Lauri Lee enthusiastically. "Let's measure the house, then we'll discuss the price. You can *select* a price, and I can get started right away, fair enough?"

"Fair enough," said the Dyers, simultaneously.

"Zingo!" thought Sam. "Eight ball in the side pocket. Just like she said."

55

EIGHT BALL IN THE SIDE POCKET
IS WORTH A LISTING EVERY TIME

An hour later, over a late lunch, Lauri Lee explained her system that had resulted once again in a well-priced listing with good terms from motivated sellers. "You see Sam, my eight ball in the side pocket is when I get a strong, unreserved 'Yes!' to my final question which is, 'I've got a great idea! Let's measure the house, then we can discuss price. You can select a price and I can get started right away. Fair enough?' To set that technique up. . .to make sure I'll get a strong yes there, I like to ask a very special question just before that. And that question is, 'What kind of salesperson would you like to have representing you to sell your home, someone who understands the problems and has solutions or someone who just puts a sign on the lawn, an ad in the paper and waits for a buyer to come?'

"Now, to make sure I get a strong, correct answer to that question, I always build my listing presentation around the problems of getting a home sold in the current market and my solutions to the problems. To make sure they are listening to my listing presentation with a completely open mind, I always ask a special question, which is the fourth step in my qualifying sequence, before I start my listing presentation. That question is, 'If you felt you could get the most money, the quickest sale and the fewest problems by giving me an exclusive listing today, would you do so?' That question will smoke out a valid reason someone might have as to why, in his mind, he couldn't give me the listing today. I'd much rather have objections out in the open before I tell him what I'm going to do for him, rather than after. Also, if he says yes to the question, as most people do, then it's very hard for him to have a strong objection when it's time to sign the listing and let me get started. Are you still with me?"

"You bet. That's terrific!" said Sam.

"Ok," continued Lauri Lee. "I'm still backing up. In order to make sure I get a strong yes to my fourth step in the qualifying sequence, I always ask two special questions in my third step. Question one is, 'Would it be in your best interest to have this home sold *and* closed in the next ninety days?' Everybody says yes, even if he actually doesn't have a specific deadline. Remember Mr. Dyer said he didn't *have* to be in Florida in ninety days, but it turned out that he sure *wanted* to be there. Well anyway, then, with the second question, I take thirty days away from them by saying, 'Since it normally takes about thirty days from the time someone agrees to buy your home until the time you get the money, we should have this home sold in sixty days so you can have the money in ninety days, isn't that right?' That makes the seller aware, very acutely aware, that he has thirty days less than he thought. Most people don't stop to think about the thirty days between the time someone agrees to buy and the time they actually close the deal.

"Ok," she continued, "I'm still backing up some more. In order to make sure that I get the right response to the two questions in my third step in my qualifying sequence, I ask a whole bunch of questions in my second step. And almost all of those questions start with, "What happens if. . ." Actually, what I do is probe for costs, problems and inconveniences. I make sure the sellers really understand what it's going to cost them if the home doesn't sell on time. I don't let up until they start saying 'Ouch!' I don't let up until we've piled up a big cost, or a big problem, or a big inconvenience or all three. When the cost is big enough, or the problems are big enough, or the inconveniences inconvenient enough, they will always say yes when I ask if it would be in their best interest to have the home sold *and* closed in the next ninety days. Any questions?"

"Nope," said Sam. "That's beautiful. And I suppose the first step in your qualifying sequence is just like breaking the rack and picking off the first easy shots."

"Exactly," she replied. "Step one questions are the basics: why are they selling; where are they going; when do they need, or want to be there; and if they are buying another home, do they need the money from this one to buy the next one. Their answers to those questions lead me to my 'What happens if. . .' questions."

Back at the airport, Sam was just saying thank you and goodbye when a local real estate salesman, returning from a trip, recognized Lauri Lee and said, "Are you still batting a hundred percent? I don't know how you do it."

"Eight ball in the side pocket," said Sam, "will get you a listing every time."

CHAPTER 7

EFFECTIVE
QUALIFYING

Most salespeople don't like to qualify prospects. For one thing, most of us were conditioned in childhood not to pry into other peoples' affairs and not to ask personal questions. Additionally, some of us, especially in the beginning of our sales careers, have a great fear of rejection. We are reluctant to ask. Finally, most new salespeople don't have enough prospects. Since qualifying can turn up reasons the prospects will not buy, the inexperienced salesperson feels inclined to tell his story first and let the prospect qualify themselves by accepting or rejecting.

Highly successful salespeople, such as Lauri Lee in the preceding chapter, have discovered that not only does a highly refined qualifying procedure prevent them from wasting the time of making a full presentation to an unqualified or uninterested prospect, it also increases the probability of a sale to a qualified prospect. Lauri Lee's record is rare, but not at all unique. There are a great number of salespeople who seldom, if ever, fail to get a listing from a qualified prospect. Their success, like Lauri Lee's, is based on a sound procedure and sound questions. Let's analyze Lauri Lee's techniques.

EFFECTIVE QUALIFYING

As I mentioned in a previous chapter, Ben Feldman, one of the greatest salesmen of all time, maintains that when selling becomes a procedure, it ceases to be a problem. Lauri Lee and thousands of other successful salespeople have discovered that same truth. Lauri Lee took the idea one very important step further by looking at the target, a well-priced listing with good terms from a motivated seller, and asking, basically, "What do I have to do to make that happen?" Then she designed each step in the procedure so that it not only accomplished an important task but also made the next step easy.

Her qualifying techniques actually began with her prospecting calls. Her first question on the telephone, "I see your ad says 'No Agents', but if I could find a buyer that would pay a decent price, would you accept the offer through me?", actually functions as a qualifying question as well as a prospecting technique. A seller who is reasonable and motivated is not likely to reject a good option, and a buyer willing to pay a decent price is a good option. A "yes" answer tells Lauri Lee that the seller is reasonable, logical and open-minded.

Her second question on the telephone also qualifies the prospects. "Are you *absolutely* serious about selling your home?" will result in answers such as "Of course we are. Why do you think we put the ad in the paper," and "Yes, we have to sell?" and "Yes, if we can get our price." As you can see, the second question measures the level of motivation to sell.

In a restaurant in Boyne City, Michigan, there is a sign which reads, "With these two rules to live by, you've pert-near got life skinned: never whittle towards yourself and don't spit against the wind." I can't make them rhyme, but two rules for real estate selling are, "Never take rejection personally" and "It's better to get objections out in the open before you make a listing presentation."

Like a lot of experienced salespeople, Lauri Lee does not take rejection personally; therefore, she asks questions. Lots of questions. Additionally, her procedure in asking the questions leads to a specific point that will bring any valid objections out in the open and make it difficult for the prospects to bring up minor, inconsequential objections.

Her procedure has four steps: 1) Basic questions; 2) Problems and cost questions; 3) Time and urgency questions; and 4) Eliminate objections and indecision questions. Note how each set of questions leads to the next. Her basic questions include: why are you selling? where are you going? when do you have to be there? and if you are buying another home do you need the money from this home to purchase the next one? These do not have to be asked in any fixed order, and they are not the only basic questions that can be asked. Additional questions could include: have you been out looking for a new home? have you found a new home? have you selected an area where you want to go? have you made a deposit? does your offer have to be contingent on the sale of this home?

Some years ago, an experienced and successful salesman said that he had two basic questions in the back of his mind any time he was asking qualifying questions. The first question was, "Do I understand their problem?" and the second question was "Do *they* understand their problem?" Like Lauri Lee, this man saw two groups of questions. In the first group were basic questions that helped him understand the prospect's problems and in the second group were problem and cost type questions that made sure the prospects understood their problems.

Lauri Lee's problems and costs questions almost always start with: "What happens if this home does not sell in ninety days, what are you going to do?" She then explores all of the costs, problems and inconveniences that could result from a delayed sale. Since there are four basic reasons why people sell - transfer, retirement, upgrading, and estate - let's analyze them one at a time. Incidentally, upgrading catches everything that isn't transfer, retirement or estate. (Someone once noted that even divorce could be upgrading from someones point of view.)

Regarding a transfer, explore all the costs, inconveniences and problems that may relate. Where will they live? Who pays the rent? Is a person now living in a $80,000 home likely to find a suitable place for $200 a month? How much will the rent add up to in sixty days? Ninety days? Who pays for meals? How long will the company pay? How about phone calls home? How often will he/she call home? Who pays? Can he/she always make the calls from the office? What happens if the spouse or children need to talk for a whole hour? How much will the phone calls add up to in sixty days? Ninety days? And how about air fare? Who pays? How many trips will the company pay for? How much will that add up to in sixty days? Ninety days?

Regarding a retirement, explore the costs, inconveniences and problems that relate. Where are they going? Do they already own a retirement home or condo? If yes, what are the costs of carrying the home to be sold? How much will that add up to in sixty days? Ninety days? If they don't *have* to be someplace else by a specific date, when would they *like* to be there? Why would they like to be there on a specific date? In the minds of some people a fishing tournament starting January 20th can be just as strong a motivator as a closing date on a new property. Analyze the seasonal influences on appreciation in your own area and in the area your prospects plan to locate. Appreciation tends to accelerate in the spring and flatten in the fall in the north and has just the opposite cycle in the deep South. It could be much better to take the best price possible in November in the northern Midwest and buy before the rest of the snowbirds head for the sunny South and push prices upward.

In the case of estates, how many heirs are involved? If the home sells for a thousand more or less, how much will that affect each heir? Is it better to reduce the price for a quicker sale to expedite settling the estate? Will delay in sale of the home delay disbursements of the rest of the estate?

In the case of upgrading, have they been out looking for another home? Have they found one? Have they made an offer? Did they make a deposit? When does that home close? Is it a conditional offer? What happens if that home closes before this one, what will they do? If they have to back out of the new home deal, will they lose anything? Do they really, really want that new home? How long did they look for it? How many other homes did they look at and reject before they found the home they selected? Is it their dream home? If they back out or if the owner has a right to accept a better offer because of the conditional offer that was made, will they be disappointed? How disappointed? If the move is to a smaller home to reduce costs now that the .family is grown and gone (this is not downgrading; they are upgrading their situation), how much less are the taxes, insurance, and utilities likely to be? How much will that add up to in sixty days? Ninety days?

At the end of the problems and costs questions, most prospects should be fully conscious of the size of their problem and be fully aware of all the costs, problems and inconveniences if the home does not sell on a timely basis. They should feel the full weight of the problems, just as if someone placed an extra fifty pound load on their shoulders. Keep in mind that you have not "created" the problems. You have only made them aware of the full scope of the problems.

If you have done a good job of exploring the potential problems, costs and inconveniences with problems and costs questions, you should receive, as Lauri Lee does, very positive answers to the third group of questions, the time and urgency questions. Note the powerful relationship between the second and third group of questions. With the second group of questions you have made people think about the consequences of a slower sale. The consequences are all negative and unpleasant. Then when you ask, "Wouldn't it be in your best interest to have this home sold *and* closed in the next ninety days?", it's pretty difficult to conceive of someone saying "no". You will much more likely receive very positive answers, much as "You bet!", "Absolutely!", and "Without question!"

Just by way of comparison, visualize asking the basic questions of the first group followed by the first question of the third group. "Why are you selling?" As noted in the beginning of this chapter, there is a tendency to avoid asking personal questions that seem to pry into the affairs of others. But just as a doctor must ask personal questions in order to do his or her professional job, so must we.

A very positive answer to the question, "Wouldn't it be in your best interest to have this home sold *and* closed in the next ninety days?" makes it easy to get a very positive answer to your next question, "Since almost any kind of financing takes almost thirty days to process, we should have this home sold in *sixty* days so you can have the money in *ninety* days, isn't that right?"

Again, analyze the power. With group two questions you have had the prospects think about the problems if the house takes an extra thirty or sixty days to sell. Now you're having them think about another problem: the time between a sale and a closing. Often, prospects have not considered this time period. You have just made them aware that they have thirty days *less* then they thought they had. And by so doing, you have made it easy, as Lauri Lee did, to get a positive "Yes!" to the fourth step in the procedure, eliminating objections and indecision.

Consider the dynamics of this question at this moment. First, reasons to object or hesitate may pop into the sellers minds, but now the reasons must be valid.

The human mind has an exciting ability to sift data and make fast decisions. At this moment, and in a fraction of a second, a seller's mind could analyze, "Well, if I had to list, I was going to list with that real estate fellow down the street, but he's only part time and I have a lot at stake. I wanted three opinions before I signed anything with a real estate person, but this person seems competent and professional and I doubt I'll get any more useful information from someone else. I'm still not sure that I can't do it myself, but the risk of a slow sale is greater than I thought. I could put my own time to better use. Anyway the question is, 'If I felt that I could get more money, a quicker sale and fewer problems by signing an exclusive' - that must mean they would get the commission no matter who sold it. Well, that's OK; they are doing the work. Listing today - I guess there's no real reason I couldn't sign up tonight if I decided to. And then, out loud, "Yes I would."

All that thinking in an instant!

Here are the various qualifying questions. Keep in mind that the questions in the costs, problems and inconveniences group are to stimulate your thinking. You would never ask all of these questions to one prospect.

BASIC **QUESTIONS**	**"Why are you selling?"** **"When do you have to leave/ be there/ close on the new house?"** **"Where are you going?"** **"Do you need the money from this house to buy your next home?"**

COSTS, PROBLEMS AND INCONVENIENCES QUESTIONS

"What happens if:
your new home closes before this one is sold?"
the interim (bridge, swing) financing runs out?"
you must leave for (destination) before this home sells?"
you have to come back from (destination) to close this sale?"
this home isn't sold in 60 or 90 days?"

"Who pays for:
rent until this home sells?"
interim financing?"
air fare?"
phone calls?"

TIME AND URGENCY QUESTIONS

"Would it be in your best interest to have this home sold and <u>closed</u> in 90 days?"

"Since it takes almost 30 days to close, we should have this home sold in 60 days so you can have the money in 90 days, isn't that right?"

ELIMINATE OBJECTIONS AND INDECISION

"If you felt that you could actually get the <u>most</u> money, the <u>quickest</u> sale and the <u>fewest</u> problems by giving me an exclusive listing today, would you do so?"

NOTE: Some experienced salespeople believe it is easier to get a prospect to say no than to say yes. Instead of finishing the question by saying, ". . .would you do so?" they finish by saying, ". . .is there *any* reason you wouldn't want to do so?" I have tried both ways and both ways always work.

CHAPTER 8

NOTHING SERIOUS. . .
I JUST DIED!

Joe Tusco stumbled into the office and dropped heavily into his chair. His face was ashen, his eyes bewildered, his shoulders slumped forward in utter defeat.

"How'd it go?" boomed the cheery voice of Jayson Stubbs, the branch manager, walking over to Joe's desk.

"It didn't go," replied Joe. "I felt like a jerk. I don't think I belong in real estate; I'm, a fish out of water. I never felt more stupid in my life. I'll never go through that again. This is not for me."

Jayson just smiled as Joe kept pouring out his feelings of inadequacy and defeat. When Joe finally stopped, Jayson said, "Don't worry, Joe. That happens to most everybody on their first call or two. You'll get the hang of it. Just don't give up."

"Oh no, man," responded Joe. "Never again. No way."

"What's going on?" interrupted Leo Carnes, the top salesman in the branch.

NOTHING SERIOUS . . .
I JUST DIED

"Nothing serious," replied Jayson. "Joe just made his first call on a For-Sale-By-Owner and got hit with a few questions he couldn't handle."

"Nothing serious?" blurted Joe. "I get my ego shredded, my intelligence questioned and my heredity challenged, and you say 'nothing serious'. I just died. . .and you say 'nothing serious.' You're out of your mind. I'll *never* go through that again."

"And besides," he continued, "I made two calls. On the first one, I only felt stupid because I couldn't answer some of his questions. The second guy had all kinds of reasons why he could do a better job of selling his own house than we could. I left his house almost convinced he was right. Nope - I'm not *ever* going to call on a For-Sale-By-Owner again. There's got to be a better way."

"Joe," said Leo "come with me. I have a call to make. I'd like to show you an idea."

Once outside the office and in Leo's car, Leo said confidentially, "Jayson doesn't think much of 'canned' sales pitches, but I sure do. Not 'canned' in the normal way where a sales presentation goes rigidly from 'A' to 'Z', but canned in a random sort of way."

"What do you mean?" asked Joe. "You've lost me."

"Think like a musician," responded Leo. "Let's make you a solo piano player. To get a job, or a series of jobs, where you would be able to make $20,000 a year, how many tunes or songs do you think you would have to memorize?"

"I don't know," said Joe. "Maybe. . .I don't know."

"Well," said Leo, "I have a few friends who make a living as · professional musicians and the consensus is between 500 and 1500. The more tunes you can play. . .and the better you play

70

them. . .then the more money you make."

"What's that got to do with real estate?" asked Joe.

"Watch," answered Leo, as he pulled to a stop in front of a home with a large, nicely painted For-Sale-By-Owner - By Appointment Only sign prominently displayed on the front lawn.

"This is strictly a cold call," said Leo, as they walked up the sidewalk. "By the way, stand a little back of me, be as unobtrusive as possible and don't say one word."

Leo rang the bell and stood fairly close to the front door. When he saw a face peer through the little window in the door, he took a step backward. When the door opened he took another small step backward and said, "Hi, I saw your sign. May I ask, are you co-operating with real estate?"

"No, we are not," was the curt reply, "and I wish you real estate people would just stay away."

"Well," responded Leo quickly, "may I ask you just one quick question? If. . .*if* I had a qualified buyer, *willing* to pay a price *acceptable* to you, would you accept such an offer through our company?"

"No, I don't think so. We need all the money we can get."

"I appreciate that," said Leo, "but if you felt that you could actually get more money, a quicker sale and fewer problems by doing business with real estate, would you do so?"

"Well yes, if I felt that way, but I don't feel that way."

"So if. . ." persisted Leo, "*if* I had a qualified buyer *willing* to pay a price *acceptable* to you, would you accept such an offer through my company?"

NOTHING SERIOUS . . .
I JUST DIED

"Yes, I guess we would. As long as we came out ahead."

"Fine," said Leo. "It will take just a few minutes to see enough of your home so I can tell potential buyers about it. Could I do that now?"

"Well, I suppose so. Come on in."

Leo introduced himself and Joe and quickly toured the house. The man's wife joined them to help point out features. Leo asked a few questions and found that they had to sell within seventy days because their new home was almost ready.

"Folks," said Leo, "in selling this house, do you want to net the most money possible?"

"Of course," responded the husband, "that's why we're selling it ourselves."

"But," countered Leo, "if you felt that you had the best chance to net the most money by listing with me, is there any reason you wouldn't want to do so?"

"No," responded the husband again. "I want the most money. If you can prove to me that you can get me more money, sure, I'll list with you. But you will have to convince me, because I don't see how you can do it."

"Ok, Leo," thought Joe, "show him. . .and me. . .how you are going to charge a six percent commission and still net him more money."

"Ok, Mr. Salesman," thought the seller's wife, "show my husband. . .and me. . .how you are going to charge us a six percent commission and still net us more money."

72

"Folks," said Leo, "right now, today, in this area, there are a certain number of people who are absolutely serious about finding and buying a new home. Would you agree with that?"

"Yes."

"One of the ways they look for a new home is in the newspaper. Isn't that right?"

"Yes," they both agreed.

Leo then showed the sellers a Sunday newspaper with an "X" on every home advertised for sale by a real estate firm and an "O" on every one for sale by an owner. "When they open up the paper," he explained, "here's what they see: 88.2% of all homes for sale are in the hands of real estate firms. Only 11.8% are for sale by owners.

"Basically," he continued, "there are four kinds of people who look at homes. The first kind are in a hurry. They have a sense of urgency. They may have been transferred, or have already sold their present home, or they may just be the kind of people who like to make quick decisions.

"The second kind are serious, but not in a hurry. They have no sense of urgency. They may be young people, or other first time buyers, proceeding cautiously. Or, they may be second or third time buyers looking for a special home.

"The third kind are looking for a real bargain. Their idea is to save the commission that goes to a real estate firm, or worse. . . they want to find someone who is desperate to sell so they can buy the home for thousands of dollars less than fair market value.

"Finally the fourth kind will never buy. They can't afford to buy, or they just don't want to buy, but they sure enjoy looking

NOTHING SERIOUS . . .
I JUST DIED

at homes for a pastime.

"Now folks, if real estate firms have 88.2% of all the homes for sale, where do the serious buyers *have* to go?"

"To real estate firms, I guess," said the husband. His wife nodded her agreement.

"So what kind of people are left over for you. . .bargain hunters and casual lookers, isn't that right?"

"Yes," they both agreed.

"Do you see how the odds are stacked against you? Do you see how you have the best chance to net the most money by listing with a professional real estate agent?"

The sellers answered yes to both questions, but the husband added, "but actually, we had planned to give the listing to a salesman who lives down the street if we did decide to sell through real estate."

Joe's heart thumped and he suddenly felt uncomfortably hot, as his own feelings of inadequacy in handling this objection caused him to flush. "Blast," he thought, "it doesn't make any difference how much you know about selling houses. If the sellers have a friend, you can't get the listing anyway. This is no way to make a living."

But Leo continued, unperturbed. "In addition to that is there any other reason you would hesitate to have me represent you to sell your home?"

"No."

"May I ask, if you felt that someone else could actually get you more money, a quicker sale and fewer problems, would you still be committed to giving the listing to your neighbor?"

"Oh, we're not committed," he said.

"Folks," responded Leo, "you will always be glad you took action with me today. I don't believe you can find anyone who will work harder, or more professionally, to get you the most money, the quickest sale and the fewest problems, which I know you want. Isn't that right?"

"You're right," said the sellers. "You can list our home. How much do you think we should be asking?"

Thirty minutes later, as Leo and Joe drove back to the office with a ninety day exclusive listing at a good market price, Joe said, "I don't believe it! I don't believe it! You made it look so simple."

"Joe," said Leo, "every word I said was memorized, just like a musician memorizes music. I just 'played the songs' they needed to hear in order to make a good decision. That's what I mean by the random selection of 'canned' presentations. What a musician needs is a hundred or so songs completely memorized so he can play what the audience wants to hear. And what you and I need is a hundred or so completely memorized language techniques covering everything from prospecting to handling objections. Then your ego won't get shredded, and you won't ever feel like a jerk."

"Yeah," responded Joe dejectedly, "but you were lucky. That pitch won't work every time. For-Sale-by-Owners still look like the hard way to go."

"I'll answer all three of your points," responded Leo. "First, I have as much good luck as I have bad luck. Second, you are right, those points don't work every time. That's why you need to have a lot of points. Third, For-Sale-By-Owners are sometimes a little more difficult to deal with, but they are a highly visible source of prospects. That's why I work them. Also, even though a lot of real estate salespeople call private sellers on the phone, very few go to the house, and fewer still get in the house. Actually, I figure I have very little competition. Let's make another call. You pick the house this time."

Leo drove down a few streets that Joe selected until they spotted a private seller sign. The owner was cutting the grass and shut off the motor as Leo stopped in the drive and got out of the car.

"Hi," said Leo, "I saw your sign. . ."

"If you are in real estate, the answer is no!" said the owner curtly.

"May I ask just one quick question?" responded Leo.

"No!" was the abrupt reply, and starting the lawn mower to end further conversation, the owner turned his back and resumed cutting. Leo raised his right hand and, with a broad smile on his face, gave the man a church-like blessing.

"You went down in flames," said Joe, as they drove away. "I told you this stuff wouldn't work all the time."

"I didn't say it would work every time. But it works often enough for me to make a lot of money every year. Let's find another house and try it again."

"Did I see you bless that guy?" said Joe.

"Yes, you did," said Leo. "I only have two things to work with: my time and my attitude. I don't let anyone mess them up. If I can't do business with someone, I excuse myself as soon as possible. If they are rude, I bless them. It does wonders for my attitude."

Three blocks later Joe selected another private seller. The sign bore the notation "By Appointment Only." Leo range the bell and stood close to the door.

"Hi!" he said when the door opened. "I saw your sign. May I ask, are you co-operating with real estate?"

"What do you mean co-operating?" asked the owner.

"Well, if I had a qualified buyer, willing to pay a price acceptable to you, would you accept such an offer through my firm?"

"Sure, if you add your commission onto the price I'm asking, why not." The seller's face had the smug look of victory. It was obvious that he had used this ploy before to get rid of other salespeople. Again, Joe's heart thumped as he felt the agony of defeat. Although new to real estate, he had been in long enough to know that an overpriced listing was not too likely to result in a commission.

But Leo was unperturbed. He had had this response before and knew that the place to deal with this particular objection was in the house after he decided that he wanted the listing, after he had made a listing presentation, and even after a price had been selected. So all he said was, "Fine, it will take just a few minutes to see enough of your home so we can tell prospective buyers about it. May we do that now?"

The owner, Jim Elek, agreed and conducted Leo and Joe through the house. As Elek pointed out various features, Leo asked qualifying questions and found out that Elek was being transferred and had to be there in ten weeks.

"It's very showable, and I have it priced right, so it should sell pretty quick," said Elek. "Frankly, I don't see how you can add your commission and be competitive."

77

NOTHING SERIOUS . . .
I JUST DIED

"Mr. Elek," responded Leo, "if you felt that you could *net* the most money by listing your home with a professional real estate agent, would you do so?"

"Of course, but how can I net more if I pay you a commission, unless you add your commission to my price which will over-price my house and then it won't sell at all?"

Leo smiled. All he wanted to hear was the "of course" which told him the man would list if new evidence gave him a new insight into the problems that face all private sellers. And Leo had the evidence.

"May I ask," said Leo, "what is the single *greatest* advantage you would have in selling your home directly to a buyer?"

"Save the commission so I net more, what else?" responded Elek.

"Right," said Leo. "May I ask, what is the single *greatest* advantage a buyer would have in buying the home directly from you?"

The look on Elek's face told Leo that Elek hadn't thought about the buyer's point of view. When he didn't answer, Leo said, "The buyer's single greatest advantage is to save the *same* commission you are hoping to save, isn't that right?"

"Yes, but. . .well, I can split the commission with a buyer and we'll both save three percent," responded Elek with a little less confidence than he had shown up to now.

"May I ask, is there any possible *dis*advantage you would have in continuing to try to sell your home yourself?" asked Leo, avoiding the commission splitting debate.

"Nothing serious. I'll probably miss a few golf games, that's all."

"Mr. Elek," said Leo, "how long have you had your home advertised for sale?"

"Only for about two weeks. That's all," he responded confidently.

"How many calls did you have last week?"

"Quite a few. I don't remember exactly."

"How many were from real estate people?"

"Only about half. I had quite a few good calls from people who sounded serious."

"Of the calls that were not from real estate, how many people came out to see your home?"

"Uh, let's see. Oh yes, there were two."

"And did either of them make an offer?"

"No."

"Mr. Elek, ninety percent of all *direct* buyers are not qualified to buy the homes they look at. Ninety percent of all *direct* buyers will not be qualified to buy your home when they come here."

Elek sat down heavily in his favorite chair. Leo's incisive questions had laid bare a truth he had been hiding from himself. Why should a buyer buy directly except to save the commission? And the fact that no one had made an offer in two weeks wasn't proof that he couldn't sell successfully, but two weeks *had* passed and there were no offers.

"Why will most buyers be unqualified?" he asked Leo.

NOTHING SERIOUS . . .
I JUST DIED

"Mr Elek," responded Leo, "when a buyer is *serious* and intends to buy directly from an owner, the first thing he does is qualify himself. He goes down to the bank and finds out how much he can afford to pay. If he finds out that he can afford a fifty thousand dollar home, he doesn't look at fifties, he looks at sixties and seventies. If he finds out that he can afford a hundred thousand dollar home, he doesn't look at hundreds, he looks at one ten, one twenty, and one thirty. Remember, he's a bargain hunter.

"Now, when he goes through the house, he sizes up the home and he sizes up the seller. If he finds out that you have just begun to sell, or that you are not willing to accept an offer, he will usually not make one. But if he finds out that you are open to an offer, maybe getting desperate, he will make an offer. However, it will usually be ten percent, twenty percent, even thirty percent below fair market value because. . .that's all he can afford."

Leo watched Elek's eyes and face for a few seconds looking for some indication of how Elek was accepting this information, but no clue was forthcoming. Finally, Elek said, "Well, you have explained why people who have seen the house haven't made an offer, but I still have a few weeks. Somebody out there wants a house like this, and if I keep on trying, I'll find them."

"Mr. Elek," responded Leo, "if you do find a buyer, statistically, you will lose three to five percent. That means that you will net three to five percent *less* than if you listed with a real estate agent and paid a commission."

"That's hard to believe," responded Elek.

"Here's why," said Leo. "First, most owners accept less. Direct buyers are usually bargain hunters looking for desperate sellers. In fact, a ten year study showed that owners selling directly

80

to buyers grossed 9.5 percent less than when similar homes were sold by real estate firms. Mr. Elek, anytime you. . .or I. . .or anyone. . .buys something where a salesperson or firm is involved, we expect to pay fair prices. But anytime you. . .or I. . .or anyone. . .buys something directly from the owner, we expect to pay less, isn't that right?"

Elek had to agree and Leo continued. "Second, the owner pays for all of his own advertising. And it's quite easy for an owner to spend one percent of the value of the home in advertising.

"Third, it usually takes an owner longer to get a sale, and that often results in extra taxes, extra interest, extra utilities, extra insurance and sometimes extra travel and long distance phone calls. All of that can add up to a percent or two.

"Fourth, the owner usually pays higher attorney fees. Mr. Elek, when you sell through a real estate firm, the attorneys *check* our work. When you sell directly to a buyer, the attorneys *do* the work. It could take an attorney half an hour to check my work. It could take him five hours to do the work, and you get billed accordingly.

"Add them all up, Mr. Elek. Accept less; pay for the advertising; pay extra taxes, insurance, interest and utilities if you wind up owning more than one home for a time; and pay extra attorney fees. It's quite easy for the total to exceed the commission we ask. Mr. Elek, do you see how the odds are stacked against you?"

"It looks like I'd have a better chance of hitting a hole-in-one than I would of saving the commission by selling this house myself," he said.

"What's your handicap?" asked Leo.

"Nine," said Elek.

81

NOTHING SERIOUS . . .
I JUST DIED

"Why don't you work on your handicap while I work on finding a buyer?" asked Leo.

"You have yourself a deal," said Elek. "Sign me up."

"Well Joe," said Leo, when they were back in the car, "what did you learn today?"

"Well," responded Joe, after a long silence, "mostly, I learned how to swim."

"Run that by me again," said Leo quizzically.

"When I was four," explained Joe, "my granddad took me swimming in the river behind his farm. Mostly the river was shallow enough to walk across on the rocks, but in certain parts there were deep pools. The swimming hole behind the farm was 10, maybe 12 feet deep. I jumped right in. . .and began to sink to the bottom. Granddad pulled me out, put me over a log to get the water out of my lungs and, when he was sure I was all right, said, 'Joey boy, it would be a good idea for you to learn to swim before you go jumping into deep water.'

"So to answer your question, today I learned that it's just as dumb to run off calling on prospects before you know what to say as it is to jump in 10 feet of water before you know how to swim. I was in deep water this morning. . .and I was dying. This afternoon, I learned what I need to learn. I'm ready for lesson two. Where do I start?"

EPILOGUE

Napoleon said, "We rule men with words."

Words that communicate effectively are the weapons that defeat ignorance, the persuaders that sell, the tools that build successful lives.

The inability to communicate effectively is a crippling handicap in this fiercely competitive world. The inability to say what is necessary to be said at the precise moment it is needed holds many at the bottom rungs of income - for life.

Joe Tusco "died" in his first attempt to function as a salesman for lack of the right words to say. Leo Carnes "lived," and most likely lived very well, because he communicated effectively. And Jayson Stubbs' casual dismissal of a very serious problem with the oft-expressed advice to "just don't give up" was not the correct solution. "Practice does *not* make perfect. Perfect practice makes perfect." Vince Lombardy said that to his football teams and turned them into champions.

You can accept Lombardy's advice. . .and the truth that "every word counts". . .and through perfect practice, climb the ladder of successful, effective communication; or you can keep on ad-libbing, continuously groping for something to say, and stand with the masses on the lower rungs of achievement. Today you can chose to live abundantly. . .or die in agony. Choose to live!

CHAPTER 9

LISTING
PRIVATE SELLERS

A broker friend of mine once said, "In the beginning, everything is hard. Once you have learned it, everything is easy." He went on to point out that when he was learning to fly, just keeping the wings level was difficult, but now, after many hours of training, he was comfortable flying into Chicago's O'Hare Field at rush hour in a rainstorm.

For many real estate salespeople, obtaining a listing from a private seller is extremely difficult, even traumatic. For others, like Leo Carnes, it's quite easy. What makes the difference? Skills. . .and attitude.

In order to be highly effective in listing private sellers, you must have three things going for you. First, you must have an unshakable belief that the prospect will benefit by listing with a real estate professional. You must also have an unshakable belief that you are, indeed, a professional in the true sense of the word. Second, in order to have and sustain an unshakable belief, you must have a total understanding of the problems and challenges. Third, you must have the ability to communicate confidently and effectively that which you know and believe.

85

LISTING PRIVATE SELLERS

Over the years, I have met a great many salespeople who do not call on private sellers because they, the salespeople, do not believe they can net the seller more money. They don't understand why the seller cannot sell the home for as much as a real estate firm. Tragically, many real estate salespeople feel that a house will sell for X dollars regardless of who sells it, but that's not true. Statistically, real estate firms gross more for a house than private sellers, and some real estate salespeople know how to get more for a home than other real estate salespeople.

The purpose of this chapter is to take you step by step through the problems, challenges and obstacles that statistically prevent a private seller from netting as much money by selling direct rather than selling through a professional real estate agent. As we progress, you will see that Leo Carnes' sales techniques, as demonstrated in the previous chapter, are built around those problems and challenges. This information will help you gain, and sustain, an unshakable belief that the private seller will benefit most by having you represent him to sell his home.

Additionally, this chapter will pinpoint specific things you can say that will cause most private sellers to understand why the odds are against them. Once you learn to communicate those ideas confidently, you will have the skill to list many more private sellers.

Let's begin by exploring two words, odds and statistically.

If you put your own home up for sale privately today, I cannot say that you will not net more money than by selling through real estate. But I can say that the *odds* are against you. I can say that *statistically* you will lose.

The best way to demonstrate the truth of that statement is to share with you an analogy we call "The Las Vegas Concept."

Every year, a few people go to Las Vegas, put a dollar in a slot machine and hit the jackpot, but the odds are against that happening for most people. Don't you agree? Every year, some people go to Las Vegas and then come home with more money than they started with, but the odds are against that for most people. Isn't that right? And every year, some people break even, but the odds are even against that for most people. Why? Because somebody has to pay for all of the lights and glitter, for the high priced entertainment and the low priced drinks. If most people didn't lose money in Las Vegas, then Las Vegas, as we know it, would not exist.

Every year, a few people put a "For Sale By Owner" sign on the lawn, overprice the home by five or ten percent and find a cash buyer in three days. They literally hit the jackpot. But I think you will agree that the odds are against that happening for most people. Every year, some private sellers net more money than if they sold through real estate, but the odds are against that. And every year, some private sellers break even. They neither gain nor lose. But the odds are even against that. Why? Because 85.8% of all homes listed for sale in the entire United States are listed by real estate firms. (In Canada it's 85.9%·) Experience has shown that half of the people attempting to sell privately today will list with someone in real estate within the next thirty days. If the average individual could stay home for a few weekends and net an extra thousand dollars by selling privately, the real estate industry would not exist as we know it today. If the average seller could net more money by selling privately, then we, the real estate profession, would have 14.2% of the listings, and 85.8% would be private sellers.

I cannot say that if you go to Las Vegas you will absolutely lose money, but I'd be most willing to bet that way. And if you choose to sell your home privately I cannot say you will absolutely lose money, but I'd also be willing to bet you would.

One of the problems a private seller has is that the very reason for selling directly is exactly the same reason to buy directly, that is - to save the commission that goes to real estate firms. Leo Carnes vividly brings this point to the attention of the sellers with a technique we call "Single Greatest Advantage."

"May I ask, what is the single. . .*greatest* advantage. . .you would have in selling your home directly to a buyer?" Notice the emphasis on the word greatest. That emphasis causes most sellers to respond with something regarding saving the commission or getting more money. The second question looks at the situation from the buyer's perspective. "May I ask, what is the single. . .*greatest* advantage. . .a buyer would have in buying the home directly from you?"

Experience has shown that most sellers have not stopped to consider the buyer's perspective. That second question causes some sellers to gasp and acknowledge that the buyer is after the same goal they are - saving the commission.

Some sellers, of course, won't readily see or acknowledge the buyer's advantage so when someone doesn't answer the question or answers incorrectly, a good response is, "The buyer's single greatest advantage is to save the commission you hope to save. Isn't that right?"

A few years ago, one of the agents attending my five day course in Edmonton obtained a referral. The prospect had just received notice of transfer to Toronto. That evening, after class, the agent hurried out to the home of the prospect. As he was walking up the porch steps, the owner came out the front door, a "For Sale By Owner" sign in one hand and a hammer in the other and said, "If you are in real estate, save your breath. I'm selling it myself." The agent asked the first question and got the expected reply. Then he asked the second question. The seller said, "D--- I never thought of that. Come on in and list the house."

The third question of this technique is dynamic. Not for the answers it gets, but for the control it gives the salesperson. When Leo Carnes asked the second question, "What is the single greatest advantage the buyer would have in buying directly from you?" his prospect answered by saying he and the buyer could split the commission. Well, that's a possibility, if in fact, the seller can find a buyer who is willing to split the commission. In any event, it is not a subject that bears much discussion. The third question permits you to avoid any such discussion and continue the presentation along the lines you wish. The third question is, "Is there any possible disadvantage you would have in continuing to try to sell your home yourself?"

Notice the words "continuing to try." We never acknowledge that the private seller will be successful, only that they may continue to try.

It is important, at this point, to go off a bit on what may first appear to be a tangent. This third question has caused some of the students in my courses a great deal of difficulty until they have thought out the whole situation.

The words "listing presentation" are frequently misused in real estate. Many salespeople go to a home, spend an hour discussing price and terms and say they have made a listing presentation. From our perspective that is a "pricing presentation." As we see it, there are eight separate selling functions involved in securing a listing. Those eight functions are: prospecting, qualifying, private seller presentation, listing presentation, pricing presentation, feed back question, closing and handling objections or indecision. A full discussion of those eight functions appears in Chapter 12, but for the moment I want to concentrate on the difference between a private seller presentation and a listing presentation.

In the listing presentation, you tell the seller why he will benefit by having you represent him to sell the home. The private seller presentation, on the other hand, is intended to tell the seller why the odds are stacked against him as a private seller. It is intended to focus on problems, obstacles and inconveniences, but not on solutions to the problems.

One man put it this way, "The private seller presentation convinces the sellers to list with a real estate firm and the listing presentation convinces them to list with me."

Another salesperson said, "If I don't convince the sellers that the odds are against them and that their best hope lies with a real estate professional before I start telling them what I will do for them, they almost always discount my efforts by saying, 'I can do it myself'."

So in the private seller presentation, all we want to focus on are the problems and obstacles. The third question of "Single Greatest Advantage" allows us to do just that. Keep in mind that how the prospects answer this question is immaterial. It makes no difference if they say there aren't any disadvantages or they say they can't think of any disadvantages, or they mention a mild or strong disadvantage. What they say *may* influence our answer, but it doesn't have to.

Consider how this worked for Leo Carnes in the preceding chapter. Leo asks Mr. Elek, "Is there any possible disadvantage you would have in continuing to try to sell your home yourself?" It is hard to think of a single possible answer that would have prevented Leo from asking how long the home had been advertised as the next question.

Now, let's consider the problems and obstacles. One obstacle is that most potential buyers who call on private sellers are not qualified to buy the house. My experience is that nine out of ten people will not be qualified. Common sense tells us why. The direct buyer wants a bargain. Anytime we buy from a store or through a salesperson, we expect to pay fair price. But anytime we buy directly from an owner, we expect to pay less. In effect, we expect to save the commissions or profits that would normally go to the salesperson or store owner.

Some years ago, my brother was being transferred from Florida to Michigan. When I arrived for a visit, I found a "For Sale By Owner" sign firmly planted on his front lawn. In the discussion after dinner, I told him that ninety percent of all direct buyers were not qualified to buy his house. He said, "You're wrong. It's only eighty percent." I asked how he had determined the eighty percent figure. He said, "Every time a potential buyer comes to the door, I tell him that the fair market value of the home is $85,000 and I ask him if that is in the ballpark of what he can afford. There have been exactly twenty potential buyers, and sixteen said eighty-five was outside their budget. Sixteen out of twenty is eighty percent."

I asked him if the other four had then inspected the house. He said yes. Then I asked if any of them had shown a high interest in the house. He said they all did. Then I asked if any of them had made an offer. He said no and I asked if he knew why. He said no. I asked, "Do you suppose at least two of the four lied about being able to afford $85,000?" He allowed that that was possible, and I allowed that I'd stick with my original statement; that ninety percent are not qualified to look at the house.

Another obstacle is that most homes for sale are already listed with a real estate firm. A comprehensive study by myself and members of my staff, covering an eighteen month period and sixty-six cities and towns in the United States showed that 85.8% of all homes listed for sale are listed by real estate firms; only 14.2% are listed by owners. (This study was published under the title "Statistics That Sell" in *Real Estate Today*.) A similar study done in Canada showed that 85.9% of all listed homes were listed by real estate, a tenth of a percent difference.

LISTING PRIVATE SELLERS

As was well expressed by Leo in the preceding chapter, still another hurdle for the private seller is the reality that there are four types of people who look at homes. In brief: buyers in a hurry, buyers not in a hurry, bargain hunters and casual lookers.

Putting these last two problems together brings forth some tough questions. If someone has been transferred and 85% of the homes are listed by real estate, where, statistically, is he most likely to go to find a home? If someone sells his present home and has given thirty days occupancy, and 85% of the homes for sale are in the hands of real estate firms, where is the most likely place he will go? How about the buyer who just likes to make quick decisions? He has no eternal urgency, but he has other, more important things to do in life than shop for a new home. If 85% of the homes are listed with real estate, where is he most likely to go?

How about the first time buyer? Young people, or other first time buyers "proceeding cautiously," as Leo put it. Often, they need the security of a professional. And 85% of the potentially acceptable homes are listed by real estate. How about the second or third time buyers looking for that very special home. They may look for two weeks or two months or two years. Sure, they will take the time to look at privately listed homes, but 85% of the potentially suitable homes are listed by real estate firms. And once an agent finds out exactly what it is the specialty buyer wants, he watches new listings for that perfect match. Again, with 85% of the new listings, month after month, going to real estate firms, where is that second time buyer most likely to go?

Which now leaves us, or rather the private seller with bargain hunters and casual lookers. The bargain hunters avoid real estate listings because they want to save big money. And the casual lookers, bless them, can't afford to buy or don't want to buy, but they sure enjoy looking at homes as a pastime, and private sellers are ever so nice. They offer coffee and say nice things like, "take your time."

One sales lady put it this way. Eighty-five percent is the same as seventeen out of twenty. Suppose there are twenty homes for sale in a specific area, and a buyer needs a home with three bedrooms, two baths, attached garage, walking distance to school, priced in the low seventies and thirty day occupancy. The buyer has a choice, he can contact a real estate salesperson, who can determine the buyer's needs, study the seventeen listings, eliminate those that don't come close and make appointments to see two or three - or he can contact the three private sellers and ask if they have three bedrooms, two baths, etc. The question is why should he do the work if he can't save a substantial amount of money? Why do the work and pay full price?

Yet another problem is that the seller, by selling privately, pays for all of his own advertising. He cannot get group rates. He cannot make one ad do the promotional work for three or four listings. And it is easy to spend one percent of the value of the house in advertising.

Still another problem is that, as a result of all of the above problems, it usually takes an owner longer to sell privately. Very often this means the owner winds up paying extra taxes, extra interest, extra insurance, extra utilities. And for a transfer situation, it can mean extra travel, extra rental costs, extra long distance phone bills.

And how about this challenge? A few years ago, the Salt Lake City FHA (Federal Housing Administration) office disclosed that fourteen percent of all FHA applications submitted through real estate firms were declined. They also reported that eighty-seven percent of all FHA applications submitted by direct buyers were declined. So when a private seller finds a direct buyer who needs FHA assistance, the seller may be caught up in a game called "Now you see it - now you don't." I don't know about you, but I'd much rather be looking at odds of eighty-six percent in favor of success than odds of eighty-seven percent in favor of failure.

Finally, the private seller usually pays higher attorney fees. As Leo Carnes states so well, "When you sell your house through a real estate firm the attorney *checks* our work. But when you sell your home directly, the attorney *does* the work. It could take an attorney half an hour to check my work. It could take him five hours to do the work, and you get billed accordingly."

So there you have it, problem after problem; and because of all of those problems, a private seller statistically nets three to five percent less by selling directly than by selling through real estate firms. Add them up, the private seller accepts less because the direct seller offers less; the private seller pays for his or her own advertising; it takes longer and he pays extra taxes, etc; and he usually pays extra attorney fees.

One salesman clinches his private sellers this way, "How much is three percent of your home? Would you take three percent of the value of your home today and hand that money over to a complete stranger? Isn't that exactly what you are doing by selling your home yourself and netting three percent less?"

Another says, "Would you take three percent of the value of your home, in cash, and lay it on a crap table in Las Vegas for one roll of the dice? Aren't you taking the same risk by trying to sell your house yourself? Do you really want to do that?"

As I said at the beginning of this chapter, to be effective with private sellers, you must start with an unshakable belief that the seller will benefit most by listing with real estate and particularly by listing with you. In order to have, and sustain, that kind of unshakable belief, you have to have a full understanding of the problems confronting the private seller. The problems we have discussed so far are the key problems used by Leo Carnes in the preceding chapter. There are other problems for the private seller, but we have found these few to be the most potent.

The visuals we use in our "Visual Aid" to illustrate and reinforce these points are shown on the sample pages printed at the end of the book.

Just to round things out, here are a a few additional points that have been used successfully by real estate agents to obtain listings from private sellers. The private seller cannot qualify a prospect very well. He cannot help an indecisive buyer make a decision. He cannot help a buyer compare two or more homes. Any effort to close usually weakens the seller's position of strength. He cannot help the buyer find mortgage money.

Here now, in review, are the key techniques used by Leo Carnes to list private sellers. Remember, as the broker said, "In the beginning everything is hard. Once you have learned it, everything is easy." Develop the skill to communicate these points confidently and you will soon be listing a lot more private sellers.

SINGLE GREATEST ADVANTAGE

"May I ask, what is the single. . .greatest advantage. . .you would have in selling your home directly to a buyer?"

"May I ask, what is the single. . . greatest advantage. . .a buyer would have in buying the home directly from you?"

"Is there any possible disadvantage you would have in continuing to try to sell your home yourself?"

CALLS AND OFFERS

"How long have you advertised your home for sale?"

"How many calls did you receive last week?"

"How many of those calls were from real estate people?"

"Of those not from real estate people, how many came out to see your home?"

"How many made an offer?" (Usually the answer is none.)

"Do you know why no one made an offer?" (Usually the answer is no, which leads us to the 90% technique - 90% of all direct buyers are not qualified, etc.)

NOTE: If the prospect says that someone did make an offer, your next question is "Did you accept it?" The answer is no. (If he did accept it, you wouldn't be there.) Your next question is, "May I ask why you didn't accept it?" The prospect's response is almost always that the offer was too low. Your next question is "Do you know why the offer was too low?" The usual answer is no, which leads you to the 90% technique as above.

ADDITIONAL NOTE: Sometimes the prospect has to say that there were no calls last week, or that all the calls were from real estate salespeople. Your next question is, "Do you know why there were no calls from prospective buyers?". The usual answer is no, which leads you to the 85% technique which essentially says that if we, real estate people, have 85% of the listings, we get the calls from the serious buyers.

**90% NOT
QUALIFIED**

"90% of all _direct_ buyers are not qualified to buy the homes they look at. 90% of all _direct_ buyers will not be qualified to buy your home when they come to see you. Here's why.

"If a buyer is serious. . .and intends to buy the home directly from a buyer, the first thing he does is qualify himself. He goes down to the bank and finds out how much he can afford to pay. If he finds out that he can afford to pay $70,000, he doesn't look at $70,000 homes. He looks at $80,000, $85,000 and $90,000 homes. Remember, he's a bargain hunter.

"When he goes through the house, he sizes up the home and he sizes up the seller. If he finds out that you have just begun to sell or that you are not willing to accept an offer, he will usually not make one. But, if he finds out that you are open to an offer, maybe getting desperate, he will make an offer, but it will usually be 10%, 20%, even 30% below fair market value because that's all he can afford."

"If you do find a buyer, statistically you will lose three to five percent. That means that you will _net_ three to five percent _less_ than if you sold through a real estate agent and paid a commission. Here's why.

"First, most owners accept less. Direct buyers are usually bargain hunters. A ten year study showed that owners grossed 9.5% _less_ when selling directly than when selling through real estate firms. Anytime you. . .or I. . .or anyone. . .buys anything where a salesperson or store is involved, we expect to pay fair prices. But, any time you. . .or I. . .or anyone buys something directly from an owner, we automatically expect to pay less, isn't that right?

"Second, the owner pays for all of his own advertising. . .and it's quite easy for an owner to spend one percent of the value of a home in advertising.

"Third, it usually takes an owner longer to get a sale. That often results in extra taxes, extra interest, extra utilities, extra insurance, and sometimes extra travel and long distance phone calls. All of that can add up to a percent or two.

99

"Fourth, the owner usually pays higher attorney fees. When you sell through real estate firms, the attorney checks our work. When you sell directly to a buyer, the attorney <u>does</u> the work. It could take an attorney half an hour to check my work. It could take an attorney five hours to do the work. . . and you get billed accordingly.

"Add them all up - accept less; pay for the advertising; pay extra taxes, utilities, interest, and insurance; and pay extra attorney fees. It's quite easy for the total to exceed the real estate commission.

"Do you see how the odds are stacked against you?"

85% LISTED WITH REAL ESTATE

"Right now, today, in (city) there are a certain number of people who are absolutely serious about finding and buying a new home, would you agree?

"One of the ways they look for a home is in the newspaper, isnt that right?

"And when they look in (name of paper) here's what they see:_____% of all homes for sale are in the hands of real estate firms, only _____% are for sale by owners.

"If real estate has _____% of the listings, where do the <u>serious</u> buyers have to go?"

FOUR KINDS OF BUYERS

"Basically, there are four kinds of people who look at homes. The first kind are in a hurry. They have a sense of urgency. They may have been transferred, or already sold their present home, or they may just be the kind of people who like to make quick decisions.

"The second kind are serious, but not in a hurry. They have no sense of urgency. They may be young people, or other first time buyers, proceeding cautiously.

"The third kind are looking for a real bargain. Their idea is to save the commission that goes to a real estate firm or what's worse, they want to find someone who is desperate to sell so they can buy the home for thousands of dollars less than fair market value.

"And the fourth kind will never buy. They can't afford to or just don't want to, but they sure enjoy looking at homes as a pastime.

"Do you see how we can save you from having unqualified strangers going through your home?"

CHAPTER 10

THE LISTING
MACHINE

Dick Woodfin was known in his company as "The Listing Machine." The title was well deserved because Dick had maintained between seventy-five and one hundred listings each year for the past three years. His sales to listing ratio exceeded the local average by anywhere from thirty to fifty percent. This year, for example, with the local economy way off, the board average showed that only twenty-two percent of the listings had sold. Seventy-eight percent had expired. Dick's average was still almost sixty percent sales. And his income had increased for the year because he had already listed an extra twenty homes.

Dale Willis, owner of the company where Dick was licensed, was frustrated and angry. When he broke into sales twenty-eight years ago, his manager had told him that in order to be good at selling, one had to be a good talker. Dale saw himself as a good talker and, following his manager's instructions, made a great many prospecting calls, did a lot of talking and succeeded well beyond his expectations. Later, as a sales manager, he hired salespeople based on their ability to come across as good talkers and, for the most part, found the strategy to be effective. Most of the people he recruited were at least modestly successful and some had proven to be outstanding.

THE LISTING MACHINE

Then he became a broker, and over a period of five years, had built a business of fourteen offices with over three hundred salespeople. He had selected managers who were good talkers, and had instructed them to find good talkers as salespeople. The managers had done as instructed and for most of the five years listings and sales increased steadily. Many of the areas top producers were with his company and as a result Dale had become wealthy.

Now times had changed. The economy was having devastating results on the real estate industry. Business volume in units sold for his area had fallen over fifty percent, and his good talkers weren't talking so good anymore. Many had quit real estate altogether. Others had transferred to other companies hoping to find greener grass, but as usual had found the grass just as hard to cut. Still others hung on, complaining instead of selling. And as the year progressed, office after office turned from profit to loss. The pinch was beginning to hurt.

Now, studying the latest financial reports, Dale showed his frustration and anger. Only one office showed a decent profit. And only one salesperson in that office was doing an outstanding job. What was wrong with the other three hundred? If one person could still list and sell, why not the rest? Especially since this one person, Dick Woodfin, wasn't even a good talker.

Suddenly Dale knew what he had to do. Quickly he found Dick Woodfin's agent file folder and reviewed his history. Woodfin had been accepted as a representative five years ago with reservations. "Not a good talker. Too shy. Doesn't speak up. Not much success with previous firm. Probability of success slim, but worth a chance. Draws and advances not recommended." The cryptic notes by the then current branch manager pretty well told how the manager felt, but the manager was wrong. The semi-annual activity summary showed steady growth with no reversal when the economy changed. This non-talker must have a system. A system that works when talking doesn't. Dale invited Dick Woodfin for a fishing weekend at his island retreat in the Georgian Bay.

Dale and Dick each popped the top on a can of beer and settled down in the chairs on the screened in porch just as the sun began to set behind the pines to the west of the cabin and long shadows darkened the water in the bay. The day's fishing had been good, and Dick had turned out to be a fair fisherman for an amateur. Fresh pan fried lake trout, walleye and northern pike had made an excellent dinner and an excellent conclusion to a great day. Now however, Dale was anxious to find some answers to the questions that had been forming in his mind.

"Dick," he began, "for a lot of years I've had some views about selling that worked very well, up until now. Since you have been able to continue your high listing and sales production all during this down cycle, I figure you must have a pretty good system that I've overlooked. Can you tell me what it is?"

"Gee," replied Dick, "I don't know that I have a specific system. I just have a bunch of things I always do when I make a listing presentation and I have a bunch of things I do to make sure my listings have the best chance of selling over the competition."

In the silence that followed Dick's reply, Dale analyzed the problem. All day Dick had proven to be a non-talker. He very seldom showed the kind of enthusiasm that Dale was accustomed to. He seldom started a conversation. He answered all questions directly and without elaboration. "How in the world," Dale asked himself, "does someone this reserved set·the kinds of sales records he has? He's *got* to have a system, even if he doesn't think he does." Dale took a deep breath and said to himself, "I'm going to get the answers if I have to ask one thousand questions and suffer through one thousand short answers." Out loud, he said to Dick, "How did you get started in selling in the first place?"

"My uncle was a salesman and made lots of money. I figured I could too."

"How did you happen to discover the bunch of things you do to get a home to sell?"

Suddenly, a near miracle took place. Dick sat up straight in his chair and was transformed from a quiet, reserved, unemotional non-talker to a gesturing, animated, excited salesperson. From a follower, he became a leader.

"You'll never believe it," he responded with enthusiasm, "but I discovered the underlying principle at the Indy 500 about 5 years ago. I forget who the drivers were, but the winning car was about twenty lengths ahead of the second car and the fellow next to me said it wasn't even close. But he was wrong. It looked like a big lead, but in fact, it was only four seconds. Then they announced that the race officially took three hours, five minutes and nine seconds. I worked out in my head that three hours and five minutes is eleven thousand one hundred seconds. I figured out that every twenty-seven hundred seconds, he had gained just one second. And I thought of all the places they could have gained or lost a second. The pit crew could have been one second slow on each pit stop and lost the race. They could have lost all four seconds at one pit stop just by dropping a bolt, or getting in each other's way. Or the driver could have lost the four seconds somewhere. And they could have lost the four seconds by having a loose spark plug lead and the engine not running at top speeed. In fact, the engine and the car are made up of a thousand nuts and bolts and pieces, and any piece that wasn't exactly right could have caused the car to run four seconds slower.

"And then I thought about selling a house and that all the houses for sale at the same time were in the same race and the winner was the house that sold. And I decided to examine every detail that could cause a house to sell or not sell and make sure that my listings had the best chance. By the way, Dale, how many cars does the winner of the Indy 500 have to beat?"

"Thirty-three," answered Dale.

"Nope," said Dick. "Guess again."

"Oh," said Dale, "I forgot to subtract all the cars that crash or break down. On the average probably fifteen to twenty finish the race, so the winner has to beat fifteen to twenty."

"Nope," said Dick again. "One. The winner has to beat the car that comes in second. He has to beat just one car. And any listing I have only has to beat one other listing in order to sell. But the listing it has to beat is the second best home for sale."

"I'm not sure I follow that analogy," said Dale.

"Look," said Dick, "on the average, buyers inspect twelve homes before making a buying decision. That means that if a buyer looks at five homes and my listing is one of them, then in that buyer's mind my listing is competing against four other listings, isn't that right? And if the buyer looks at twenty homes, then in that buyer's mind my listing is competing against nineteen other listings. But out of those nineteen homes, some are definite no's and one or two are strong maybe's and so finally my listing has to compete with just one other listing. So my listing can't just be a good listing, it has to be the best. I don't want to compete. I want to win!"

"Well," said Dale thoughtfully, "there are a lot of variables. How do you control all the variables?"

"I made a list of everything that could affect the sale. And I mean everything. Then I just set about making sure that I was best on every point. Let me give you an example. Visualize two houses side by side, both the same style and both for sale. Everything else is equal, but one has a great looking lawn with edged walks and trimmed shrubs and the other has overgrown shrubs and uncut grass. Which will sell first?"

"The one with the good looking lawn."

"Everything else is equal, but one has freshly painted trim and the other has a front door that needs paint and trim that needs paint. Which will sell first?"

"The one with the fresh paint."

"Dale, if we walked through an average house, in five minutes I could name over one hundred individual items that could make the difference between a house coming in first or second in the buyer's mind. And coming in second in this market means a one thousand dollar loss in commissions to me. I can't afford to come in second."

"So your main thing is to prepare the house so that it shows well, is that it?" asked Dale.

"There is no 'main thing,' Dale," responded Dick. "Which is the 'main thing' on a race car; the motor, the tires or the steering wheel? None of them. They are *all* vital. Preparing the home for sale is not the 'main thing,' but it's just as important as everything else. Another potential problem is the price. If it's too high most salespeople won't even show it, so I have to get the sellers to pick a price that will cause most salespeople to think this is a good buy. I try to get all my sellers to list just a little below the average asking price of similar homes, so that other salespeople will be at least a little excited about the bargain. If I can get the sales people excited, I get more showings and when I get more showings, I have an edge over houses that aren't being shown as much."

"How about terms?" asked Dale.

"Absolutely critical," responded Dick. "The seller has to accommodate to the realities of the current market. If he won't make the necessary concessions, I don't take the listing. If there are twenty similar homes and ten of them have better terms, the ones with good terms sell first. I can't afford to come in second. I don't believe my customers can afford to come in second. I don't let them come in second if I can help it. So if they don't want to do everything necessary to win, I don't want to be their agent.

"Look," he continued, "if I was a professional race car driver and the owner of a car didn't want to do everything necessary to give us a chance to win, I don't want to be the driver. If a house needs paint to meet the competition, then I get the owner to paint it or I don't take the listing. If the carpets need to be cleaned to compete, I get them to clean the carpets. If the price has to be lowered a thousand or two from what they want or think it's worth, then I get them to lower the price, or I don't take the listing. And if we have to offer special terms to meet the competition, we offer the special terms. I don't want to be *in* the race, I want to *win* the race."

"Ok," said Dale after a thoughtful silence, "so your main thing is to get the house in perfect shape for showing, price it exactly right and get the terms right, right?"

"Sometimes," said Dick with a smile, "you sure learn slow. There is no 'main thing'. You get the race car perfect. Everything is right. Engine. Tires. Steering. Body. But no gas or no driver. How are you going to win? You can't even get started! Look, if people want a listing to sell in this market as a result of anything else but dumb luck, they are going to have to pay attention to every detail."

"I have a feeling," responded Dale, "that if I asked, 'What else is there?' I'd get hit on the head with something I have not thought of."

"You would too," agreed Dick. "There are a few more problems to solve. For example, when buyers inspect five homes, eight homes, ten homes, or even two homes, they often get confused. They get home at night and can't remember what they saw. They say, 'Which home had the picture window in the kitchen?' or 'Which home had the new carpeting in the bedroom?' Can you see that kind of thing happening?"

"Yes," agreed Dale.

"So I make up special information sheets that highlight the features and benefits of a home. I print enough so that I can leave a dozen or so in the house. Then anytime there's a showing, the buyers can take one home. And. . .Dale, think about this! On the average, real estate salespeople inspect five to fifteen homes every week. At the end of thirty days, the average person has seen twenty to sixty homes. They get back to their offices, and they can't remember what they saw. So I make up enough extra special information sheets so that all the salespeople who inspect my listings can take one with them. I even mail the sheets to top salespeople in other companies who don't come to my inspection. I figure there are about eighty active salespeople in my area, and I want every one of them to know that my seller's house is priced right, has good terms, has a lot of good features and shows well. The more salespeople who know about my listings, the more gas I have for winning the race."

"But a lot of our people use feature sheets," objected Dale.

"Did I say I used 'feature sheets'? No, I said I use special information sheets that highlight the features *and* benefits. People don't buy features. They buy benefits. So I highlight the benefits as well as the features. And I don't print them on company letterhead. I want salespeople in other companies to use the sheets and show the sheets to their buyers. Who's going to show their buyer a fact sheet with some other company's letterhead on it? Not the sharp salespeople, that's a fact. And I want *all* the salespeople I can get talking about my listings, showing my listings, getting excited about selling my listings."

"Anything else?" asked Dale.

"It'll cost you another beer," replied Dick.

"Okay," resumed Dale as he handed Dick the beer. "Let's see if I have it straight so far. You tell the seller that if they want to win the race, everything has to be perfect. You go through the house and check about a hundred items. Anything that needs fixing has to be fixed or you bow out. The price has to be right, and the terms have to be right. You print special information sheets that show both features and benefits, and you get these sheets in the hands of salespeople in every competing office as well as our own. You also leave sheets at the listing so potential buyers can take them home. It's hard to believe there can be anything else to do besides advertising."

"Dale," responded Dick thoughtfully, "the reason that most people don't win races is that they don't really believe they are going to win. So they rationalize that since they aren't going to win, why bother with every little detail. Man, if you want to win, you have to beat whoever is going to come in second next to you. You've got to figure he's going to be great and you have to be better. And in selling a house, that means you pay attention to *everything* that can go wrong. And do you know what can go wrong now?"

Dale just shook his head as Dick continued, "Like I said before, there are about eighty active salespeople in this area. Any one of them could find a potential buyer for my listing, and the problem is that not all salespeople show a house the same way. They bring the buyers *to* the house, but they don't always show them all the features *in* the house. Why? Maybe because it's their first time in the house, and they don't know about all the features and benefits. Maybe they don't know how to show a house. Maybe no one ever taught them. Maybe they look at one good feature and overlook another one. Maybe they'd prefer to sell a different house to this buyer. Maybe they think the other listing is better for their buyer. Who knows? And maybe the buyer says, 'Look Charlie, don't try to sell me the house. If I like it, I'll buy it. You just stay here in the living room and the Mrs. and I will look around.' So Charlie doesn't even get a chance to show the house. And the buyers don't find all the features and benefits. So do you know what I do Dale? I make up sharp little cards that highlight the features and benefits. And I put them inside closets and cupboard doors. I put them up in the attic and down in the basement. I put them everywhere that's necessary. The cards are five by seven, not three by fives. Big, with a nice border. Like a miniature billboard. And I use a fat felt-tip pen that writes big. I want the buyers to be able to read every card without putting their bifocals in low gear. I want the buyers to *find* all the good features, regardless of how well or how poorly another salesperson may show the house. I play to *win!*"

"I've seen your cards occasionally," responded Dale, "and they do look good. But do the sellers all like the cards?"

"Heck no!" Dick responded. "But a lot of sellers don't like a sign on the lawn. And some don't like open houses. And some don't like you to have a company tour and have 'all those people' going through their house. But I tell them all the same thing. I tell them, 'Do you want to *win* the race or do you just want to be *in* the race?'

"Look, Dale," he continued, "when times were good and the

market was hot a couple of years ago, I didn't have to do all of this stuff to the same degree I do now. When every decent listing will sell within ninety days and half of them will sell in the first two weeks, who needs to pay attention to every little detail? If the buyers will grab anything that's halfway decent, then the listing only needs to be halfway decent. But now, things are different. In our MLS report last week, the summary sheet showed that there were 7,270 homes for sale and only 111 sold. Do you know what that means? It means that every buyer had 65 choices, that's what. If every buyer has 65 choices, we are in a tough race."

Dale tapped a rhythm on the arm of the chair with the beer can for a few minutes while he digested the logic and power of Dick's ideas and procedures. There was nothing spectacular about any one item. There was no 'main item,' just like Dick had said. Maybe it wasn't a system, but it sure functioned like a well oiled machine.

"Dick," said Dale, "I've heard people refer to you as 'The Listing Machine.' After listening to you tonight, I believe that's a very well-deserved compliment. If I can get just one person in each office to learn to use your system, I'll turn this company around in sixty days."

"Are we going fishing in the morning? I have a feeling there's a good size northern pike in those lily pads in the cove at the north end of the bay. I'd like a crack at it."

"You bet," said Dale. "Let's hit the sack."

CHAPTER 11

LIST MORE
SELL MORE
PART I

Dick got the northern pike. And Dale turned the company around. And you can turn your career around. This chapter and the next will help you develop a listing presentation that will get listings. It will help you develop a method of making sure that most of your listings sell.

Actually, the two are intertwined. A good listing presentation is one that convinces the prospects that you can do the best job. The best way to convince people that you know what you are doing is to tell them what you are going to do and why those activities are important. The race is not always to the swift, but that's the way to bet. And top listing and sales production is not only achieved by salespeople who have a good procedure, but that also is the way to bet.

Dick Woodfin became known as "The Listing Machine" not only because he could get seventy-five to one hundred listings every year, but also because most of those listings sold. They sold because Dick understood the problems and challenges to getting a sale in a tough market and had solutions to those problems.

115

LIST MORE - SELL MORE
PART I

Over a ten year period, I analyzed the sales techniques of more than one hundred top producers in many different fields of selling. I began to see a constant pattern. First was a discussion of problems. Second was a discussion of solutions. One top salesman said, "If they (the prospects) don't understand the problem, they won't understand my solution." Another said, "If they discount the problem, they will discount my solution."

Dick Woodfin understood the problems. The problems relate to human psychology. Most people prefer clean things to dirty things, fresh paint to dull paint, dull paint to peeling paint. They prefer less work to more work, more value for their dollar to less value for their dollar. Given a choice, they will select the clean, the shiny, the new, the less work and the more value.

Dick understood that his fellow salespeople were one of the problems, that given the choice, they would rather sell the clean, the shiny, the new and the better value for the dollar. He understood that if they didn't "buy" his listing, they wouldn't sell his listing.

Finally, Dick understood that when there are more buyers than sellers, even a halfway decent house will sell quickly, but when there are hundreds of hopeful sellers and only a few buyers, then the competition becomes tough, very tough indeed. And it's not enough to be in the race. To get paid, you have to win the race.

Billy Kidd, who won an Olympic gold medal for the United States in skiing, said, "The winner is the one who makes the fewest mistakes." In a tough real estate market, the home that sells will be the one that has the fewest imperfections. The imperfections fall into two categories. First, the condition or showability of the home. Second, the price and terms.

Here's how to improve the showability and salability of your listings. Select one of your listings as the vehicle for your next race. Find three other homes that potential buyers would also most likely inspect, and take a long, careful tour of each home. Look for little details, such as cleanliness and organization of the garage, fingerprints around light switches, worn or dirty spots in carpets, condition of the kitchen sink. Use the check list in the back of the book.

Rate each room or area separately. Then rate every home. Use a point system of one to ten, with one being very bad and ten being good. Add up the points. Compare price and terms the same way. Determine which of the other homes is the best of the three. Then determine what has to be done to your listing to beat the best of the competition.

In every aspect of life there is a certain amount of luck. Through no one's fault, the leading car can blow an engine or tire on the final lap and lose the race. Through no oversight on your part, a buyer can buy a similar home that costs more, or has less desirable terms or doesn't show nearly as well, just because he likes the dining room wallpaper, or a swing set in the garden or the floor plan. As stated before, the race is not always to the swift, but that's the way to bet. A buyer won't always buy the most showable home with the best price and terms, but that is also the way to bet.

Let's review every problem, then we can develop a listing presentation that provides a solution to the problems.

According to a Minnesota study some years ago, the average buyer inspects twelve homes before making a buying decision. That means, on the average, your listing is competing against eleven homes in the mind of the buyer. Keep in mind that if the seller does not understand that this is a serious problem, he or she will not be willing to fix, paint, clean or adjust the price or terms to beat the competition.

A continuous study by myself and members of my firm over a

LIST MORE - SELL MORE
PART I

twelve year period shows that in average years, only 60% of all listed homes sell within ninety days. That means 40% do not sell within ninety days or do not sell at all. Our data also shows that in some years 80% will sell within ninety days, while in other years as few as 10% or 15% sell. The worse the market is, the more critical it becomes for a house to be prepared for showing and a price selected that will cause other salespeople to get excited about showing your listing.

Experience shows that when a buyer inspects several homes, even two homes, he can forget what he saw after he gets home. Logic, as well as experience, tells us that if a salesperson inspects ten new listings every week, that at the end of thirty days he would have seen forty new listings, and at the end of sixty days he would have seen eighty new listings. It's not hard to summarize that even the most experienced salesperson is going to forget certain important details in most of those homes.

Experience also proves that most salespeople, even very active ones, do not have a chance to inspect every new listing that comes into the market place. When a salesperson doesn't know much about a home, it's not too likely he will include it in the list of homes he plans to show a prospective buyer.

Experience has also shown that most salespeople show a home in different ways. Some salespeople are new and don't know how to show a home. Others, even experienced salespeople, have never had any specific training on how to show a home, and many have developed some bad techniques. One very large man, for example, always stood in the middle of the room to allow prospects the most room to move about. No one ever told him that he made the room look much smaller. Another salesperson always pointed out the features in the home, but never mentioned any benefits. But people buy features to get benefits. And most pros know that it's dangerous to assume that people always understand the benefits.

In summary, the key problems are:

1)   There are usually more homes for sale than there are buyers.

2)   In very slow markets, there could be as many as sixty homes for sale for each buyer.

3)   The average buyer inspects twelve homes before making a buying decision.

4)   The more homes a buyer inspects, the more chance there is of forgetting about an important feature.

5)   The average salesperson inspects ten to fifteen homes a week.

6)   The more time that goes by, the more new listings a salesperson will see, and the more chance they will forget an important feature in your listing.

7)   Salespeople come in all sizes and shapes, with all levels of training and experience and with an infinite variety of personal likes and dislikes. Accordingly, not all sales people who show your listing will do it well or completely.

Now, let's look at the solutions to these problems. To improve the odds that a home will sell in a tough market, don't depend on luck. Rather, convince the sellers to spend the extra money or take the extra time to paint and clean and fix. The challenge lies in the fact that most people don't want to invest in something they are getting rid of. Also, when most people buy a new home, the cost is almost always higher than they anticipated, so there's a natural tendency to conserve. Additionally, and maybe the worst part, there is no guarantee that the effort or money spent will produce a sale. We are only attempting to improve our chances. So a most valid question is, how do I get more of my sellers to invest the time and money?

Let me answer that question this way. If I come to your home to obtain your listing and your basic question is why should you list with me rather than someone else, my challenge is to convince you to believe in me. But if I don't believe in me, why should you believe in me? If I am not sure that I can do the best job for you, why should you believe I can do the best job for you? If I don't believe, and I mean unshakably believe, that every buyer having thirty choices is a serious problem, that when a specific buyer looking at two other homes, five other homes or ten other homes is a serious problem, that buyers forgetting what they saw is a serious problem, that salespeople forgetting what they saw is a serious problem - in short, that every problem is a serious problem - then why should you believe they are serious problems? And if you don't believe that the problems are serious, then you won't feel my solutions are important.

Using a check list to make sure that you have not overlooked *anything* to prepare the home for sale will only seem important if you *and* your seller believe that the problems of competition are serious. Using "Highlight Sheets" to make sure buyers and salespeople remember all of the good features will only seem important if you and your sellers feel that the problem of buyers and salespeople forgetting what they saw is a serious problem.

Thousands of successful real estate salespeople from coast to coast maintain a higher sales-to-listing ratio than other salespeople in their area because, like Dick Woodfin, they believe the problems of competition are serious, and they convey that belief to the seller, who then takes action on recommendations to clean, fix, paint, or adjust price and terms.

Now, here is a listing presentation that has proven effective for thousands of salespeople, in big cities and small towns, from coast to coast, for over ten years. This presentation is based on a problem-solution formula.

EIGHT GOOD REASONS

"There are <u>eight</u> good reasons why <u>you</u> will benefit by having <u>me</u> represent you to sell your home. What you want is the most money you can get. . .as quickly as you can get it. . .with the fewest problems possible, isn't that right? Here's how I can help you do that."

REASON 1 PREPARE FOR SHOWING

"First, I can make almost any home a litle more attractive to potential buyers. Through my experience I know the reasons people do <u>not</u> buy, as well as the reasons they do. For example, most buyers are concerned about getting ample closet space, but most people keep so many clothes in the closet that it makes the closet look small and unsatisfactory, turning away an otherwise interested buyer. Can you see that kind of thing happening?

121

**MORE TO
SELLING**

" _____, there's more. . .there's a lot more to selling a home than just putting a sign on the lawn, an ad in the paper, and waiting for buyers to come. Here's why. . .

---

12 LOOKS

"On the average, buyers inspect twelve homes before making a buying decision. That means eleven other homes are competing against yours. The result is. . .

60/40

"In average years, only 60% of all listed homes sell during the original listing period, 40% do not. That means, of any ten homes for sale in this area, only six will sell within ninety days, and four will take longer than ninety days to sell, or will not sell at all."

**I'M
DETERMINED**

"I'm absolutely determined to make sure your home competes successfully against all of the other homes for sale in this area. I am determined to make sure that your home has every sales advantage possible. So. . .

CHECK LIST

"I work from a check list that contains twenty-one items. As soon as you give me the go-ahead, I'll give you a copy of this check list and go over it with you very carefully, step by step. That's one way you will get the most money, the quickest sale, and the fewest problems, which I know you want. Isn't that right?"

HIGHLIGHT SHEETS

"Here's something else I do. I'll make a list of all the good features in your home. I'll print enough copies so that buyers can take them home. Here's why I do this. When buyers inspect five homes, eight homes, ten homes, or even two homes, they often get confused. They get home at night and cannot remember what they saw. They say, 'Which home had the picture window in the kitchen, which home had the cedar closet?' Can you see that kind of thing happening?

BENEFIT QUESTIONS FOR HIGHLIGHT SHEETS

Can you see how the highlight sheets will help a buyer remember all the good features in your home?

123

**BENEFIT
QUESTION**

Can you see how they will help us compete against homes that don't have highlight sheets? That's a terrific idea, isn't it?"

**HIGHLIGHT
SHEET**

"Here's something else. There are about __(80)__ active salespeople in our area. Any one of them could bring a potential buyer to your home. The problem is that not all salespeople show a home the same way. Some salespeople bring a buyer to the home, but they don't always point out all of the good features in the home. Sometimes they look at one good feature, but overlook another. And sometimes it's because the buyer doesn't let the salesperson point out the features. Mr. Seller, I am absolutely determined to make sure that all of the good buyers find all of the good features in your home, so I make up highlight cards. If you have a _____
I will highlight that feature. (Or, I noticed that you have a _____, so I will highlight that feature.)

**BENEFIT
QUESTION
HIGHLIGHT
CARD**

Do you see how highlight cards will help the buyers <u>find</u> all of the good features in your home?

**BASIC
BENEFIT
QUESTION 1**

"Do you see how you will benefit by having me represent you to sell your home?"

NOTE: A positive answer to the final benefit test question is your cue to close. See Chapter 19 for your options on closings.

CHAPTER 12

LIST MORE -
SELL MORE
PART II

In the spring of 1969 a young man named Mike attended one of my courses. At the time I was teaching people how to prospect. We focused on how to be more effective on personal calls and phone calls. I taught techniques for canvassing, surveys and, of course, For Sale By Owner. Someone in Mike's office told him that selling was a numbers game, that if he just called enough people and asked them if they wanted to sell their home, sooner or later someone would say "yes." Mike made 300 phone calls and 300 people said "no."

I taught Mike several techniques for contacting private sellers and made sure that he understood them all and had learned them well. A week after the course I called him on the phone and asked how he was doing.

"Fantastic!" he replied.

"What's 'fantastic'?" I asked.

"Fantastic is that I made 50 calls and got 33 appointments!"

"That is fantastic," I said. "Congratulations! I'll call next week."

LIST MORE - SELL MORE
PART II

A week later I called again. "How's it going?" I asked.

"Terrible," he said dejectedly.

"What's 'terrible'?"

"Terrible is that not one of those 33 appointments became a listing, that's what."

"Mike, don't move a muscle. I'll be right there."

It took me twenty minutes to get there. On the way I asked myself over and over, how in the world could anyone blow 33 appointments. When I got to Mike's office, I found out how. Mike was totally unprepared to tell anyone why he would benefit by having Mike represent him in the sale of his home. He didn't begin to understand how to go about selling a house. I asked him why I should list with him if I decided to sell. "Because I'm in real estate," was his answer. When I pursued what he would do for me, he essentially said that he would put a sign on the lawn, an ad in the paper, send the listing into the MLS and then wait and see what happened.

During the next few weeks I talked to over 50 salespeople, managers and brokers to see what they felt were the key reasons a seller would benefit by listing with an agent. We came up with eight key benefits.

First, we can prepare a home for sale by giving the owner tips on making the house and grounds more showable.

Second, we can help the owner select the best marketing price.

Third, we can expose the home to potential buyers through the salespeople in our own company, our multi-listing and national re-location services and through our advertising ("for sale" signs and other marketing activities.)

Fourth, we can pre-qualify buying prospects to minimize unproductive showings.

Fifth, we can help a prospective buyer make a decision.

Sixth, we can negotiate on behalf of the buyers.

Seventh, we can help the buyers arrange financing.

Eighth, we can expedite the paperwork for a closing.

I taught these eight reasons to Mike, but, tragically, within a few months he was out of real estate. Part of the problem was personal. As one of his fellow salesmen told him, "If you want to soar with the eagles in the morning you can't hoot with the owls at night." But more importantly, Mike didn't make it because he failed to understand that real estate brokerage is a service business and that there is a lot more to selling a home than just putting an ad in the paper and a sign on the lawn and waiting for the buyers to appear. Brokerage is not a get-rich-quick-without-work scheme.

I also taught these eight reasons to thousands of others who did understand that the eight reasons are not just a pitch, but a course of action to get the home sold. A list of names of people who increased their incomes by more than $5,000 with these eight reasons would take many pages. And testimonials of individuals who doubled and tripled their incomes, or who increased their incomes by $10,000 or $20,000 would take still more pages. These eight reasons are the eight key services we have to offer. Presented correctly, they will produce listings. If the steps are actually followed, the listings will sell.

Here is how Bob C. , one of our graduates, uses all eight reasons to make an effective, short listing presentation. Notice that in each case there is reference to a problem and a claim that the salesperson can solve the problem, but no detail as to how.

LIST MORE - SELL MORE
PART II

"Mr. and Mrs. Seller, there are *eight* good reasons why you will benefit by having me represent you to sell your home. What you want is the *most* money, the *quickest* sale and the *fewest* problems, isn't that right?

"First, I can make almost any home a little more attractive to potential buyers. Through my experience, I know the reasons people don't buy as well as the reasons they do. Since the average buyer looks at twelve homes before making a buying decision, I will help you highlight the best features. Do you see how highlighting the best features and preparing your home for sale would help us compete better?

"Second, I can help you determine the right price to put your home on the market. Surprising as it may seem, people sometimes price their home far below current market value. Usually, however, the price is set too high, and the home does not sell. It takes a lot of work on my part, but I can help you determine the best asking price.

"The third reason you will benefit by having me represent you to sell your home is that I can expose your home to a great number of potential buyers. First is through the salespeople in my office, in the other offices of my company and through our multi-listing service and national re-location service. Next, we advertise almost every home we list and that creates additional prospects. Then we continuously receive calls from qualified buyers because we have been in business over 15 years and because we have a great number of "for sale" signs on our other listings. And finally, I do some specialized work to develop additional buyers.

"The fourth reason you will benefit is that I can qualify prospects. Basically there are four kinds of people who look at homes: serious, in a hurry; serious, not in a hurry; bargain hunters; and casual lookers. My job is to make sure that prospects are serious so I can save you from having unqualified prospects just looking at your home.

"Fifth, I can help a buyer make a decision. Even a good prospect may need urging to make a commitment. We frequently are working with first time buyers who need a home, like a certain home, want to buy the home, and qualify to buy the home, but are just scared to death to make a decision. My job is to help them over the fear of making that decision.

"The sixth reason you will benefit by having me represent you to sell your home is that I can negotiate on your behalf. I will be doing my very best to get you the most money possible. . . without losing a serious, qualified buyer just because he started with a low offer.

"Seventh, I can help the buyer find mortgage money. With today's conditions we have to do that quite often.

"And the eighth reason you will benefit by having me get started right now is that I can cut through the red tape. Once an offer has been accepted by you, there is a lot of red tape and it seems that more and more lenders and government agencies are cutting red tape lengthwise. Since I live with this every day, I have learned how to eliminate or minimize problems at the closing.

"Mr. and Mrs. Seller, you said that you wanted the most money possible, as quickly as possible and with the fewest problems possible. Do you feel that a salesperson should touch all eight steps to give you the best possible service?

"Since that is the way I work, do you see how you will benefit by having me represent you to sell your home?"

There are a number of very interesting points that can be made concerning that presentation. First, it takes only about three and a half minutes. Experience has proven that a listing presentation doesn't have to take a half hour. In fact, the shorter the better. As someone once said, a presentation should be like a mini-skirt - short enough to be interesting and long enough to cover the subject.

Notice the constant repetition of the phrase, "The (number) reason you will benefit by having me represent you to sell your home is. . ." Bob believes that a prospect should hear the words "you will benefit by having me represent you" at least a dozen times in a presentation.

Notice also that the eight reasons are a logical sequence of events. First, we help prepare the home for showing and help select a good price. Then we expose the home to as many potential buyers as possible. Having exposed the home to a lot of potential buyers, we qualify to make sure showings are scheduled only for people who can afford to buy if they like the home. Having shown the home to qualified buyers, we can help them decide if there is a problem. If the offer is less than the asking price, we negotiate to help the seller realize the most money without losing a serious buyer by insisting on too much. Having negotiated a price that is acceptable to both buyer and seller, we then assist the buyer in obtaining financing. And finally, we expedite the paperwork to make the closing as smooth and trouble free as possible.

I use the word "we" in most of the above because some of these steps are things we do in co-operation with other salespeople, for example, when we secure the listing but they find the buyer.

Each of the eight reasons could be expanded into more detail if necessary and some of the reasons can be expanded to the point that they become the primary presentation as illustrated with "Reason One - Prepare for Showing" in Chapter 11.

Incidentally, when making a listing presentation, you will be

132

making your points from a competitive position in which you will be telling the prospect the things that you can do or actually do that your competitors can't do or don't do. Or you will be making your presentation to a private seller, in which case you will be explaining the things that you can do that the private seller can't. Each of the eight reasons can be tailored to fit the situation.

Here's an assignment that will take about an hour, but will pay dividends of thousands of dollars in commissions every year. (If you are a broker or sales manager, this will make an excellent workshop-sales meeting.) At the top of a sheet of paper, write the words, "Here are the reasons you will benefit by having me represent you instead of (name three competing firms)." Now take each of the eight reasons and write down as many points as you can think of. Brainstorm with some of your associates. You should fill at least two pages with valid reasons. Remember that many salespeople do not do things they can and should do. Remember also that in life, success is not doing something different: it's doing it better. Every driver at the Indianapolis 500 puts his foot down on the gas and turns left at the curves. The winner does it best. The winner makes the fewest mistakes.

Now, take another sheet and at the top write the words, "Here are the reasons you will benefit by having me represent you instead of trying to sell your home yourself." Again, take each of the eight reasons and write down as many points as you can think of. Some of the points will be the same, some different.

When you are done, match your list against this book. Any points you have come up with that are not covered here, but which you believe to be strong and valid sales points, should be developed into your presentation.

If you can develop an unshakable belief that your prospects will benefit most by having you represent them to sell their homes - and you can convey your belief with solid, convincing information, you will seldom miss getting a listing from a motivated seller. And when you can get almost every listing you go after, you will find that prospecting for appointments becomes a lot more fun, as well as a lot more productive.

CHAPTER 13

LIST MORE -
SELL MORE
PART III

I turned on the yard lights so I could watch the gusting wind of this late December blizzard blast the heavy snow around the trees in my back yard. I like a good blizzard; especially when I'm inside looking out. It's even better when I'm standing by a roaring fire with nice hot grog in hand.

About the only thing that can improve that situation is someone handing me a really great present, and that night I got one of the best presents one could hope for. It came in the form of a phone call from Jim M. of Ohio.

"Jerry," he began, "I don't know if you remember me, but I took your course about 18 months ago in Columbus. I'm calling to tell you that because of your system, I am giving my family the best Christmas present ever. We are leaving first thing in the morning to spend the holidays in Bermuda. I'm taking all seven kids, and the reason I can afford it is that in the last 15 months I have made 78 listing presentations and got 78 listings. All but 17 have sold, and of those, 6 are still active."

Jim went on to tell me that he had developed a special three step
system out of the various techniques covered in the course
which was getting him listings and getting them sold. He
finished up by saying, "Jerry, if anyone will give that three step
presentation, I think he can get a listing every week, just like
me. And if they will do everything that is promised in the
presentation, almost all of his listings will sell."

"Any chance of getting an outline of your three step plan?" I
asked.

"Better yet," he responded, "I made a tape recording of the whole
plan and I sent it off to you today. That's my Christmas present
to you."

Needless to say, I watched the mail every day for the next week
with great expectations. And when the tape arrived, I was not
disappointed. Jim's plan was simple but thorough and with his
permission was incorporated into our full program. Now, I am
pleased to pass it along.

As Jim pointed out, his plan was developed out of many of the
components of the entire system. "The Three Step Plan," as we
now call it, is a conclusion to several other steps. Jim first
qualifies his prospects carefully and thoroughly using the
techniques covered in Chapter 7, "Effective Qualifying." He
then makes a listing presentation that is almost identical to
what we call our standard listing presentation which is covered
in Chapter 11, "List More - Sell More, Part I."

On completion of the standard listing presentation, Jim asks for
the listing. If the prospects agree, he then makes a pricing
presentation, discusses and selects a price, gets the listing signed
and then presents his three step plan.

If, on completion of the standard listing presentation, the prospects hesitate or object when he asks for the listing, he then presents the three step plan as his answer to the stall or objection. On completion of the three steps, he asks for the listing again and says he always gets an O.K. at that point. Then he discusses and selects the listing price.

Now, here is the dialogue for "The Three Step Plan."

"Mr. and Mrs. Seller, as I mentioned earlier, there is a lot more to selling a home than just putting a sign on the lawn, an ad in the paper and waiting for buyers to come. But the conventional method of marketing a home is to put a sign on the lawn, an ad in the paper, turn the listing into the Multi-Listing Service and then wait and see what happens. Quite a few salespeople also hold an open house, if necessary.

"But I use an extra effort three step marketing plan that goes like this:

"My first level of effort has eight steps. First, I use the 21 point check list that I showed you earlier, to make sure that your home is very, very showable and will compete very well against all the other homes also for sale at this time. Remember, the average buyer looks at 12 homes, so we have to look sharp to beat the competition.

"Second, I use the "Highlight Cards" to make sure that all of the potential buyers who see your home will remember all the good features and benefits.

"Third, I print "Highlight Sheets" to make sure that all of the potential buyers who see your home will remember all the good features and benefits.

137

"Fourth, I will be using a "Comparative Market Analysis" to compile all the current market data you will need to select the right market price. I don't want my clients to underprice a house and lose any money, and I don't want them overpricing the house and not getting any action.

"Then, I put the sign on the lawn, ads in the papers, turn the listing information into the Multi-Listing Service and schedule an inspection and evaluation tour by all the salespeople in our branch.

"Now, if we don't have a buyer in 30 days, I move along to my second level of effort, which has 4 steps.

"First, I contact 20 neighbors. I usually contact 5 homes to the right, and 5 homes to the left, and 10 across the street. I will be asking them who they know who might possibly be interested in buying your home.

"Second, I will be contacting you to review the "Check List" and the "Comparative Market Analysis" to make sure we haven't overlooked anything because my third step is to begin holding "Open House" on a regular basis.

"And the fourth part of this step is. . . I will re-contact all of the 20 neighbors and invite them to an "Open House" because they might know someone who would buy your house but not think of the person until they saw some special feature of your home.

"Okay, if we do not have a buyer in the next 30 days, I then begin my third level of effort, which also has four steps.

"First, I will review the "Comparative Market Analysis" and update it to include any changes in the market.

"Second, I will continue to hold "Open House" on a regular basis.

"Next, I will be contacting an additional 50 to 100 families in the area. I will invite them to an "Open House" and I'll be asking them who they know who might be interested in your home.

"My final step is to hold a special open house for the top agents in our area. I have coffee and donuts, wine and baked ham, or Bloody Marys, as required, to get a big turn-out. I send each top agent a personal invitation, and include a copy of the "Highlight Sheet" and a copy of the menu. You'd be surprised how far a salesperson will drive for a free ham sandwich.

"Now, Mr. and Mrs. Seller, that is my basic three step extra-effort marketing plan. I can make adjustments in the timing and sequence, but before we talk about any adjustments, may I ask this question: What kind of salesperson do you want to have representing you to sell your home. someone who knows how to merchandise a home and has a plan of action, or someone who just puts a sign on the lawn, an ad in the paper and hopes for the best?"

Isn't that terrific?

Jim says that everyone gets excited and gives him the listing right away. It's easy to see why.

In the years since the blizzard, I have taught this system to everyone who attended our courses and we have since had a great many people report successes similar to Jim's. Lots of listings and a high sales-to-listing ratio is a great idea. As one man said, "it's legal, it's moral, and fattening of the wallet."

When I teach this system in the course, I always get some questions, so, anticipating that you may have some, let me review the logic behind the system.

First, notice that Jim said that this plan is not presented until he has first qualified the prospects. That means he knows why they are selling, where they are going, when they have to be there and if they need the money from this house to buy their next one. He also has discussed the potential problems if the home does not sell on a timely basis. Additionally, he has made a complete listing presentation, explaining why it is important that the home be carefully prepared for showing. He has explained the problems of the "Highlight Cards" and the "Highlight Sheets." Then he asks for the listing.

At this point, I'd like to recommend that you review Chapters 7 and 11 to get a sense of the flow. Keep in mind that some people make decisions faster than others. Some need more information to make a decision, and some need less. If the prospect is a fast decision maker, you don't want to "oversell" by making too long a presentation.

That's why, as Jim pointed out, he asks for the listing after completing what we call our standard listing presentation as covered in Chapter 11. If the prospects are agreeable, he then prices the house, gets a signed listing agreement and after everything is wrapped up tells his prospects about the "Three Step Plan."

You may be asking - why tell them about the plan if you don't need to? That's a valid question. While the greatest number of experienced salespeople tend to agree not to tell more than is necessary to get the listing, Jim Miller and quite a few others feel that they want the sellers to be so sold on them that they will go out of their way to develop referrals.

If the prospects are slower decision makers and need more information, Jim finds that out by making the listing presentation and asking for the listing. If they hesitate, he then offers the "Three Step Plan" and asks for the listing again.

Many people have asked why the "Three Step Plan" is laid out as it is. The answer is that if the market is brisk and most homes are selling quickly, the first level of effort may produce the sale without the extra effort. The greatest effort is reserved for the final 30 days.

Nothing says you can't hold the special "Open House" for other salespeople the first week. But our experience shows that it's best to reserve that effort. It's best if you can sell it yourself, or within your own company, and keep both ends of the commission. Also, if you immediately hold the special "Open House" for each of your listings, you may find attendance dropping on all your listings.

Most people who use this plan see it as a very flexible sequence. In some cases, when a seller is in a panic to move, the first level of effort is started immediately; the second level is started a week or two later; and the third level is started a week or two after that.

On other occasions, I have had reports where a salesperson used the first level of effort for 60 days before starting the second level of effort, because the sellers could not move into their next home for 150 days and didn't want too quick a sale.

The main key is to have a plan to explore different ways to prospect for buyers and merchandise the listed home. You can always adjust the timing or the sequence.

"One last point; this kind of planning is far more effective when presented along with a visual aid of some sort. The one we offer with our courses is printed in the back of the book. Many salespeople, however, feel more comfortable by writing out the entire program on one or two sheets using a felt tip pen for easy readability. Their reasoning is that they want to look completely organized and prepared, but they want the plan to look as if it is theirs exclusively, rather than a standard plan as would be indicated by the printed sheets.

Jim Miller made 78 appointments and listed 78 homes with this system. Only 11 listings expired. Skeptics always point out that those were probably the hot years. Yes, they were. But a lot of others have used this system to maintain sales-to-listing ratios of 80% or better while the area averages were falling to 20% and below. The truth is that a trained, professional salesperson can maintain a listing a week in most markets, and a trained professional can maintain a very high sales-to-listing ratio even in the worst markets.

Jim Miller averaged a listing a week with this system. He earned enough to take his family to Bermuda for the holidays. Jim says that anyone who will make the presentation should get every listing they go after. And if they do what the system promises, most of their listings will sell. What more can you ask?

I like a good blizzard. Especially when I'm indoors looking out. But even better, I like to read about one back home while I'm on a nice, warm, sunny beach in the Bahamas. How about you?

CHAPTER 14

THE
THOUSAND
DOLLAR
TICKET

If you study the techniques of consistently high producers, you'll soon discover that they ask a lot of questions and that their questions generally fall into three main groups:

> Tie downs

> Benefit Questions

> Logic checks.

Tie downs are little tag lines at the end of statements that check to see if the prospect agrees with the point that has just been made.

Some examples are:

> Isn't that right?
> Does that make sense?
> Would you agree with that?
> Can you see that kind of thing happening?

143

THE THOUSAND DOLLAR TICKET

These very simple techniques serve a most important function. They make you money - lots of money. More correctly, they save you money. Here's why.

When you drive about town, you're on the alert for traffic lights. Sometimes it's conscious, but mostly subconscious. Long established habit keeps you tuned into the light situation. Why do you watch so diligently? Because if you run a red light you could get killed. Or injured. Or get a ticket.

Today, in most cities, the cost of a ticket for running a red light is about $30 to $50. Darned expensive, right?

If you make a listing presentation to a prospect and you make one statement after another without checking to see if the prospect agrees with your point, or even understands your point, you could run a red light. At the end of your presentation, you get a ticket. It's called "no listing" and it costs about $1,000. Some people get three or four a week.

When we make the statement: "There are eight good reasons why you will benefit by having me represent you to sell your home. What you want is the most money you can get, as quickly as you can get it, and with the fewest problems possible. Isn't that right?" we add the tie down to give the prospect a chance to respond. If he says "Yes" he is giving us a green light. If he says he's not in a hurry, he is giving us a caution signal. We should now determine his urgency or lack of it.

The important point is. . .if we had not asked. "Isn't that right?" and the prospect did not feel a sense of urgency, he could then discount every good point we made in the listing presentation on the basis that he is not in a hurry. At the end we wind up with a ticket for running a red light.

SELF-IMPOSED
TICKET

Whereas_____
did violate one or more of the following rules:

☐ **SPEEDING**
Talk too fast

☐ **RECKLESS DRIVING**
Ad lib presentation
Disorganized and erratic

☐ **RAN OUT OF GAS**
Couldn't think of what to say to:
    Qualify the prospect
    Explain a problem
    Explain a solution
    Make a presentation
    Overcome an objection

☐ **OBSTRUCT TRAFFIC**
Failed to show enthusiasm

☐ **VEHICLE DEFICIENT**
Listing overpriced and/or
not showable—expired

☐ **OVERTIME PARKING**
Failed to try—busy
doing nothing

AT_____
(ADDRESS)

Value of Lost Listing
$_____

© Jerry Bresser 1978

As a rather interesting aside, you can look at almost every step of selling in the same light. Failure to prospect is a parking ticket. Talking too fast is a speeding ticket. A rambling, disjointed, unorganized presentation is reckless driving. Lack of enthusiasm could be looked at as obstructing traffic. In each case, the cost of the ticket is the value of the listing commission.

Here's a sample of a "Self Imposed Ticket" we often give to salespeople with the challenge to fill one out every time they fail to get a listing or at the end of any day they failed to try. We then suggest that they add up the losses to see what their poor selling techniques are costing them every week.

The listing presentation in Chapter 11 is a good example of making a point and then checking with "Tie Downs" to see if the prospect understands or agrees.

In the first of the eight reasons, we make the statement that we know the reasons people do *not* buy as well as the reasons they do. We give an example: "Most buyers are concerned about getting ample closet space, yet many people keep so many clothes in the closet that the closet tends to look small and unsatisfactory, turning away an otherwise interested prospect. Can you see that kind of thing happening?"

Consider the importance of the "Tie Down" right there. If we do not ask the prospect if he or she can see "that kind of thing

145

happening," we could lose our credibility. The prospect could think, "I looked at three homes yesterday and I didn't look in a single closet. That's crazy. If you like a house, buy the house. The closets will be there."

By asking the question, we give the prospect a chance to express his belief in our point and example. If he agrees, we get a green light to continue. If he disagrees, we get a red light. So we stop, find out the reason for the disagreement, and restate the point more clearly or use a different example.

Benefit questions are a form of feed-back that relate to benefits to be gained or losses to be avoided. For example, in Chapter 11, we tell our prospects about the "Highlight Sheets," and at the end we ask, "Do you see how the 'Highlight Sheets' will help a prospect *remember* all the good features he saw in your house?" A positive "yes" is a clear green light. A "maybe" or "I think so" is a caution light telling us that the prospect missed something.

Also from Chapter 11, we tell our prospects about the "Highlight Cards" and when we are done, we ask, "Do you see how the 'Highlight Cards' will help a buyer *find* all the good features in your house?"

Again, the purpose is to make sure the prospect agrees with the point and sees how he or she will benefit. A positive "yes" is a green light to proceed with the presentation while an "I think so" type of answer is a caution light telling us to slow down and make sure the prospect clearly sees the benefit before we proceed.

Now, please read this next statement slowly - maybe even twice. A "Benefit Question" is any question, a positive answer to

146

which indicates that the prospect understands the benefit to be gained.

If you show someone a "Highlight Sheet" as outlined in Chapter 11, and when you are done, say, "Isn't that exciting?" and your prospect says, "It sure is!", you have just asked a "Benefit Question."

As you might expect, a series of affirmative answers to "Benefit Questions" is a good sign that the prospects like what they are hearing and a good way to measure how much further information you need to give them in order to make a sale.

"Logic Checks" are simply questions that make sure the prospect is logical. More often than not, they serve a dual purpose. For example, one of our prospecting techniques for private sellers is also a logic check: "If I had a qualified buyer, willing to pay a price acceptable to you, would you accept such an offer through my company?" A "no" answer is illogical. An evasive answer could mean we have an illogical prospect.

Another example is the question, "If you felt that you could get the most money, the quickest sale and the fewest problems by giving me an exclusive listing today, would you do so?" A "no" answer is illogical unless there is a valid reason for the prospect not being able to sign a listing.

In Chapter 8, Leo Carnes, the private seller expert, expressed a most important point of view. We only have two things to work with - our time and our attitude. Don't let anyone mess them up. I cannot sell an illogical person, and I don't think you can either. The purpose of logic checks is to find out quickly if the prospect is illogical; if he is, split.

147

THE THOUSAND DOLLAR TICKET

Dennis, one of our graduates, mastered what we call the basic listing presentation as well as the art of asking questions. As a result, he has an extremely effective system.

After he has qualified the prospect, Dennis asks a series of questions that helps the listing presentation to "unfold," as he puts it. His procedure sounds like this:

Dennis: "In choosing a salesperson to represent you, Mr. Seller, what characteristics do you feel would be important?"

Prospect: "Well, I'd like a real professional."

Dennis: "Does it sound reasonable to you that a home that shows well would sell faster and for more money than one that doesn't show as well?"

Prospect: "Yes, it does."

Dennis: "So would you like to have someone who knows how to prepare your home for showing so that it will compete successfully?"

Prospect: "Yes, I would."

Dennis: "Does it sound reasonable to you that the average buyer would look at a dozen homes or so before making a decision?"

Prospect: "Yes."

Dennis: "So would you want a salesperson who knows how to make buyers notice your house better?"

Prospect: " Yes."

Dennis: "Do you think it is possible that most buyers would tend to forget some of the features they saw in a home, especially if they looked at several more homes afterwards?"

Prospect: "Yes, I'm sure they would. I would."

Dennis: "So would you want a salesperson who knows how to make sure that good prospects *remember* all of the good features that you have in your home?"

Prospect: "Yes. That would be very good."

Dennis: "Mr. Seller, do I look like I understand how to get a home sold?"

Prospect: "Yes, you do."

Dennis: "Why don't you let me get started tonight?"

Prospect: "OK."

Dennis' system works because the seller feels completely involved in identifying the important characteristics of a professional sales person to represent him in the sale of the home. Dennis gets the listing because, by asking these questions, its obvious to the prospect that Dennis has those important characteristics. That makes sense, doesn't it?

CHAPTER 15

WHAT I THINK
YOUR HOME IS WORTH
HAS NO MERIT

I met Paris O'Reilly just after 9 o'clock one rainy night. As part of my research program to find good language techniques and procedures for listing and selling real estate, I had been out talking to a salesman who was tops in his company. I don't remember if he gave me a good technique, but he sure gave me a good lead. Paris, he said, had been top salesman in their Board almost every month for 9 years. This was a man I would have to see. I took a chance and drove right to his office. . .and scored. He was in and could spend some time with me just as soon as he finished the paperwork on another offer.

Paperwork done, he took me to a local pub where he told me that his French mother had taught him to look successful and work hard, and his Irish father had taught him to work smart and enjoy life to the brim. "A man's entitled," he said.

"Paris," I began, "the secretary at your office told me that you were top salesperson for your Board 116 out of 122 months. She told me you only missed 6 times and those were usually your vacation months. She also told me that you list between 50 and 75 homes a year and that you have never had less than 80% of

WHAT I THINK YOUR HOME
IS WORTH HAS NO MERIT.

your listings sell, and that in four of the nine years you had 100% of your listings sell. How do you do it?"

"Glory be," he said. "Did she tell you that I hardly made a living for the first ten years? Did she tell you that I nearly quit five times? No, nobody wants to remember the bloody trip to the top. They just want to make a hero out of a body for doing a decent job."

I asked him if he thought a new salesperson could avoid a bloody ten year trip to the top if that person was to learn, really learn, his current techniques. He said yes, and I told him that I was looking for exactly that - techniques and procedures to save people from reinventing the wheel. Here's what he told me.

"For the first ten years," he said, "when sellers asked me how much I thought they could get for their house, I told them. When people asked me to give my opinion, I gave it, and I had all the bloody troubles that everybody else had because of it.

"Then, after ten years, it suddenly occurred to me that, in spite of ten years' experience, what I *thought* a home was worth had absolutely no bloomin' merit. The *only* thing that counts is-what are people willing to pay, for that kind of a home, in that area, and at that time. If it's priced right, a house will sell. Price 'em right in the first place, and they will sell faster. Turn down the bloody buggers that think you can work miracles. Stick with sellers who use their God-given common sense and you'll have most of your listings sell. Do you want another ale?"

Experience had taught me that to get some salespeople to give you their best secrets, it's good to let the hair down a bit, so to speak. On the other hand, I was taking notes on the back of a placemat and I wanted to read my writing in the morning, so I allowed him to get one ahead of me and said, "Paris, why don't you start at the beginning and walk me through a specific situation. Let's say that you get a lead on someone who wants to sell. How do you start, and what do you tell him so he prices the home right in the first place?"

"Well, laddie," he said, "when I get a lead, the first thing I do is look in the company files to see if we have sold that home before. If we have, it saves me a trip. If not, I jump in my car and dash over. I look it over from the outside and make an educated guess as to what's on the inside. Then I go back to my office and make up a market analysis.

"Let me tell you something about my market analysis. About ten years ago, I began showing people information on several similar homes that had recently sold. Since recent sales tell us what buyers are willing to pay, I figured that a few recent sales would be enough information. But the sellers always wanted to leave some negotiation room and so most of 'em still insisted on a price that was too bloomin' high. I decided to show them information on several similar homes that were currently on the market, but then they always felt their home was better than everything else and they still insisted on picking a price that was too bloody high. Then I hit on the idea of also showing them several expired listings so they could see what people are *not* willing to pay. If they still insisted on listing too high after that, I told them to bugger off."

"You didn't really. . ." I started to say.

"Nah," he responded quickly. "My mother taught me to be 'diplomatique.' So I just tell 'em I can't take the listing. Anyway, now I make up a complete market analysis that has two or three similar homes that have recently sold, two or three currently for sale, and a couple of expireds."

"Do you ever find a time when there are no expireds?" I asked.

WHAT I THINK YOUR HOME
IS WORTH HAS NO MERIT.

"Sure, laddie. Lots of times. Then I use reductions. They work just as well. Sometimes better. In fact, I always carry one market analysis that has one house listed on it three times. First it shows the high price where it didn't sell for about 90 days, then it's listed in the "currently for sale" section at a competitive price, and finally it's listed in the "recent sales" which shows that it sold for a thousand less than any other house. . .and it took 150 days to do it. I don't show it much, but when I need to, I always get a good listing."

"OK," I said. "I like that idea. Let's go back to the beginning. You get a lead and you make up a comparative market analysis. Then what happens?"

"Well, I go out to my appointment. When I arrive at the home, about half of the people ask me right away how much I think they will get for the house. My answer is always the same. I say, 'The pricing of your home is far too important to guess at. Let's go through the house first.'

"I can usually tell what kind of situation I am going to have by how they ask the question. If someone says, 'How much do *you* think you can get us for this house?' with a strong emphasis on the word 'you,' and a demanding tone of voice, I know he has had a price from one or more other salespeople, and I know he is not happy with what he was told, and I know that he is planning to give the listing to the highest bidder.

"Sometimes, tone of voice tells me that they don't have much respect for real estate salespeople and that they don't think we know what we are doing besides sticking a sign in the lawn and hoping for a bit o' luck. Bloody right they are at times, too. I didn't deserve most of the commissions I got for my first five years. Anyway, I adjust to fit the situation.

"As we go through the house, I find out why they are selling, where they are going and how soon things have to happen. I

154

also try to point out the difference between experienced, professional salespeople and salespeople who take listings at any price
and don't know how to sell a home anyway. You have to be
careful doing that because you don't want to get caught running
down anyone or making the real estate profession look bad."

"How do you handle that?" I asked.

"Well," he responded, "I like to set the stage so they understand
that picking a price is more than just making an educated guess.
If they are the kind of people that seem real sure of themselves,
you know, cocky or smug, I like to disturb their false sense of
security. So as we are going through the house and talking
about the various features, I will usually say, 'You know, people
are funny. About half the people think they should give the
listing to the salesperson who is willing to take the listing at the
highest price, as though the one who asks for the most will get
the most. And the other half think that a house will sell for x
dollars regardless of who sells it. But that's not true either. Real
estate firms almost always get a lot more for a house than a
private seller, and some real estate firms can get more for a
house than other real estate people.'

"Now I've got them thinking. I've already set the stage to bump
off any other salesperson who's trying to get the listing by
bidding high, and I have also set the stage so they want me to
tell them why some salespeople can get more for a house than
others. In fact, almost everyone asks me that next.

"Well, it's bloody simple. I just tell them, 'Look, if one salesperson takes your listing 10% or 20% over current market value,
and hardly anyone comes to see it, and no one makes an offer
until three days before you have to leave, and you don't have
any negotiating time left, you're going to wind up with a lot less
money than if you had listed with someone who helped you
pick the right price in the first place, and you got a lot of action

155

WHAT I THINK YOUR HOME
IS WORTH HAS NO MERIT.

and you got your offers early when you still had plenty of time to negotiate.'

"When we have been all through the house, and I've seen everything I need to see, I get them to sit down at the kitchen table..."

"Why the kitchen table?" I interrupted.

"Some old guy told me that years ago. He said that he got a 6% commission so 94% of the money belonged to the sellers. He said he wanted the sellers to pick the price and he wanted them to be as comfortable as possible and that most people were most comfortable making big decisions at the kitchen table. I tried it and it works."

"What about letting the sellers pick the price? Don't most sellers want to pick a price that's too high?"

"Sure they do, laddie. We all want to get a fortune for our junk. We all want the most we can get and it always seems logical to start high. You can't get it if you don't ask for it, can you? But my job is to show them how to get the most people to look at the house so they will get the most offers. I always have them pick the price, but I make bloomin' sure they pick the right price or I don't take the listing. That's how I get most of my listings to sell. I just don't take bloomin' overpriced listings - period.

"You know," he continued, after ordering two more ales, "most salespeople don't understand that. But the way I look at it, it's their house. They have the *right* to select the price. . .and they have the *responsibility* to select the price. On the other hand, I have the *responsibility* to give them the information they need to pick the right price. . .and I have the right to refuse the listing if I don't think it will sell.

156

"And another thing. . .one of the reasons so many of my listings sell is that for 10 years I worked bloomin' hard to get the reputation that my listings are always priced right. Other salespeople don't question my prices anymore so I get extra showings. I can't afford to ruin that reputation and one bloody overpriced listing could do it.

"Anyway, getting back to what I do - I sit them down at the kitchen table and then I say, 'Folks, a little while ago you asked me how much I thought your house was worth. Well, what *I* think your house is worth has absolutely no merit whatsoever. The *only* thing that counts is - what are people *willing* to pay, for *this* kind of home, in *this* area, at *this* time, isn't that right?' And I bloody well make them say 'yes.' Some of them just sit there like bloomin' stones cause they don't want to admit to that logic, but I just keep saying, 'Isn't that right?' until they say 'yes.'

"Then I say, 'The best way to determine what people are willing to pay for this kind of home is by looking at similar homes that have recently sold.' Then I take out a *blank* Comparative Market Analysis and I say, 'In a minute I'm going to show you the market data I have on your house, but first I want you to understand what the information will be telling you. First, I will show you several homes that recently sold. These will tell us what people are *willing* to pay, for *this* kind of home, in *this* area, at *this* time. Next, I will show you several similar homes that are currently for sale. These will tell us what we are competing against. The buyers for your home will be looking at these homes too. And last, I will show you a couple of expired listings. These will be similar homes that did not sell for 90 days or longer. They will tell us what people are *not* willing to pay for this kind of home.'

"When I'm sure they understand that, I show them the figures I put together. I go slow and explain my reason for picking each

WHAT I THINK YOUR HOME
IS WORTH HAS NO MERIT.

house as a comparable. I repeat that the current recent sales tell us what people are willing to pay, that the current listings tell us what we are competing against, and that the expireds tell us what people won't pay. Then I ask them, if they were looking, what price they would be willing to pay, based on the competition.

"Now," he continued after telling me not to let my ale destroy itself by running out of bubbles, "we come to the most critical part. They may not like the information I just gave them, but I want them to like me. The problem is that most people don't like the bearer of bad news. In the old days, the Phoenician kings used to cut the head off the messenger that brought the news that there were 10,000 enemy troops coming towards the city. The messenger didn't *create* the problem, he just told the king there was a problem. But he lost his head. I'm in the same bloomin' predicament. The seller wants to believe he has the best home in the area. He wants to believe that someone will pay extra just because he could use the extra money. He wants to score big, but the information I just gave him is bad news. And I brought it. And he knows I'm right. But he wants me to be wrong. So the most natural thing is to lash out at me by challenging my experience or my information or my intentions.

"There are a lot of different personalities out there, so there are a lot of different reactions. Some people say, '&?¢$%!, I was hoping to get more than this shows we will get, but facts are facts.' And then they pick a good price that will sell and it's all over. But most people don't make such quick decisions. Some of them ask me if it wouldn't be ok to start high and come down if we need to. Others beg me to agree that some special feature of the house is certain to get an extra thousand or so. Others just sit there and don't say anything. Some get angry - and that's what I try to avoid."

"Paris," I said, "you have just come to a critical point. There are thousands of different people and thousands of different

158

personalities. You have been in sales 19 years so you have learned how to react to different people. Most likely, you do it intuitively now. How can new salespeople learn that without taking 19 years?"

"Actually, it's easy the way I do it. I only see four kinds of personalities - friendly leaders, friendly followers, unfriendly leaders and unfriendly followers. Everybody is in there somewhere. But what makes it real easy is that I have one technique that I always use next, regardless of the type of personality. I say, 'Do you want the most money possible?' They all say yes. I say, 'Do you want it as quickly as possible?' They all say yes. And then I say, "Where do you want to price it?' And most of them pick a good price right off. Bloomin' simple, it is."

I thought about that for a bit, and then I had a question. "What do you do when people won't pick a good price? Don't some people ask you what you recommend? Don't some of them say, 'You're the expert. You tell me.'?"

"Hold on, laddie," he came back. "Why do you want to plow hard ground? If something works all the time, why do you want to worry about the few times it doesn't work? Just make a few extra presentations and find the bloomin' easy ones. Let your competitors deal with the bloody tough ones."

"Your point is well-taken," I responded, "but I'm taking notes and I'm looking for good techniques. I'm sure a lot of people still want you to tell them what price you think they should ask. I'd like to know how you deal with that. I can't believe you don't take a listing just because the seller can't make the decision for themselves."

"You're right, laddie," he retorted, "but you're still missing my

WHAT I THINK YOUR HOME
IS WORTH HAS NO MERIT.

point. My point is that you don't get concerned about advanced calculus until you have learned basic arithmetic . . . and you don't get concerned about methods for handling tough prospects until you have learned how to get lots of listings from the bloody easy ones."

He banged his fist on the table when he said "bloody easy ones" and the waitress took that as a signal for two more ales. I figured it would be best if we kicked some other ideas around for a while.

As we talked, the conversation drifted back to rights and responsibilities. He reiterated his position - the seller owned the house, 94% of the money would be his, he had a right to pick the price, yes, even a responsibility to pick the price. And Paris had the right to reject the listing if it was overpriced. Suddenly, I saw my opening.

"Paris," I asked him, "what other information can you give a person who just cannot seem to make a decision and keeps asking you to tell them where to price it?"

"Laddie," he said, "everything is so bloomin' simple. When someone says, 'You're the expert, what do you think we should ask?' I say, 'How would you like to get a little more for your house than the other people have been getting for their houses?' They all say, 'Yeah! That's what we want.' Then I say, 'Some people are doing it by using the 'Slightly Less - Slightly More' principle. It works like this. To get the most money, price your house slightly *less* than the competition and slightly *more* than recent sales - about half way in between. Here's why. By pricing your house slightly *less* than the competition, more salespeople will show your home, and as a result more buyers will see your home. And because of the increased activity and excitement, we stand a much better chance of getting a full price offer that is

160

slightly *more* than what the other people have been getting.'

"Then I ask them to figure out what half way between the highest recent sales and lowest current listing is. When they name the price I say, 'Does the idea make sense?' They all say yes, and I say 'Do you want to do it that way?' And they almost all say yes."

It was still raining when I said good night to Paris and drove away with the backs of three placemats jammed full of what I call writing. I sorted it out the next day and came up with one very bothersome question. How could a 19-year veteran say that his opinion had no merit? I called him on the phone.

"Laddie," he said, "in spite of 19 years experience, my *opinion* has no merit. What I *think* your home is worth has no merit. That's a crucial point. Facts have merit, my opinion has no merit. My experience has merit, but my opinion has no merit. Why? Because when I say, 'What I think your home is worth has no merit' and when I say, 'The *thing* that counts is: what are people willing to pay,' I'm not only rejecting my opinion, I'm getting rid of their opinion and everyone else's opinion. Now we can focus our attention on facts.

"My experience is," he continued, "that houses sell faster and for more money if they are priced right in the first place. My experience is that using current market data gives us the facts so we can price right in the first place. My experience has merit. My opinion has no merit. Got it?"

"Yes."

"Good. And may you be in heaven 20 minutes before the devil knows you're dead.

"Merci."

161

CHAPTER 16

PRICING PROPERTY
PROPERLY

Paris O'Reilley's track record of selling more than 80% of his listings is not unique. Many other professional real estate salespeople have duplicated that feat year after year. All of them agree, however, with his basic philosophies. . .if the house is priced right it will sell faster, and if you don't take overpriced listings you will have a higher percent of your listings sell.

Using Paris' techniques and a number of other techniques given to us by other successful salespeople, we have developed a pricing presentation that can be learned by anyone and which has proven to be extremely effective.

This presentation, like all of our presentations, follows a procedure. The goal, as always, is to create a flow of events that will keep you in control of giving the information, while it lets the prospect stay in control of making the decision. If you were watching for that when you read the previous chapter, you probably noticed that Paris felt very strongly that the prospect has the right - and the responsibility - to make the final decision. If you were watching for a flow of events that keeps the sales-person in control, you may have noticed that Paris was good at that, too.

163

PRICING PROPERTY PROPERLY

Now, let's take a look at the sequence we developed by linking good techniques together. Each of the techniques has now been given a title, so I'll be referring to these titles as we go along.

The first technique in the system is one we call "Help You Price" or "Reason 2," because it's the second of the eight reasons. It sounds like this:

"One of the reasons you will benefit by having me represent you to sell your home is: I can help you select the right price to ask.

Surprising as it may seem, people sometimes set the price much lower than fair market value. Usually, however, the price is set too high and the home does not sell. It takes a lot of work on my part, but I can help you select the best price to ask."

The purpose of this technique is to establish your professional knowledge. The first statement basically says: "Here's what I'm going to do for you. I'm going to help you pick a good price to put your home on the market." The second statement immediately identifies a potential problem. Some people price too low. They're not getting all the money their house is worth because they didn't ask enough. But it also says that most people price too high and the home does not sell right away. The third implies that there is work to be done and restates your initial claim.

The next technique in the system is called "Comparative Market Analysis Concept" or "CMA-C" for short. In this technique, we do exactly what Paris discovered many years ago. We present a blank CMA in order to make sure the prospects understand the concept, or the purpose, of the market data before we show them the actual numbers. Our "Comparative Market Analysis" is shown at the back of the book.

If you have ever shown a prospect a comparative market analysis only to have them completely disregard your carefully

164

prepared data and say, "I don't care about that. I want X for my house," and X is 20% more than current market, then you'll appreciate the effectiveness of showing a blank CMA first. Here's how we present a blank CMA.

"I work from a Comparative. . .Market. . .Analysis that contains three important parts. First are similar homes recently sold. These will tell us what people are *willing* to pay. . .for *this* kind of home. . .in *this* area. . .at *this* time.

"Second are similar homes for sale now. These will tell us what we are competing against. Buyers for your home will also be looking at these homes.

"Third are expired listings. These are homes similar to yours that went *unsold* for 90 days or more. These illustrate the problems of overpricing. As a matter of fact, these tell us what people are *not* willing to pay. . .for this kind of home, in this area, at this time.

"Do you see how this approach will help you select the best price to ask?"

Notice the deliberate pauses (three periods. . .after a word means to pause) after the words "Comparative," "Market" and "Analysis." We recommend that you say those words slowly and clearly because it is an unfamiliar term to most non-real estate people. When your listener misses key words, part of his attention is directed toward trying to figure out what it was you said, and as a result he often misunderstands what you say next.

Did you ever get a speeding ticket that you deserved? Even though you deserved it, you didn't like it. And it cost a lot. But did you ever get a speeding ticket because you didn't slow down fast enough on entering a slower speed zone? When you get a ticket for inadvertent speeding, it's even more aggravating. And it still costs a lot. Now, consider this: If you miss getting a listing because you spoke too fast, even for a brief moment, you got a "speeding" ticket that costs about $1,000. . .or whatever the listing commission was worth.

Present the rest of the Comparative Market Analysis the same way - clearly and slowly enough so that the prospects clearly understand everything you are saying. If you use a CMA like the one illustrated, you will find it is quite easy to cover each point. Actually, all you have to do is read each section with emphasis.

At the end, it is important to make sure your prospects understand the information you have just given them. We do this by asking the question, "Do you see how this approach will help you select the best price?" Notice the words, "will help you". Saying it that way clearly implies that the final decision will be the sellers. That's important, remember, because we want the ' seller to select the price. It's his right. . .and responsibility.

Now, once the seller agrees that this approach will help, we then present the actual Comparative Market Analysis that we have prepared on his home. Our language sounds like this:

"Here's the Comparative Market Analysis that I prepared on your home before I came out today. Here's your home. . .and I think you will agree that all of these homes are similar to yours. Do you agree?" As you say that statement, first point your index finger at his address, then run your finger down the left side of the page to direct his attention to the other addresses on the CMA.

If you have presented CMA's before and had people discount your information by saying that they felt the other houses weren't anywhere near as good as theirs, you are in for a delightful shock. If you follow our procedure, you will seldom get an argument from this point on. Why? Most people follow the lead of positive people. If you have done a good job of qualifying the prospect, and you have made a good listing presentation, and the prospect was impressed enough to agree to measure the house, and you have professionally presented a blank CMA so they understand why you are showing the date on the CMA-when you now say, "I think you will agree that these homes are similar to yours. Do you agree?" they are going to say yes!

Now we present the figures on the CMA. We present it just as if it was the blank one, only this time we show the numbers. It sounds like this:

"Okay, here are similar homes that recently sold. Again, these tell us what people are *willing* to pay, for this kind of home, in this area, at this time: $78,300, $80,990, and $79,600.

"Here are the similar homes for sale now. Again, these are what we are competing against: $87,000, $89,000, and $85,500.

"And here are the expired listings. Again, these tell us what people are *not* willing to pay, for this kind of home, in this area, at this time: $90,300 and $93,900."

At this point, I suggest that you lean back and do not say one word. Nothing. Watch the seller. Different people need different amounts of time to absorb information. Don't get impatient. As long as your prospect studies the CMA information, say nothing. Only when they raise their eyes should you continue. Remember, you are providing professional leadership at this crucial time. Remember that most people don't like to make decisions, especially decisions that happen infrequently and could be costly if a mistake were made. At this critical point, we add Paris O'Reilley's excellent technique, which we call "Price Tie Down."

"John, (you should be on a first name basis by this time, if possible and if appropriate) do you want the most money possible?"

"Yes."

"As quickly as possible?"

"Yes."

"And with the fewest problems possible?"

"Yes."

"The best way to do that is to price your home *right* in the first place, isn't that right?"

"Yes."

And now you close: "Based on the information I have just given you, what price do you think will get you the most money, the quickest sale and the fewest problems?"

Your prospect has three choices: name the right price, which will be in the competitive range; name the wrong price, which will be over-priced; or ask you what you think the price should be. Before I discuss these alternatives, I'd like to go back and analyze the techniques I have just presented.

The sequence of events, or the flow of events, that we have just covered is an exciting, proven procedure. If every graduate who now uses this procedure effectively and profitably was to submit a one page report on his success, I could probably publish a book the size of "War and Peace." To summarize the procedure by titles, we have:

Help You Price
Comparative Market Analysis - Concept
Benefit Question - Help You Price
Comparative Market Analysis - Actual
Price Tie Down
Close

Think about that sequence. We began by making an important claim: We can help you select a good price. We brought out two possible problems: pricing too low and the more frequent pricing too high. We said it took a lot of work, but we had a solution. We told how we would solve the problem. We worked from a Comparative Market Analysis. We explained the three important elements of the CMA. We made sure they understood how the CMA would help. We presented the actual figures. We asked them if they wanted the most money, the quickest sale and the fewest problems. They said "yes, yes, yes." We told them that the best way to do that was to price right in the first place and asked them if they agreed. They said "yes." Finally, we asked them where, based on the CMA information, they thought their house should be priced in order to get them the most money, the quickest sale and the fewest problems. If you learn to do this smoothly, you should seldom get a serious objection to pricing right in the first place.

If your prospect rejects all this and firmly indicates a desire to overprice, you can use the techniques in the next chapter. However, the most frequent response from decisive people is to pick a good, competitive price and let you get started, which was your original objective. The most frequent response from indecisive people is to ask you what price you think they should ask. Our answer here is the effective answer given by Paris O'Reilley, which we call "Slightly More - Slightly Less." It sounds like this:

"How would you like to get a little more money for your home than other people have been currently getting for theirs?" Almost everyone says that's exactly what they want. You continue, "Some people are doing it by using the 'Slightly More-Slightly Less' pricing concept. It works like this: to get the most money, the quickest sale and the fewest problems, price your home slightly *less* than the competition, and slightly *more* than recent sales. Here's why. By pricing your home slightly *less* than the competition, more salespeople will come to see your home. As a result, more buyers will see your home. And because of the increased activity, interest and enthusiasm, we stand a much better chance of getting a *full price* offer that is slightly *more* than recent sales. Does that make sense?"

Now, here are the techniques listed for ease of study.

HELP YOU
PRICE

"One of the reasons you will benefit by having me represent you to sell your house is. . .I can help you select the best price to ask. Surprising as it may seem, people sometimes set the price much lower than current market value. Usually, however, the price is set too high and the home does not sell. It takes a lot of work on my part, but I can help you select the best price to ask."

**CMA-C
COMPARATIVE
MARKET
ANALYSIS
CONCEPT**

"I work from a Comparative . . . Market . . . Analysis . . . that contains three important parts. First are similar homes recently sold. These will tell us what people are <u>willing</u> to pay . . . for <u>this</u> kind of home . . . in <u>this</u> area . . . at <u>this</u> time.

"Second are similar homes for sale now. These will tell us what we are competing against. Buyers for your home will also be looking at these homes."

"Third are expired listings. These are homes similar to yours that went <u>un</u>sold for 90 days or more. These illustrate the problems of over-pricing. As a matter of fact, these tell us what people are <u>not</u> willing to pay . . . for this kind of home, in this area, at this time.

**BENEFIT
QUESTION
HELP YOU SELL**

"Do you see how this approach will help you select the best price to ask?"

171

**CMA-A
COMPARATIVE
MARKET
ANALYSIS
ACTUAL**

"Here's the Comparative Market Analysis that I prepared on your home before I came out today. Here's your home. . .and I think you will agree that all of these homes are similar to yours, do you agree?" As you say that statement, first point your index finger at your seller's address then run your finger down the left side of the page to direct his attention to the other addresses on the CMA.

"OK, here are the similar homes that recently sold. Again, these tell us what people are <u>willing</u> to pay, for this kind of home, in this area, at this time: $87,000, $89,000, and $79,600."

"Here are the similar homes for sale now. Again, these tell us what we are competing against: $87,000, $89,000, and $85,000."

"And here are the expired listings. Again, these tell us what people are <u>not</u> willing to pay for this kind of home, in this area, at this time: $90,300, and $93,900."

**PRICE TIE
DOWN**

"Do you want the most money possible?" (Wait for "yes" answer.) **As quickly as possible?"** (Wait for answer.) **"And the fewest problems possible?"** (Wait for answer.) **"The best way to do that is to price your home right in the first place, isn't that right?"**

**CLOSING ON
PRICE**

1

"Where do you want to price it?"

2

"Based on the information I have just given you, what price do you think will get you the most money, the quickest sale, and the fewest problems?"

3

"I'll take your listing now at a price you are comfortable with, then I'll go back to my office and prepare a comparative market analysis and bring it back later. You can use it to raise the price, lower the price, or leave it alone, as you feel best. Fair enough?"

NOTE ON #3: This technique is excellent when you have gone to a home without a CMA, or, for some reason, you decide it's best not to show the one you have.

SLIGHTLY MORE-SLIGHTLY LESS

"How would you like to get a little more money for your home than other people have been currently getting for theirs?" (Wait for answer.) **"Some people are doing it by using the 'Slightly More-Slightly Less' pricing concept. It works like this: to get the most money, the quickest sale, and the fewest problems, price your house slightly _less_ than the competition, and slightly _more_ than recent sales. Here's why. By pricing your home slightly _less_ than the competition more salespeople will come to see your home. As a result, more buyers will see your home. And because of the increased activity, interest and enthusiasm, we stand a much better chance of getting a _full priced_ offer that is slightly _more_ than recent sales. Does that make sense?"**

CHAPTER 17

BUT I WANT
AN EXTRA MILLION

You have just presented current market data to a listing prospect. Your information shows that recent sales of three similar properties were $78,300, $79,600, and $80,990. Your information shows that three similar homes currently for sale are priced at $85,500, $87,000, and $89,000. You also showed two expired listings that were priced at $91,000 and $93,000. The sellers say they think their house is much better than others (it's not); they say they need $95,000 in order to buy their new home which is being built and will be ready in 90 days and is costing them $135,000; and they say that if you don't think you can get them $95,000, maybe they should give the listing to someone else.

In the previous chapters you have seen how different people, like Paris O'Reilly and Lauri Lee McKier, have prevented this kind of situation from developing. I would like to suggest now that your highest goal is to develop a listing appointment procedure that gets you the listing before you discuss price - that sells your professional abilities so well that most sellers will not be saying maybe they should find another salesperson who can get them 10% or 15% more than market value.

BUT I WANT AN EXTRA MILLION

However, in spite of the best procedures, the situation in the first paragraph will occur, and the question is, what do you do now? We have found two excellent procedures that seem to work equally well.

The first procedure begins with four questions and ends with an assuring, professional suggestion. Keep in mind that we believe the seller has the right to make the decision, and that you have the right to reject the listing if you don't want it. The procedure is:

> "What information do you have that leads you to believe someone will actually get $95,000 for your home?
>
> "What happens if no one will pay $95,000?
>
> "Suppose the best offer you get is $81,000. Will you accept it?
>
> "May I ask, what is the absolute least you will take for your home at this time?
>
> "I sincerely believe that you will get the most money, the quickest sale and the fewest problems by pricing your home in the competitive range in the first place."

Let's analyze this procedure. The first question is asking them to give some justification for selecting the price they think they should get. It is important that your tone of voice not be demanding or "parental." Remember when you were a teenager and your parents or some parent substitute said something like, "And just where did you get the information that said you could stay out until 3 a.m.?" That's the tone of voice we *don't* want to have.

176

Some people are more comfortable changing the words around to ask, "Do you have some information that leads you to believe you can actually get $95,00?"

Actually, there are two ways to ask this same basic question. Some of our graduates find it effective to ask both questions. The alternative question is, "What information do you have that leads you to believe someone will actually pay $95,000?" Notice the difference. The one question focuses on what the seller can get and the other focuses on what a buyer will pay.

Now, here's a most interesting discovery. No matter how a person answers the first question, you can always proceed to the second question. Let's look at most of the answers we could get to the first question. We ask, "What information do you have that leads you to believe that someone will actually pay $95,000?" The answers could be:

> "My neighbor got $95,000 for his home."
> "I had it appraised."
> "I have that much in it."
> "Another salesperson told me I should be able to get it."
> "I think it's worth it."
> "I need $95,000 to buy my next home."
> "I paid $95,000 last year and I'm not taking a loss."

There is no answer that would prevent you from proceeding to the second question, which is, "What happens if no one will pay $95,000. What are you going to do?" Here too, no matter how a person responds, you can proceed to the third question. Let's take a look at the answers we could get to "What happens if no one will pay...?"

> "I don't know."
> "I'll cross that bridge later."
> "I'll keep on trying."

"I guess I'll have to reduce it."
"I'll rent it."
"I'll burn it."
"I'll get another agent."

Again, there is no answer that will prevent you from asking the third question, which is, "Suppose the best offer you get is $81,000. Will you accept it?" They can only say "yes" or "no."

If they say "yes," you give them your professional recommendation by using the fifth technique of the procedure: "I sincerely believe you will get the most money, the quickest sale and the fewest problems by pricing your home in the competitive range in the first place."

If, on the other hand, they say "no," you can use the fourth question, which is: "May I ask, what is the *absolute least* you would accept for your home at this time?"

If the answer is in the competitive range, something below $87,000, for example, you can finish with, "I sincerely believe, etc."

If the answer is less than their original objective ($95,000 in this case) but still higher than the competition, you can go back to the second technique and proceed through the system again. For example, if the answer to "Absolute Least" was $93,000, you could then repeat, "What happens if no one will pay $93,000 for your home, what will you do?"

Again, it makes no difference how they answer the question, you can always logically ask the third question of the procedure, which is: "Suppose the best offer you get is . . ."

Now, please note carefully, we have found it best to select a price approximately equal to the *highest* recent sale for the first time you ask this question, and approximately equal to the *lowest* current listing for the second time you ask. In this case, the first price mentioned would be $81,000, as we did above, and the second price mentioned would be $85,500 or $86,000.

And again, the prospects can only answer "yes" or "no." If he answers yes, you can say, "I sincerely believe, etc." If he says no you can repeat the 4th question of the procedure, which is, "May I ask, what is the *absolute least* you will take for your home, etc." Generally, we have found it is best to focus on the least they will accept *right now* for the first time we ask the question, and on the least they will accept in 90 days the second time we ask the question.

Once more, the prospect can only answer with a price that is competitive or one that is not. If it is competitive, you can say, "I sincerely believe, etc." If it isn't, you can reject the listing, or you can take the listing by saying something like, "Okay, it's your house. Let's see what we can do." You could take the listing by using the techniques listed in our second procedure for dealing with prospects who want to overprice the listing. This procedure will give you another shot at reducing the price before taking the listing.

To summarize the first procedure, the five steps are:

 "What Information"
 "What Happens If"
 "Suppose"
 "Absolute Least"
 "I Sincerely Believe"

If you will memorize not only the language for each technique, but also the five step sequence and then practice this procedure at least 10 times with a partner who plays the part of a seller, I believe you will find you will become very, very effective in a real situation.

179

BUT I WANT AN EXTRA MILLION

The second procedure we have found to be extremely effective in dealing with situations where the prospect wants to ask 10% to 20% above current market prices. This procedure focuses on the four problems of over-pricing, which are:

> Hard To Get Salespeople Excited
> Hard To Get Good Buyers To Look
> Hard To Get An Offer
> Hard To Get Financing

We start this procedure with a technique we call, "Price Problems Opening Statement," or "PPOS" for short.

"I will take your listing at $_____ if you want me to . . . and I'll do my very best. But before we put that price on the listing agreement, let's discuss the problems of overpriced listings."

If you will look at the Comparative Market Analysis illustrated, you will see the four problems of overpriced listings printed in bold type. We have found it to be a good place for them. I believe a lot of prospects read them as they look at the market data and as a result decide to price correctly in the first place.

It's also a good place to have the four problems printed because they become a handy reference when it becomes necessary to explain them in detail. Now, here they are.

"First, it's very hard to get salepeople excited. And it doesn't make any difference who you give the listing to, the problem remains the same, it's hard to get salespeople excited.

"The salespeople in my office *know* what people are willing to pay for this kind of home, in this area, at this time. If I take your listing in at $_____, their reaction will be that it's overpriced. They won't get excited because they know they can't get their buyers excited.

"Your listing will go into our Multi-Listing Service. The active salespeople in this area know what people are willing to pay for this kind of home at this time, and their reaction will be that it is over-priced. They won't get excited because they know they can't get their buyers excited.

"Now, on the other hand, if you price it in the competitive range, watch what happens. The salespeople in my office get excited because they know they can get their buyers excited, and the active salespeople in our Multi-Listing Service get excited because they know they can get their buyers excited. Folks, excitement is contagious! So is apathy. Which situation would you rather have?"

That's a very effective technique. And it's nothing more than the truth.

There are several points worth noting. A most influential phrase is this one, "and it doesn't make any difference who you give the listing to, the problem remains the same . . . it's hard to get salespeople excited." When a prospect is trying desperately to believe his house is worth more than the evidence is telling him, he must also be wondering if another salesperson might do better. This phrase eliminates your competition.

The second critical point is that we don't blame the salespeople for not showing the house. The blame is fixed on the buyers. It's important to say that the salespeople don't get excited *because* they can't get the buyers excited.

Notice also the sequence. First we give the bad news and second the good news. And to reinforce it, we give the bad news twice and the good news twice. If the listing is overpriced, our

181

company salespeople won't get excited. If it is overpriced, the MLS salespeople will not get excited. If it's priced right, our sales-people will get excited. If it's priced right, the MLS sales-people will get excited.

The final important point is the phrase, "Excitement is contagious! So is apathy." When you ask people to make a choice, it's hard for anyone to make the wrong one.

In many cases, you won't have to give the other three problems. This first problem is a big one and most sellers now have enough information to select a good price right now. If you decide to close at this point, a good technique is: "Based on the information that I prepared for you on the Comparative Market Analysis, what price do you think will get the most salespeople excited, so we can get the most buyers excited?"

The second problem is that it is very hard to get good buyers to look at overpriced listings. A serious buyer doesn't want to waste time. If the sellers are asking 10% or 20% over other current listings, a serious buyer often declines to look because his reaction is that he can get as much house elsewhere for less money. If he is willing to spend the amount asked, his reaction is that he can get more house for his money elsewhere. No matter how you slice it, it is hard to get good buyers to waste their time looking at overpriced listings.

The third problem is that even if we can get a buyer to look at an overpriced listing, it's difficult to get him to make an offer. Why? One reaction is that if the sellers are unreasonable enough to overprice it, they will be unreasonable if a decent offer is actually made. Another reaction is that even if they will finally come down, it's going to take a long time because they are so far over the current market. Why bother - there are other homes that are priced right in the first place.

The second and third problems are easily stated like this:

"The second problem is . . . it's hard to get good buyers to look. A serious . . . qualified buyer just does not want to spend time looking at overpriced listings. And the third problem is...even if we can get him to look . . . it's hard to get him to make an offer. Serious, qualified buyers just don't want to tie up their deposit money for even one day on what they think is a hopeless cause or a long, drawn-out procedure.

The fourth problem is like an ace in the hole. It's a potent reason and doesn't require a lot of explanation. It goes like this:

"The fourth reason is . . . it's hard to get financing. Even if we can find a buyer *willing* to pay $_____, *where* are we going to get it financed? You see, lenders know what people are willing to pay, for this kind of home, in this area, at this time. They have been willing to finance 70% to 80% of the *average* selling prices, but they are unlikely to finance 70% or 80% of an *inflated* selling price. So, even if we can find a buyer willing to pay the price . . . *where* are we going to get the financing?"

To appreciate the full truth of the fourth reason, you have to look at the situation from the bank's point of view. They want to know how they are going to get their money back if the borrower defaults. They also worry that the market could go down. So they like to leave lots of difference between what they lend and what they feel is a price they could get at auction if they were forced to foreclose.

The net result is that the bank sends their appraiser out . . . and he's a most conservative fellow. You know the type. Needs two green lights to cross a street. Drives 53 MPH on the freeways. Enjoys looking for tiny flaws in everything. Suffers from terminal pessimism. And when all the dust settles, the bank directly or indirectly tells the buyer he is paying way too much.

183

BUT I WANT AN EXTRA MILLION

A good close at the end of the fourth pricing problem is an extension of the one presented above. Review the problems and ask the sellers what price they think would avoid the problems. "Folks, when a home is overpriced, it's hard to get salespeople excited; it's hard to get good buyers to look; even if we can get them to look, it's hard to get offers made; and even if we could find someone willing to pay, it's hard to find financing. So what price do you think would get the salespeople excited, get the buyers to look, get the offers and get the financing?"

One of our graduates reports that on one occasion, when he had completed giving the four problems of overpricing and asked the question, "So where do we get the financing?" the seller said, "I've got a great idea. Why don't you just find a cash buyer." To which the salesman responded, "I think I understand my assignment. You want me to find someone who was smart enough to accumulate $90,000 in cash . . . and dumb enough not to shop around."

Now, here are the techniques for dealing with pricing problems arranged for easy study.

WHAT INFORMATION	"What information do you have that leads you to believe that you will actual- ly get $_____ for your home?"
	"What information do you have that leads you to believe that someone will actually pay $_____ for your home?"
WHAT HAPPENS IF	"What happens if no one will pay $_____ in 90 days, what will you do?"

184

SUPPOSE

"Suppose the best offer you get is $_____, will you accept it?"

***

ABSOLUTE LEAST

"May I ask, what is the absolute least you will accept for your home at this time?"

***

I SINCERELY

"I sincerely believe that you will get the most money, the quickest sale and the fewest problems, by pricing your home in the competitive range in the first place."

***

PRICE PROBLEMS OPENING STATEMENT

"I will take your listing at $ _____ if you want me to . . . and I'll do my very best. But before we put that price on the listing agreement, let's discuss the problems of overpriced listings."

**PRICE
PROBLEM 1**

"First, it's very hard to get salespeople excited. And it doesn't make any difference who you give the listing to, the problem remains the same, it's hard to get salespeople excited.

"The salespeople in my office <u>know</u> what people are willing to pay for this kind of home, in this area, at this time. If I take your listing in at $ _____, their reaction will be that it's over-priced. They won't get excited because they know they can't get their buyers excited.

"Your listing will go into our Multi-Listing Service. The active salespeople in this area know what people are willing to pay for this kind of home at this time, and their reaction will be that it is over-priced. They won't get excited because they know they can't get their buyers excited.

"Now, on the other hand, if you price it in the competitive range, watch what happens. The salespeople in my office get excited because they know they can get their buyers excited, and the active salespeople in our Multi-Listing Service get excited because they know they can get their buyers excited. Folks, excitement is contagious! So is apathy. Which situation would you rather have?"

186

**PRICE
PROBLEM 2**

"The second problem is . . . it's hard to get good buyers to look. A serious . . . qualified . . . buyer just does not want to spend time looking at over-priced listing."

**PRICE
PROBLEM 3**

"The third problem is . . . even . . . if we can get them to look . . . it's hard to get people to make an offer. Serious, qualified buyers just don't want to tie up their deposit money for even one day on what <u>they</u> think is a hopeless cause or long, drawn-out procedure."

**PRICE
PROBLEM 4**

"The fourth problem is . . . it's hard to get financing. Even if we find a buyer willing to pay $_____, <u>where</u> are we going to get it financed? You see, lenders know what people are willing to pay . . . for this kind of home . . . in this area . . . at this time. They are willing to finance 70% to 80% of $(<u>market value</u>), not $(<u>inflated asking price</u>). So, where . . . are we going to get it financed?"

**PRICE
PROBLEM 1
CLOSE**

"Based on the information that I prepared for you on the Comparative Market Analysis, what price do you think will get the most salespeople excited, so we can get the most buyers excited?"

187

PRICE PROBLEM CLOSE

"Folks, when a home is overpriced, it's hard to get salespeople excited; it's hard to get good buyers to look; it's hard to get offers made; and even if we could find someone willing to pay the price, it's hard to get financing. So what price do you think would get the salespeople excited, get the buyers to look, get the offers and get the financing?"

CHAPTER 18

LIST FIRST –
PRICE SECOND

You hear that John and Nancy Cummings of 4888 High Street are moving. You call to verify and are granted an appointment for 7 o'clock this evening. During the conversation you determine that John has accepted a promotion and is being transferred to a distant city.

Your broker remembers that the Cummings bought the house through another agent who has since left the company. You search the files and find all the information you need to do a good market analysis.

Your research effort discloses that three similar homes in the area have recently sold for approximately $70,000, $71,000, and $72,000, four similar homes are currently for sale between $74,000 and $78,000 and that two similar homes priced at $80,000 and $82,000 have gone unsold for more than 90 days. You prepare a "Comparative Market Analysis" showing the various addresses, prices and other pertinent data.

At 7 p.m. John answers the door, cordially invites you in and asks you how much you think he will be able to get for the house and also informs you that he has an appointment elsewhere at 7:30 and must leave in 20 minutes.

Before you can answer, Mrs. Cummings volunteers that housing is much more expensive in the city to which they are moving, that it is a good thing they have the best home in the area because they will need all the money they can get, and she hopes that you will appreciate the nice features of the house better than the salesperson who was there at five o'clock and suggested a listing price that was $5,000 less than she knows someone will pay in a minute. Her discourse consumes five minutes.

At this point you should: a) Ask how much the other salesperson thought the house should be listed for; b) Ignore your market analysis and ask the Cummings how much they want for the house and take the listing at that price, knowing that they will come down quickly because they are under pressure to move; c) Suggest that Mrs. Cummings find something else to do while you show Mr. Cummings your "Comparative Market Analysis" and tell him about the realities of the current market; d) None of the above.

If you chose "d" I would agree...for several important reasons.

1. If you ask how much the other salesperson suggested the house be listed for, you corner yourself into a lose-lose situation. You lose if you agree with the other salesperson and you lose if you take an overpriced listing.

2. If you ignore your market data and take an overpriced listing, you not only damage your own professional reputation, you do the sellers a disservice because overpricing reduces showings and robs them of important negotiating time.

3. If you immediately show Mr. Cummings your market analysis, you have not had time to establish any valid reasons

why he should trust your judgment. If he agrees with Mrs. Cummings about how the home is the nicest in the area, you are in another lose-lose situation.

I was recently explaining all these reasons not to discuss price before getting a commitment from the sellers, when one real estate salesman said, "Nice speech, Jerry, but the sellers expect us to give them the price before they agree to list with us. How do we get them to change their minds?"

Good question. Easy answer. We get the sellers to change their minds by first changing our minds. Once we understand *why* we should not give out price information before we get the listing, and we become *determined* to do business on our terms instead of their terms, it is extremely easy to get the listings first and price them second.

First, a most important point: When I say "get the listing first and price it second," I don't mean that the listing should be signed. I mean only that the sellers have agreed that we can have the listing.

To clarify that point: Other than price, why should I list my home with you? If your answer is convincing, why shouldn't I agree to list with you before we discuss price?

There are several important benefits to obtaining the listing first and pricing it second. First, it gives us a chance to demonstrate our professional abilities on topics other than price, so that, when it's time to discuss price, the prospects will have more confidence in our information and judgment. Second, by getting the sellers to agree to list with us before we discuss price, we have just avoided getting into a bidding contest with other salespeople who may be offering to take the listing at an inflated price just to get a listing.

191

LIST FIRST - PRICE SECOND

Aside from the benefits of listing first and pricing second, I also believe that the seller has no right - and I mean *absolutely* no right - to any information you have regarding the current market value of his home or of similar homes until he has agreed to list with you.

Would you ask a doctor to operate on you on the basis that after the operation is over, you will decide *if* you will pay?

Would you ask an architect to design a new home for you on the basis that after the blueprints are complete and you study them for the weekend, you will decide *if* you will pay?

Would you ask a painter to paint your house on the basis that after the job is complete, you will decide *if* you will pay?

The answers, of course, are "no." Why? Because operating on people, designing homes and painting homes is the product of those individuals professional ability . . . and we have no right to the product of their ability unless we agree to compensate them appropriately.

Likewise, determining the current market value of a home is the product of our professional abilities. The sellers have no right to the information until they agree to compensate us by giving us the listing, or, if we are certified appraisers, paying us a fee.

Some salespeople say, "Well, it's not that much work to put some market information together." That's beside the point. It doesn't matter if it takes 5 hours or 5 minutes to get the information. It doesn't matter if you had to do a lot of research or whether you could pull the information out of your head as a result of 15 years of experience. *Any* information you have relative to the current market value of a seller's home is the product of your professional ability, and the seller has absolutely no right to the information until he agrees that you can list the home.

192

Now, assuming that you agree, and assuming that you are determined to list first and price second, let's take a look at some techniques to do that.

Mr. Cummings has just asked us how much we think he can get for the house. Our objective is to avoid discussing price, so the important question here is where should we attempt to go? If we look at selling as a sequence of steps, the answer is clear.

Logically, the first thing we should do with prospects is find out why they are selling, where they are going, when they have to leave here or get there and whether or not they need the money from this house to buy their next one. That's called qualifying.

Then, if we want them to agree to list with us before we discuss the price, we need to tell them why they will benefit by having us represent them to sell the home. That's called the listing presentation.

So, if the prospect immediately asks us how much we think the house is worth, our objective should be to qualify him and then make a good listing presentation and obtain his agreement that we can have the listing. (You may want to review Chapters 7 and 11 to get the full feeling for the flow of things.)

However, not all prospects have the same personality or method of relating to others. Some people are more assertive than others; some are less assertive. Some are more friendly; some less. So as a result, we need more than one way to deal with the "How much?" question.

Happily, we have, in our system, five good answers that are effective. Once you learn the answers, you will almost instinctively know which ones to choose based on the prospect's personality.

193

LIST FIRST - PRICE SECOND

The first choice is simply to begin qualifying.

Cummings: "I'm in kind of a hurry. How much do you think we can get for our house?"

Us: "Well, may I ask, why are you selling? etc."

Another choice is to respond with a great technique called "Two Important Decisions."

Cummings: "How much do you think we can get for the house?"

Us: "Mr. Cummings, when you put your home up for sale, you have two *important* decisions to make. First, what person, or firm, will you have represent you to sell your home, and second, with that person, determine the best price to put your home on the market. Does that make sense?"

Cummings: "Yes."

Us: "May I ask, why are you selling? etc."

I need to make one *very* important comment here that relates to "Every Word Counts." The prospect has two decisions to make, but he doesn't have to make them. Therefore, it is important to say "you have two important decisions to make," not "you have to make two important decisions." That is a very important distinction.

Sometimes, the "how much" question is put to us just as we enter the home. Paris O'Reilley's answer is called "Price Delay."

Cummings: "How much do you think we can get for the house?"

Us: "The pricing of your home is far too important to guess at. Let's go through the house first."

Then, as we proceed through the house, we can begin qualifying, or we can use "Two Important Deicisons" first and then swing into qualifying.

If you like humor, Phyllis D. has a neat technique when people ask her for a price just as she enters the home.

Cummings: "How much do you think we can get?"

Phyllis: "$158.50."

Cummings: "Where did you get that figure?"

Phyllis, with a laugh: "Well, all I've seen so far is the front door, and you can buy a good front door for $158.50."

After they have had a good laugh, she adds "Price Delay."

Paris O'Reilley's other excellent technique titled "What I Think" is also a good response to a "How much?" question.

Cummings: "Well, how much do *you* think this house is worth?"

Us: "What I think your house is worth has *absolutely* no merit whatsoever. The *only* thing that counts is . . . what are people *willing* to pay . . . for *this* kind of home . . . in *this* area . . . at *this* time. Isn't that right?"

Cummings: "Yes, that makes sense."

195

LIST FIRST - PRICE SECOND

Us: "Mr. Cummings, when you put your home up for sale, you have two *important* decisions to make, etc."

Still another way to handle the "How much" question is to respond with the technique titled, "Help You Price," which is also "Reason 2" of the "8 Good Reasons."

Cummings: "Look. I'm in a hurry. Just give me the bottom line. What will I get for this house?"

Us: "Mr. Cummings, one of the reasons you will benefit by having me represent you to sell your home is: I can help you determine the best price to ask. Surprising as it may seem, sometimes the price is set much lower than current market value. Usually, however, the price is set too high and the home does not sell. It takes a lot of work on my part, but I can help you determine the right price to ask because . . .

"I work from a 'Comparative Market Analysis' that contains three important parts. First will be similar homes recently sold. These will tell us what people are willing to pay, for this kind of home, in this area, at this time. Second will be similar homes for sale now. These will tell us what we are competing against. Buyers for your home will also be looking at these homes. And third will be expired listings. These will be similar homes unsold for 90 days or more. These illustrate the problems of over-pricing. As a matter of fact, these tell us what people are not willing to pay for this kind of home, in this area, at this time.

"Mr. Cummings, do you see how this approach will help you determine the best price to ask?"

Cummings: "Yes."

Us: "Mr. Cummings, when you put your home up for sale, you have two important decisions...etc."

Isn't it neat how one technique so logically flows into another? Just learn them well and the right one to use will pop into your mind.

The new technique to study for this chapter is "Two Important Decisions." All of the others were covered in Chapters 14 and 15.

TWO
IMPORTANT
DECISIONS

"When you put your home up for sale, you have two <u>important</u> decisions to make. First, what person, or firm, will you have represent you to sell your home, and second, <u>with</u> that person, determine the best price to put your home on the market."

CHAPTER 19

MAY I HAVE
THE LISTING?

The subject of this chapter is "Closing." This is the step in the selling procedure where we ask the prospect to take action, to make a decision, to sign a listing agreement. It is, to use an old, old phrase, the moment of truth.

One of the oldest questions in selling is: "When should we close?" And the answer is: "Whenever it seems right?"

Most people don't like to make decisions. Some are petrified; some are just uncomfortable. The more infrequent the decision, and the more complicated the issue, the more difficult it becomes. Some people never do decide for themselves. They let events happen, or they go along with whatever others decide.

Some people, of course, have no problem in making decisions. Given the facts they need and asked to take action, they usually do so. A small percentage of the population are very decisive. They usually "close" themselves.

For experienced salespeople, knowing when to close is no problem. They just "know." For less experienced people, it's best to have a general plan.

Here's a formula that works very well. It is based on the idea that in professional selling our job is to give the propect enough information so that he can make a good decision.

1. Prospect to find potential client
2. Qualify
3. Give listing presentation
4. Test to see if prospects see how they will benefit
5. Close
6. Respond to indecision or objections, if necessary
7. Close again

In discussing the question of when to close, it's fairly obvious that normally we would not attempt to close right after we ask a prospecting question, but there are exceptions. Here's an example.

We hear that Nick and Rita Penn have just made a deposit on a new house but have not yet listed their present home. We go directly to the home, introduce ourselves and say:

"I understand that you have bought a new home, is that correct?"

"Yes, it is."

"Great! I'd like to represent you to sell this home. May I?"

Talk about getting right down to brass tacks, there it is. It sounds like a fast close, and it is, but what's the worst thing that could happen? They could say "no." They could also say that they have a friend in the business, or they could ask us what we think we can do for them or how much we think the house is worth. And they could say "yes." Nick and Rita need to sell the house. We are there. We must feel competent or we wouldn't be asking for the listing. So they could say "yes."

We could also close right after we qualify but before we make a listing presentation. Let's go back to our lead. Let's assume that we did not ask for the listing right away but rather that Nick asked us in to talk about the listing.

Us: "Nick, when will the new house be ready?"

Nick: "We close in 90 days."

Us: "Do you need the money from this house to buy the new house?"

Nick: "Every dime."

Us: "What happens if this home isn't sold in 90 days: what are you going to do?"

Nick: "I think I have enough equity to get some swing financing."

Us: "How much do you think that would cost you for 30 days?"

Nick: "Well, I need $25,000 down, so whatever the interest rate is times $25,000."

Us: "In any event, it's money out of your pocket, isn't it?"

Nick: "Yes."

Us: "Nick, what happens if you have to make payments on both houses? How long can you handle that?"

201

Nick: "Not very long. I don't even want to think about it. The whole move is a squeeze."

Us: "Would it be in your best interest to have this home sold *and* closed in the next 90 days?"

Nick: "You bet it would!"

Us: "Since it normally takes about thirty days from the time someone agrees to buy your home until you get the money, we should have this home sold in sixty days so you can have the money in 90 days, isn't that right?"

Nick: "Holy Moses! I forgot about that! If I don't get this home sold quick, I'm going to be in a heap of trouble."

Us: "Nick, why don't you let me get started right away?"

Nick: "Why not! Let's do it!"

Why would Nick agree so quickly? Because the quality of our qualifying questions indicates that we understand the business. . .and because the questions also indicate that we understand Nick's problem.

When should you close? When it feels right.

In most cases, asking for the listing will happen after we make a listing presentation. Let's assume that we have qualifed Nick and Rita and given them what we call our standard listing presentation as covered in Chapter 11. Now, according to our formula, it's time to test to see if they understand how they will benefit by the points we made in our listing presentation.

Some people refer to this step as "Trial Close," but I don't really like that term. To me, it implies that you're "trying" to close and I am always reminded of the time when someone was interviewing Flip Wilson on television a few years back. Flip was asked what he felt was the difference between an amateur comedian and a professional. "An amateur," he replied, "*tries* to be funny and a professional *is* funny."

I have found that asking "test" questions to see if the prospects have enough information to make a decision puts me in a better position. If they do have enough information, my closing techniques work easily, and if they are not ready to decide, I can easily review important sales points or add extra ones to my presentation.

The two best "test" techniques in our system are called, "Basic Benefit Question #1" and "What Kind."

"Basic Benefit Question #1" sounds like this:

"Nick, do you see how you will benefit by having me represent you to sell your home?"

He only has a few choices, "Yes, go ahead and list it"; "Yes"; "No"; "Yes, but. . ." (offers a stall or objection).

If he says, "Yes, go ahead and list it," we don't have to ask for the listing. He's given it to us. He is highly decisive and closed himself.

If he says, "Yes," with no further comment, we can ask for the listing with favorable odds that there will be no objections or indecision.

If he says "No, not really," he is telling us we haven't given him enough information, or the right information, or he isn't convinced that we can do the job. In any event, we wouldn't try to close now but rather find out why he isn't sold on us and review important points from our listing presentation or add more points, as necessary.

If he says "Yes, but. . ." and offers a stall or objection, we have to deal with that. Stalls and objections are covered fully in Chapters 19 and 20.

The second technique for testing readiness to close is called "What Kind" and it sounds like this:

"Nick, what kind of salesperson do you want to have representing you to sell your home. Someone who understands the problems and has a solution, or someone who just puts a sign on the lawn, an ad in the paper and waits for buyers to come?"

He only has two logical choices. Either he says, "I want you," and closes himself, or he says, "The first kind," or "Someone who understands the problems and has solutions" or something else to that effect, and we can then ask a closing question.

This particular technique has proven to be very, very effective. Lauri Lee McKier used it exceptionally well, as illustrated in Chapter 6.

Let's look at our formula again:

1. Prospect
2. Qualify
3. Listing Presentation
4. Test
5. Close

OK, we got to the prospect, we qualified and found a motivated seller, we made a listing presentation, and we have tested and found that the prospect sees how he will benefit. Now, let's examine some various methods of closing.

For this part of the chapter, let's assume that we have given the listing presentation, have asked Nick and Rita "Basic Benefit Question #1" and we have obtained a positive "Yes." At this point we can close by asking for "Facts" that go on the listing agreement, such as correct spelling of his last name, or his full first name, or whatever.

"Nick, Rita, do you see how you will benefit by having me represent you to sell your home?"

"Yes."

"Good. May I ask. . .Nick, what is your full first name?"

Notice that we didn't actually ask if we could have the listing. Because of the positive "yes" answer to our test question, we just assumed we had the listing and asked for information to go on the listing agreement.

In closing on "Facts" we can either ask for information or verify the correctness of information. "Nick, how do you spell your last name?" or "Nick, your last name is spelled 'P-e-n-n', isn't it?"

Other examples of "Facts" closes are:

>"The address here is _____. Isn't that right?"
>"The lot size is _____. Isn't it?"
>"Is this property located in the _____ school zone?"
>"How much are the taxes here now?"

We can also close on "Possession Date."

205

MAY I HAVE THE LISTING?

"Nick, Rita, do you see how you will benefit by having me represent you to sell your home?"

"Yes."

"Great. May I ask, how soon after a sale could you give possession? Would _____ days be ok?"

We can close by asking about "Accessories."

"Nick, Rita, do you see how you will benefit by having me represent you to sell your home?"

"Yes."

"Good. May I ask, what accessories will be included in the sale? For example, are you taking the drapes, or will they stay?"

Some people find that it is just a bit abrupt for them to close as we have just done. There is a very nice way to soften those closes a bit by using techniques we call "Pivot 1" or "Pivot 2".

"Nick, do you see how you will benefit by having me represent you to sell your home?"

"Yes."

"Fine, for me to represent you, I need just a little information. How do you spell your last name?"

When Nick answers the question, he is actually saying, "Go ahead and represent me."

In "Pivot 1" we focus representing the seller and in "Pivot 2" we focus on getting started.

"Nick, do you see how you will benefit by having me represent you to sell your home?"

"Yes."

"Fine, I can get started just as soon as I get a little more information. How soon after a sale can you give possession?"

Notice that what we have done is simply link a "Fact" close or a "Possession" close to the "Pivot".

These two techniques are called "pivots" because they literally "pivot" or turn the conversation from the test question into the closing questions.

Another form of closing is called "Activities".

> "May I measure the house now?"
> "May I put up a sign today?"
> "May I schedule an office inspection for Wednesday morning?"
> "May I schedule an open house for this weekend?"

All of the above closes would qualify as "assumptive" closes, since we never actually asked for the listing. Keep in mind that a closing question is any question in which a positive answer indicates a willingness to buy.

"Impending Events" is a type of close in which we create a sense of urgency about something that is about to happen.

MAY I HAVE THE LISTING?

"Nick, do you see how you will benefit by having me represent you to sell your home?"

"Yes."

"If you give me the listing now, I can still include your house on our company tour for tomorrow morning, and that will save us one whole week."

Notice the urgency that is created by the phrase, "that will save us one whole week." The best "Impending Event" closes are built around activities that generally happen only on a weekly basis.

Other impending events could be scheduling an "Open House" for this weekend, and deadlines of various newspapers or local real estate publications. Since the weekends are usually the most active for buyers, you can often focus on that.

In one of our courses a few years ago there was a girl who was very, very pregnant - which means the baby was due most anytime. The evening of the day we covered the "Impending Event" technique, she went out on a listing, qualified the prospects, gave a good listing presentation, and then said, "Folks, if you give me the listing tonight, I can have the baby in the hospital because I'm not leaving without a listing!" She got it.

The "Highlight Sheet Close" and the "Deferred Price Close" are two of the most effective closes we have ever tested and used.

"Nick, Rita, do you see how you will benefit by having me represent you to sell your home?"

"Yes."

"I've got a great idea. Rita, why don't you use this "Highlight

Sheet" as a guide and make a list of all the good features we could use on the "Highlight Sheets" for your house while Nick and I measure the house. Then we can discuss the price; you can select a price, and I can get started right away. Fair enough?"

"OK."

The "Highlight Sheet Close" refers to the "Highlight Sheet" feature of our standard listing presentation which was covered in Chapter 11. A sample is illustrated at the end of the book.

Notice how this gets customer participation in the closing activitiy. Customer participation at this point is one of the best things we can do.

The "Deferred Price Close" is almost identical, except that there is no reference to the "Highlight Sheets."

"Nick, Rita, do you see how you will benefit by having me represent you to sell your home?"

"Yes."

"I've got a great idea. Let's measure the house, then we can discuss the price; you can select a price, and I can get started right away. Fair enough?"

"Sure. Let's do it."

Again, we are getting the prospects involved in the closing activity.

Notice also the sequence of events. First we measure the house, which gives us a chance to inspect the house and make sure our market data is accurate and our comparables are comparable. Then we discuss the price - that means we will be making a full "Pricing Presentation" as outlined in Chapter 15 and dealing with any price objections as outlined in Chapter 16 - and after the sellers select a price, we can get started right away. Fair enough? A positive response to that question means we have their agreement that we can have the listing.

One of the reasons this technique works so well is the phrase, "you can select a price," which gives the sellers a strong feeling of control. That is consistent with our entire system and philosophy which puts us in control of giving information and keeps the sellers in control of making the decision. And that's as it should be. After all, it's their house. They are going to get 93% or 94% of the selling price.

Our final closing technique is called "Direct Questions." When all the dust settles, sometimes the best way to get a listing is to ask for it.

"Nick, Rita, do you see how you will benefit by having me represent you to sell your home?"

"Yes."

"May I have the listing?"

"Sure, you sound good."

"Thank you."

Here are some more "Direct Questions":

> "Why don't you let me get started?"
> "Why don't you give me the listing?"
> "Would you like me to get started today?"
> "I'd like to get things started first thing in the morning. Why don't you give me the listing tonight so I can do that?"

Closing is easy when you are good at it, just like everything else in life. The key to making closing easy and natural is to follow the formula. Qualify, make a listing presentation, test for readiness and close.

In this chapter, I have covered quite a number of closing techniques because there are a lot of different prospects out there and no one technique will fit all personalities and situations, although the "Deferred Price Close" comes pretty close. Study all of the techniques, then select three that appeal to you and master those three immediately.

Develop a system to selling so that you feel in control of carrying the conversation in the direction you choose, rather than being led all around the mulberry bush by a dominant seller.

When you are good at it, selling is easy and fun. . .and very profitable. Why not become a great salesperson?

Now, here are the techniques covered in this chapter arranged for easy study.

PIVOT 1   "Fine, for me to represent you, I need just a little more information."

PIVOT 2   "Fine, I can get started just as soon as I have a little more information."

MAY I HAVE THE LISTING?

FACTS

"The correct spelling of your last name is _____,
right?"

"The address here is _____, isn't that right?"

"Is this property in the _____ school zone?"

_____

POSSESSION

"May I ask, how soon after a sale could you give possession?"

_____

ACCESSORIES

"May I ask, what accessories will be included in the sale? For example, will the _____ stay or go with you?"

_____

ACTIVITIES

"May I measure the house now?"
"May I put up a sign today?"
"May I schedule an office inspection for Friday?"
"May I start advertising on _____?"
"May I schedule an open house for __?"

**IMPENDING
EVENTS**

"If you give the listing now, I can
    - still get an ad in the Sunday
      paper,
    - include your house in tomor-
      row's company tour,
    - still schedule an 'Open House'
      for   Sunday,
and that will save us one whole week!"

**HIGHLIGHT
SHEET
CLOSE**

"I have a great idea. Why don't you use this 'Highlight Sheet' as a guide and make a list of all the good features we can use on the 'Highlight Sheet' for your house while I measure the house, then we can discuss the price, you can select a price, and I can get started right away, fair enough?"

**DEFERRED
PRICE
CLOSE**

"I have a great idea. Let's measure the house, then we can discuss the price, you can select a price, and I can get started right away, fair enough?"

MAY I HAVE THE LISTING?

DIRECT QUESTIONS

"'May I have the listing?"

"Are you going to let me go to work for you?"

"Why don't you give me the listing?"

"May I get started now?"

"Would you like me to get started now?"

"I'd like to represent you to sell your home, may I?"

CHAPTER 20

EVERYTHING YOU WANTED
TO KNOW ABOUT
INDECISION
BUT WERE HESITANT
TO ASK

Several years ago, while addressing a realtor group in Montreal, I asked one man if he would agree that some people have a harder time making decisions than others.

"I don't know," he replied. "What do you think?"

I never did find out if he was putting me on or was part of the problem.

Why do some people have such a hard time making decisions? Why can some people look at one home and say, "I'll take it," while others have to look at 30 homes and still feel they should look some more? Why do some sellers give you a well-priced listing in ten minutes while others need to get seven opinions and still aren't sure whom to list with and where to price the home?

The answer lies in habits, attitudes, feelings, self-image, self-

215

esteem. Some people have a habit of procrastinating. Others have a real fear of making decisions. Some people decide quickly for fear of looking indecisive. Others decide quickly because they have faith in their judgments and because they feel they can correct any errors before any serious damage is done.

In order to become effective in dealing with indecision, it is necessary to have a basic understanding of that part of human nature that controls one's decisiveness. Once we gain that understanding, there are some simple techniques that are extremely effective. Let's take a look at how behavior develops.

My research indicates that behavior is the outer expression of attitudes, feelings and skills. As I see it, attitudes are habits of thought. The habits of thought are the result of ideas we are exposed to on a repetitive basis. And the source of the ideas is our environment, which is made up of our families, our friends, school, church, work, books, radio, television, movies, experiences, etc. Feelings, which also affect behavior, are the result of sensations of okayness or not okayness which we experience on a repetitive basis. The source of the sensations is also our entire environment, which includes family, friends, etc. Finally, skills obviously affect behavior . . . practice, or actions repeated, is the source of skills.

Graphically, a model would look like this:

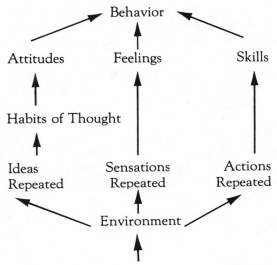

Family - Friends - School - Church - Work
Radio - Television - Movies - Newspapers
Books - Magazines - Experiences - Etc.

Let's see how this works. Suppose a boy is born into a poor family that prides itself on being honest. For the first few years, the boy isn't even aware of being poor. What is there to compare with? But at some point, he discovers that other kids and other families have a lot more things than he and his family. At some point he will begin to hear a standard justification among many poor people: "It's OK to be poor as long as you are honest."

The idea is reinforced at family gatherings, school, church, and daily living. The idea is repeated until it becomes a habit of thinking, which in turn becomes an attitude, which in turn controls behavior.

217

EVERYTHING YOU WANTED TO KNOW ABOUT INDECISION BUT WERE HESITANT TO ASK

Running parallel to ideas and attitudes are sensations and feelings. If the idea of being poor and honest is reinforced by "OK" sensations of approval - the family shows love and acceptance when the boy acts and talks poor and honest and shows strong disapproval and rejection when the boy talks about becoming rich or being dishonest in order to get ahead- these sensations will develop into strong, subconscious feelings, which also affect behavior. What kind of a job will this boy ultimately look for? One that will keep him poor and honest.

However, if the young boy somehow beings to feel that there is no reason to be poor, and that one can be rich and honest, he will begin looking for new ideas to justify the feelings. If he can get enough positive ideas, ultimately he will develop a habit of thinking and an attitude that will reinforce the feelings and change his behavior. His first change of behavior will be to acquire skills. The new skills will then affect his attitudes and feelings.

Now let's look at how this process affects decision making. Suppose a young girl is brought up in an environment where every decision she makes is challenged or ridiculed. When she tries to dress herself, at the age of three, she is laughed at for getting her shoes on left or right or her dress on backwards. She is reprimanded for going out doors or across the street without permission. Every time she makes a decision, she is made to feel "not-okay." And it never stops.

Someone finds fault with her choice of subjects in high school, with the clothes she wears, with the car she buys, with the boy she marries, with the church she joins - or for not joining a church - and one day, you get her as a lead for a listing. If she has developed a lifelong "not-okay" feeling about making decisions, you are going to get a heavy dose of indecision when it comes time to decide.

Feelings, I have found, seem to outweigh attitudes ten to one.

218

That's why it so often happens that when people say this time they will make a quick decision, when the time comes they just can't bring themselves to do it.

The key question, therefore, is: when faced with a prospect who cannot decide, what do you do? The answer lies in what the prospect *needs*. Very simply, the prospect needs assurance.

Think about it. When you ask or suggest that the prospect give you a decision, and he says he wants to think about it or he wants to talk to his mother, father, boss, attorney, priest, minister, rabbi, or guru, what is he saying except, "I need someone to assure me that this is going to be a good decision." Here's our answer:

"Mr. and Mrs. Prospect, you will always be glad you took action with me today. I don't believe you can find anyone who will work harder, or more professionally, to get you the most money, the quickest sale and the fewest problems, which I know you want, isn't that right?"

Let's analyze those words, because they are mighty effective indeed. "You will always be glad . . ." Always! When I say those words, I visualize you being 95 years old, enjoying good health, and vacationing on a beautiful sand beach on a beautiful, warm sunshiny day and saying: "Boy, I'm sure glad I made that decision with Jerry Bresser way back when . . ."

". . . you took action with me today." Action! Today! With me! We're gonna get this job done, together!

"I don't believe that you can find anyone who will work harder, or more professionally . . ." If you were not in real estate and you had just been transferred and were looking for a salesperson to represent you, would you want someone who would work hard in your behalf? Would you want someone who would work professionally? Would you want someone who believed in himself? There's power, real power, in them thar words.

EVERYTHING YOU WANTED TO KNOW ABOUT
INDECISION BUT WERE HESITANT TO ASK

Notice, by the way, that I did not arrogantly say that I was better than everybody else. I didn't say that no one else works as hard as I do or as professionally as I do. I just said that I don't believe you can find anyone who will work harder or more professionally. I have allowed that there are some others as good as me - only a few, mind you - but no one is better.

Also, if you were selling your home,. would you want the most money possible? As quickly as possible? And with the fewest problems possible? Consider then, the impact of the words, ". . . to get you the most money, the quickest sale, and the fewest problems."

Finally, we turn the statement into a question with the words, ". . . which I know you want, isn't that right?" How can anyone say no?

For dealing with indecision, that is one of the most effective techniques I have ever found.

Will it always work? Absolutely not! Some people suffer from terminal indecision. They cannot decide if they want to live or die - and you and I and the rest of the world won't be able to help them. But it works most of the time. And that's all you need.

Another good technique that can be most helpful at the point you are asking a prospect to decide is the "Depressure" technique. As you may have noticed, some prospects feel a very heavy and threatening sense of pressure when you ask them to make a decision. You are not causing the pressure. It is the act of deciding that causes the pressure. The technique sounds like this:

"Mr. and Mrs. Prospect, I am not here to pressure you into making a bad decision, but I would like to give you enough information to make a good decision. Is that fair?"

220

It is very, very hard for people to say "no" to that question. When you get a "yes" answer, you can restate some of your more important points, or give additional information. A good example of this technique in action is in Chapter 1 when John is presenting the offer to Mr. Fax.

Here's an example of how one salesman used the "Depressure" and the "Assure" technique together. The salesman had made a listing presentation explaining several special marketing techniques he would use and had concluded by asking, "Do you see how you will benefit by having me represent you to sell your home?"

"Now hold on," the prospect suddenly said, "I don't want to be pressured into signing a listing agreement just yet."

"Mr. Prospect," responded the salesman, "I'm not here to pressure you into making a bad decision, but I would like to give you enough information to make a good decision. Is that fair?"

"Well, yes," said the prospect, "I can't afford to make a bad decision. I need all the money I can get for this house."

"That's exactly my point," responded the salesman. "You need the most money possible. Do you also want the quickest sale possible?"

"Yes, of course."

"And the fewest problems possible?"

"Naturally."

"Mr. Prospect, do you want to list with someone who will work *hard* in your behalf?"

"Yes."

221

EVERYTHING YOU WANTED TO KNOW ABOUT INDECISION BUT WERE HESITANT TO ASK

"Do you want someone who will work *professionally* in your behalf?"

"Very much so. I can't afford mistakes."

"Mr. Prospect, you will always be glad you took action with me today. I don't believe that you can find *anyone* who will work *harder* or more *professionally* to get you the most money, the quickest sale and the fewest problems, which I know you want, isn't that right?"

"Yes."

"Why don't you let me get started tonight?"

"OK. You look like you know what you are doing."

Isn't that great? All the prospect needed was some assurance and an extra minute to think things out. And the key to the salesman's success was that he had memorized the language so it came out exactly the way it should at the precise moment it was needed.

Which brings me to a most important point. Some techniques can be messed up a bit and still communicate the basic message, but others can cause a bit of a challenge if they don't come out word perfect.

Dianne, one of our graduates, had only partly memorized the "Assurance" technique. The first time she had an occasion to use it she said, "Mr. Prospect, you will always be glad you had a little action with me today . . . "

Now, let's discuss another important subject. How do you know when to use certain techniques? How can you determine what techniques to use on different kinds of people?

222

Most experienced salespeople tell me it took them five to ten years to gain enough experience to become effective in determining personality traits. Now - good news! There is a way you can learn how to do that in a matter of a few days.

A Dr. David Merrill has developed an efficient way of identifying personality and behavior traits that makes it very easy for salespeople to quickly select the right kind and amount of selling techniques to be more effective.

Dr. Merrill identifies two major traits as the keys to personality. One is assertiveness and the other is emotional responsiveness.

On a scale of 1 to 100, some people will be very assertive and very decisive, and some will be most unassertive and indecisive, and others will be in between. Assertive, decisive people need *less* information to make decisions. They feel more "OK" about their ability to absorb information and make decisions. On the other end of the scale, unassertive people need *more* information in order to make a decision and feel less "OK" about their ability to decide.

The other trait to consider is emotional responsiveness. Again, on a scale of 1 to 100, some people will be very emotional, very responsive, very friendly; some will be unresponsive, unemotional, and unfriendly; and others, somewhere in between.

EVERYTHING YOU WANTED TO KNOW ABOUT
INDECISION BUT WERE HESITANT TO ASK

Dr. Merrill sees these two traits interrelating in such a way as to identify four basic personalities, or social styles. If we look at the "assertive" trait on a horizontal scale, and the "friendly" trait on a vertical scale, and draw a box around the two, we can observe these four styles, as shown in the illustration.

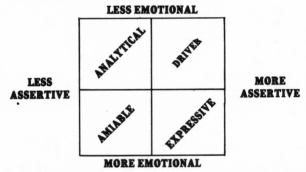

What we see is that a person who is less friendly and more assertive is a "driver" type person. One who is more friendly and more assertive is an "expressive" type. One who is more friendly but less assertive is an "amiable", and one who is less friendly and less assertive is an "analytical."

It is vitally important to understand that it is not wrong for a person to be in any position. The world needs all types of people. We need analyticals to do research. As one wit said, if Thomas Edison weren't an analytical, we'd have to watch television by candlelight.

We need amiables to be good harmonious workers. We need expressives to start and lead ambitious projects, and we need drivers when tough-minded leadership is required. I'd hate to be in combat, under heavy enemy fire, with an amiable sergeant who couldn't decide if we should attack, retreat or surrender- and who needs the opinions of three captains, two majors, and a general before making a move. I also wouldn't want to be there with an expressive who thought we were all ten feet tall and bullet-proof.

Dr. Merrill points out that drivers and analyticals need different kinds of information than expressives and amiables. The first two need more fact-oriented information, while the other two need more people-oriented information.

As you think about it, it will be the people on the unassertive end of the scale who will need and respond to techniques like "Depressure" and "Assure". For the analytical, review lots of facts. For amiables, stress how comfortable they will feel with you as their representative.

Indecisive people are a real challenge. They can be inconvenient when they simply can't decide what to eat at a restaurant and they can be costly when their indecision consumes your valuable time. Learning how to identify different types of people and learning how to respond to their needs for kinds and amounts of information to make a decision is the key to more effective selling.

Now here are the two techniques to learn.

ASSURE "You will always be glad you took action with me today. I don't believe you will find anyone who will work harder or more professionaly to get the most money, the quickest sale, and the fewest problems, which I know you want. Isn't that right?"

225

DEPRESSURE

"I'm not here to pressure you into making a bad decision, but I would like to give you enough information to help you make a good decision. Is that fair?"

Another alternative to this technique is: "I'm not here to pressure you into making a bad decision, but part of my job is to give you enough information so that you can make a good decision. Is that fair?"

CHAPTER 21

A GOOD ANSWER
FOR
EVERY OBJECTION

What impressed me about Leo was that he had an answer for every objection. What was even more impressive was his ability to prevent objections from arising. At the time I thought he walked on water, but later I realized that he just knew where the rocks were.

The "rocks" were not only answers to objections, but also his philosophy and procedure.

Leo believed that if you got the same objection three times, you were causing it. He believed that a good presentation would eliminate most objections and he believed that good procedure was the key to making good presentations.

Years later, as I was gathering effective selling techniques from successful salespeople, I was constantly impressed that so many high achievers had arrived at the same conclusions as Leo. If they got the same objections several times, they changed their procedure to prevent it from occurring again. They stressed that good procedure and a good presentation would eliminate or minimize objections. I was also impressed by the fact that they, too, had good answers for almost every objection.

227

A GOOD ANSWER FOR EVERY OBJECTION

Most experienced salespeople have found that at least 50% of all objections are not valid from the prospect's own point of view. My experience is the same. When a prospect is uncomfortable or fearful about making a decision, his indecision may be expressed with an objection. The prospect says he has a friend in real estate, but he has no such friend. He says he has another appointment, but there is no appointment.

As a result, we have taught a procedure that has proven to be very effective. The first time an objection is expressed, or if there is even the slightest suspicion that the objection is a cover-up for indecision, immediately use "Assure" or "Depressure" as covered in Chapter 19. Remember, you have a 50% chance that the objection is not valid. The worst that can possibly happen is that the objection was not a cover-up, but was valid from the prospect's point of view, and he or she will simply repeat the objection. You can then deal with it as covered in this chapter.

Now, let's see what can be done when the objection is not a cover-up for indecision and must be answered. Here's a list of the most common objections heard in listing situations. Please keep in mind that in our system, we see the listing presentation as completely separate from a pricing presentation. Dealing with price objections is the subject of another chapter. These are objections that can arise before we make a listing presentation, during the listing presentation, or as we ask for the listing, but *before* we have discussed the price.

I want to think about it - sleep on it.
I have another appointment.
I have a friend - relative in the business so I will be listing with them.
Tell me what you think the house is worth and then I'll let you know if you can have the listing.
I want to talk to my spouse - parent - relative who is in real estate in another city - attorney, etc.
I want to fix the house up first.

I want to find another house first.
Another agent says he may have a buyer.
Another firm only charges 4%.
You are too pushy.
I prefer a younger - older person.
I prefer a larger - smaller firm.
I had a bad experience with a real estate firm so I'm doing it myself now.
I can't afford a commission.
I sold my last home myself and had no problem.
I may have a buyer.
I just put the ad in the paper and I want to see how it goes.
I'll give you an open - one party - 24 hour - listing.

There are hundreds of variations to these basic objections, but the answers we are about to cover should handle just about all of them.

––––––––––––––––––

Some objections come at the beginning of our presentations, some in the middle and some at the end. For the moment, let's say that we have made a reasonably complete listing presentation, we have just asked for the listing, and the prospect says he wants to think about it.

Procedurally the best thing to do is "Isolate" the objection. Our technique sounds like this: "In addition to thinking about it, is there any other reason you would hesitate to let me get started today?"

There are two main reasons for isolating an objection. First, we are making sure that there are no other, more serious, reasons, and second, our minds are fantastic computer-like devices that can instantly search our memory banks for the best responses and this technique gives our mind a few seconds to work.

Incidentally, the "Isolation" step is one of the most useful techniques in selling. It fits any situation - listing, selling, presenting offers, making appointments, and just about anything else. The basic technique is, "In addition to (something) is there any other reason you would hesitate to (do something)." For example, "In addition to the price being offered, is there any other reason you would hesitate to accept this offer?" Or, "In addition to looking at one more house, is there any other reason you would hesitate to make an offer on this house?"

In one of my courses, a husband and wife were both attending. The man got the hang of this technique very quickly and, that evening, said to his wife, "In addition to having a headache, is there any other reason you would hesitate to go to bed early?" As I said, it's a most useful technique.

The first reason for isolating an objection is very, very important. Any objection can be a cover-up for a more serious objection, or it can be just one of several objections. In either case, it's not in our best interest to answer and solve one objection only to be hit with another one.

The objection, "I want to think about it", could be an expression of indecision, or a cover-up for the fact that the prospect has another appointment, has a friend or relative in the business to whom he feels obligated, or wasn't completely sold by your presentation and feels he should get another firm to present their story. It could also be that the prospect has a firm policy of always sleeping on big decisions before signing any commitments.

If the objection is simply indecision, you will probably be able to tell by the way the prospect answers the "Isolation" question.

The next best technique will usually be the "Assure" or "Depressure" steps we covered in Chapter 19.

If the objection was a cover-up for one or more other objections, they will usually come out and you can deal with them with the other techniques to be covered in this chapter.

If it turns out that the prospect has a firm policy of sleeping on all big decisions, the best solution might be to say OK and call them back in the morning. If you are absolutely sure in your own mind that there is no danger of losing the listing, that could be the best thing to do. However, if there is a danger that the prospect might contact another real estate firm and you don't want to walk away at this moment, then you might like the technique we call the "Delayed Listing Close". It sounds like this:

"Mr. Prospect, do you feel confident about me now?"

"Yes."

"If you feel confident about me at nine o'clock tomorrow morning, do you think I might have the listing then?"

"Yes."

"I have a great idea. Let's fill out a listing agreement and select the listing price now. That way, you will have something *specific* to think about tonight. Fair enough?"

"OK."

This is a two-step technique and that was the first part.

If you have done a good, professional job of qualifying the prospect, and of explaining how you will merchandise their

231

home so they will get the most money, the quickest sale, and the fewest problems, your prospect should have developed professional respect for you. If, at that point, they want to think about what you have said, then suggesting that the listing agreement be filled out and all the important data, including price, be set down on paper, is a most reasonable suggestion or request. There is absolutely no reason for the prospect to say "no".

While you are filling out the listing and discussing and selecting the price, your prospect will have plenty of time to think about the job you can do for him, especially if you review the most important points. Our experience is that most sellers will give you the listing by the time the agreement is filled out and the price selected. But, for those occasions where the prospect still wants to think about it or sleep on it, we have part 2 of this technique, and it goes like this:

"Mr. Prospect, what time do you leave for work in the morning?"

"Eight o'clock."

"I have a great idea. Why don't you let me take the listing with me tonight. I'll call you at seven-thirty and if you say "Go", I can get everything started right away. But if you say "No", I'll tear it up and throw it away. Fair enough?"

If you think that half the prospects would agree and half would not, you are right. The second part of the "Delayed Listing Close" works about 50% of the time. That's either good news or bad news, depending on whether you are an optimist or a pessimist. Why do so many prospects agree to sign the listing when they have not yet agreed to list? Because, again, it is very difficult for people to say "no" to a reasonable request that is made by someone for whom they have some respect. The request is reasonable.

Keep in mind that you will be dealing with "Drivers," "Expressives," "Amiables," and "Analyticals." Depending on your prospect, and how you see the situation, you can stop anywhere you feel that you have gone as far as you should.

The next objection on our list is, "I have another appointment." The answer is very similar to the "Delayed Listing Close" and is called, "Equal To Or Better Than." It goes like this:

"I appreciate that you want to talk to another salesperson, but may I ask: if I am equal to, or better than, the other salesperson, may I have the listing.?" This is a reasonable request, so the answer is almost always . . .

"Yes."

"I have a great idea. Let's fill out the listing agreement and select a listing price now. That way you will have something specific to compare. Fair enough?"

"Yes."

That's the first part. Again, our experience is that most sellers will then have enough time to think about the benefits of your service while you fill out the listing and discuss and select price to give you the listing when you are finished. However, in the event they still want to see the other firm or salesperson, we have a similar second part which goes like this:

"What time are you going to see the other salesperson?"

The prospect names a time.

"I have an idea. Why don't you let me take the listing with me

233

now. I'll call you at (allow the other salesperson one hour) and if you say "Go", I can get everything started right away, but if you say "No", I'll tear it up and throw it away. Fair enough?"

Strong? Yes! Effective? Yes!! The important point is . . . when a prospect tells you that he has another appointment and wants to talk to another salesperson after you leave, you are sitting in cheap seats. What do you have to lose by asking? The request is logical and reasonable.

One of our graduates tried this technique and the prospect's response was: "You are pretty sure of yourself, aren't you?" And the graduate's response was, "Isn't that the kind of person you want?" The prospect agreed, cancelled the other appointment and signed a listing.

This answer would also be excellent if you got the objection: "I'd like to see what another firm has to offer before I sign."

Speaking of cancelling other appointments, that is, in fact, another choice we have when a prospect's objection is that he has an appointment with another salesperson. We call it, "Cancel Competitive Appointments", or "CCA" for short.

With this technique, we do not "Isolate" the objection, but rather respond directly to it.

"Oh! If you have any other appointments, please let me cancel them for you. Here's why. If you keep the appointment, but do not give them the listing, they may be so disappointed they may not try to sell your home. But if I call them, I can give them first-hand information and give them a head start on finding a buyer. Fair enough?"

234

The salesman who gave me that technique uses it as his closing technique anytime he knows, or suspects, he is in a competitive situation. He claimed that it always worked. Strong? Yes! Effective? Yes!!

The next most frequent objection, it is generally agreed, is: "I have a friend (or relative) in real estate." For most salespeople, this is giant-sized obstacle. However, people who have learned and use our three techniques report success 80% to 90% of the time.

The three techniques are titled, "Friend #1", Friend #2", and (naturally) "Friend #3" and they sound like this:

"If you felt that someone else could actually get you more money, a quicker sale, and fewer problems, would you still be *committed* to listing with this other person?"

"Do you *feel obligated* because of the friendship, or because you truly think the other person can get you the most money, the quickest sale, and the fewest problems?"

"You owe me nothing. You owe the other person nothing. But you owe yourself the very best."

These three techniques work so well, it's uncanny. The key lies in the fact that most sellers are not *committed* to anyone in particular. They may *feel* obligated, but they are not usually committed. Let's analyze why.

There are only four ways you can get to a prospective seller. They called you; they are selling privately and you saw their sign or ad; you heard, through a friend, that they are selling and contacted them; or you were canvassing or "farming" and stumbled across them.

235

OK, some questions. If they asked you to give them a price or to tell them what you and your firm can do for them, how *committed* can they be to another salesperson?

If they have a "For Sale By Owner" sign on the lawn, or ad in the paper, how *committed* can they be?

If you heard they were selling, called and made an appointment, or went directly to their home, and they let you in and listened to your entire listing presentation, how *committed* can they be?

Likewise, if you were canvassing and stumbled on them, and they listened to your entire listing presentation, how *committed* can they be?

The answers are: Not very committed. They may *feel* obligated, but they are not committed.

Our experience is that 60% or 70% of the prospects who say they have a friend in real estate will immediately admit they are not committed when we ask them "Friend #1". For those who say they are committed, or who say they have a strong sense of obligation, we ask "Friend #2". Our experience here is that most people admit that the feeling of obligation lies in the friendship or relationship rather than the other person's professional ability.

At this point, we usually insert a simple question. "Do you need the money from this house to buy your next house?" A variation is, "Do you need or want as much money as you can get for this house?" The answers are almost always a very emphatic "Yes!" Then we very softly express "Friend #3". Most people agree and will then base their decision on professional ability instead of friendship.

Here's an interesting point. These techniques "work" even when you don't get the listing. For example: You hear that Al and Alice Jennings have just made a deposit on a new home, but have not yet listed their present home. You rush over, ring the door bell, and when Al comes to the door, you introduce yourself and say that you understand he has just bought a new home and will be moving.

He says: "That's correct, but I will be listing this house with a friend of mine."

You say: "May I ask - if you felt that someone else could actually get you more money, a quicker sale, and fewer problems, would you still be committed to listing with this other person?"

He says: "Yes I would. We went to high school together."

You say: "May I ask - do you feel obligated because of the friendship or because you truly think the other person can get you the most money, the quickest sale, and the fewest problems?"

He says: "I have total confidence in him. He's a full-time agent and has been one of the top people in his firm for almost ten years."

Let's say that at this point you graciously leave. You didn't get the listing, but the techniques worked. Why? Because in under 30 seconds you have determined that the prospect is committed to a professional agent, you have determined that the prospect has based his decision on professional ability and not just friendship or a sense of obligation, and you can now direct your efforts elsewhere.

We all have two key assets that are critical to our productivity in life. Our attitude - and our time. With these techniques, we can quickly determine the prospect's level of commitment and reason for the commitment or obligation. If we can't get the listing, we will not have wasted hours of time, and if we understand that we can't get every listing, we won't have our attitude so messed up we can't work for the rest of the day.

The next objection on our list is: "Tell me what you think the house is worth and I'll let you know if you can have the listing."

The solution to this objection is covered completely in Chapter 17, which is titled "List First - Price Second", so I won't repeat all that here. Remember, however, to "Isolate" the objection before solving it. "In addition to determining the price, is there any other reason you would hesitate to have me represent you to sell your home?"

The next objection is: "I want to talk to my husband - wife - parents - relative in real estate in another city - attorney - etc."

Our solution is a technique called, "Missing Partner" and it goes like this:

"If it was your own decision . . . if you had to make the decision by yourself . . . if (the other party) wanted you to make the decision by yourself . . . then based on the information I have given you, would *you* give me the listing?"

If the answer is "Yes", then: "Let's fill out the listing, subject to their disapproval."

If the answer is "Maybe", or "I think so", then: "If (spouse, parent, attorney, etc.) says OK, would you approve?" If the answer is "Yes", then: "Let's fill out the listing, subject to their disapproval."

238

The key here is to make absolutely sure that the person you are talking to is sold because one of the easiest ways to get rid of a salesperson is to say that you have to discuss things with someone else. If the prospect is only trying to get rid of you, they will not answer "yes" to the first question, so your job will be to sell them more thoroughly or find out what their objection really is.

A similar objection occurs when we have just made a listing presentation to a couple, and one of them says that they want to talk it over and will let you know in the morning. Our technique for this is titled, "Silent Partner."

The procedure here is very important. First, "Isolate" the objection to the person who gave it. Then, turn to the other, or "silent" partner and say:

"If it was your decision . . . if you had to make a decision by yourself . . . if (the other party) wanted you to make the decision by yourself . . . then based on the information I have given you, would *you* give me the listing?"

If the answer is "Yes", turn back to the first person and ask them. Usually, all we have to say is their name with a questioning tone. "Mr. Smith?"

The exciting part of this technique is that, if either party has an objection, you get to deal with that one objection and with that one person. For example, you have just made a listing presentation to Mr. and Mrs. Smith. You ask for the listing and Mr. Smith says he wants to talk it over with Mrs. Smith. You "Isolate" his objection:

You: "Mr. Smith, in addition to talking it over with Mrs. Smith, is there any other reason you would hesitate to have me

239

represent you to sell your home?"

Mr. Smith: "Well, actually, I had kind of committed to list the house with a fellow that lives down the block."

There! Talking it over was a cover-up. The "Isolation" technique brought out the real objection. Your next move is "Friend #1".

I tell you again, if you will memorize these techniques until you can say them instantly and confidently, you will experience a major breakthrough in your ability to get listings, sell them faster, and increase your income. If you will get these techniques down "cold", your friends will think that you walk on water.

You want to "walk on water", don't you? You want to know where the "rocks" are, don't you. Say "Yes!" Study and memorize, and you will make it.

Ready for some more techniques? The next objections on the list were: "I want to fix the house first," and, "I want to find another house first." There are a lot of possible solutions depending on market conditions, their reason for selling, and their time situation.

The key is to "Isolate" the objection, and then either demonstrate the benefit of listing now, or the disadvantage of delay, or, if there is no disadvantage in waiting, to secure their commitment that you can have the listing. Our technique is called "Ready When You Are."

"Mr. Prospect, may I represent you when you are ready?"

"Yes."

"I have a great idea. Let's fill out the listing agreement and get all

240

the paperwork done. We can even discuss the price and have a general idea now and make any adjustments necessary when we actually put your home on the market. Fair enough?"

If they readily agree, you have the listing. If they hesitate, the objection may be a cover-up. Reports from salespeople using this technique are that many prospects sign the agreement just as soon as the price has been discussed and the listing filled out. It appears that these two objections are often a cover-up for indecision. The extra time used up to discuss and select a price and to fill out the listing agreement also gives us the chance to assure the prospect that listing with us will be a good decision.

Now, here's a technique I really like. It's a good example of turning a lemon into lemonade.

You have just completed a listing presentation and maybe even the pricing presentation. You are ready to go just as soon as they sign the listing agreement. You ask them to sign and the prospect says, "Actually, I probably should have told you before, but I had an agent from another firm here earlier and they may already have a buyer. I think I should hold off signing up with you until I see how that works out."

Devastation! Your heart falls. The worst news possible. A chance for a quick sale and you aren't in the game. But can you be? Yes! If your reaction is right. Yes! If you treat this as not just good news but great news. Our answer, which is titled, "XYZ Has a Buyer", is:

"Great! Super! Excellent! We work together through our Multi-Listing service. Give me the listing. I'll call the other salesperson right away. If their buyer buys, you get a quick sale! If their buyer does not buy, you get all of my services: Highlight Sheets, Highlight Cards, Check List, (etc. etc.)! You are in a win-win situation!"

There are two reasons this technique works so well. First, the prospect is obviously not sold on the other salesperson's professional ability or he would have signed the listing already; especially if he felt the other salesperson actually had a buyer. On the other hand, the seller doesn't want to lose the buyer if there is a chance there is one. When we point out how he can sign with us and put himself in a win-win situation, that's exactly what he wants.

The second reason it works so well is because we treat it as exciting, good news. By saying, "Hey! Great!" instead of being defensive and casting doubts concerning the possible buyer, we literally have taken a lemon and made sweet, sweet lemonade.

For certain objections, the key is to paint a picture that gets the prospect emotionally involved. This next objection is a good example.

When the prospect asks you to take a lower commission rate or tells you that another firm is offering a lower commission rate, the best response is to put the prospect in the situation of getting a big pay cut. Our response, which is titled, "XYZ 4%", sounds like this:

"Mr. Prospect, if you went to work tomorrow and your boss asked you to take a 40% pay cut, what would you tell him?" I always add, "Be careful now. Not too earthy." The usual answer is, "No way!"

"If you made your living selling real estate, and there were many, many homes for sale at 7% and someone brought a listing in at 4%, would you try to sell it?" The usual answer is,

"No".

"Are you serious about selling?"

"Yes."

"Do you want a quick sale?"

"Yes."

"Pay 8%!" Wait for a reaction, then continue. "I'm serious. Do you realize how excited I can get the salespeople if you will pay them a bonus?"

"Look at it this way - suppose your boss offered you a good bonus if you worked extra hard for the week. Would you do it?" The usual answer is "Yes".

"Do you want to list at 8% . . . or do you want me to do my very best at 7%?"

This basic philosophy has helped a lot of salespeople get 10% listings on hard-to-sell properties. We call them "Extra Effort Properties." The idea is to explain why the property is an extra challenge to get sold because of location, condition, or whatever. Then use the "XYZ 4%" technique to help the seller realize that sometimes it's best to pay a bonus to get a tough job done.

Here's another situation where painting a strong word picture that gets the prospect emotionally involved is the solution. We have just made a reasonably complete listing presentation - that means we believe we have given the prospect enough information to make a decision. We ask for the listing, and they respond with an objection. We answer the objection and close again.

A GOOD ANSWER FOR EVERY OBJECTION

Suddenly, the prospect says something like, "I don't know. You move too fast. You are a bit too pushy for me."

Our answer is a technique called, "You're Too Pushy." This must be presented in a low, easy going tone of voice because we need to counteract the feeling that we were talking too fast and coming up with just the right answers a bit too fast.

"Mr. Prospect. . .two weeks from now. . .a month from now. . . we have a young couple who *need* a home. . .*like* your home. . . *want your home*. . .*and qualify* to buy your home. . .scared to death to make a decision. At that point in time. . .what kind of salesperson do you want to have representing you. . .one who can help them decide. . .or someone who will collapse with them?"

The normal answers are that they want a salesperson who won't collapse, who can help the young buyers decide, and sometimes, they even say, "You are right. I want a pushy salesman. Where do I sign?"

There is a vast difference in being professionaly persistent and in being pushy. If the prospect feels that our sense of urgency is based on our belief that taking action now is in the prospect's best interest, we will come across as being correctly and professionally persistent. If the prospect feels that our sense of urgency is for our personal benefit only, we will come across as pushy.

For example, we have found that it is important to cover all four conditions in the "You're Too Pushy" technique to avoid being seen as a pushy salesperson only looking out for our own interests. Note that the young couple must *need* a home, *like* the home, *want* the home, and be *qualified* to buy the home. If we leave any one of these elements out, we will come across as not caring if the buyer will benefit by our persistence.

244

There are quite a number of objections that can be handled with one particular technique that sounds like this: "If you felt that you could actually get the most money, quickest sale, and the fewest problems by . . ." The end of the question is adjusted to fit the objection.

"I prefer to list with an older person." "If you felt that you could actually get the most money, the quickest sale and the fewest problems, by listing with a young, energetic, well-trained salesperson, would you do so?"

"I prefer to list with a larger firm." "If you felt that you could actually get the most money, the quickest sale and the fewest problems, by listing with a small, energetic, well-trained firm, would you do so?"

"I had a bad experience the last time I listed with a real estate firm. This time I'm doing it myself." "If you felt that you could actually get the most money, the quickest sale and the fewest problems, by listing with a professional real estate person whom you could trust, would you do so?"

Obviously, none of these answers will get you a listing with nothing else added. The purpose of these answers is to open a shut door, or open a shut mind, to be more precise. It is not logical to answer "no" to any of these questions. The normal answer is, "Yes, if I felt that way, but I don't feel that way." Or, "Yes, if I felt that way, but you are going to have to prove it to me." And that's exactly what you want - a chance to prove yourself, your ability, or whatever. All the proofs you need are in this book.

A GOOD ANSWER FOR EVERY OBJECTION

For example, you call on a private seller. You hardly finish introducing yourself, when the seller says, "Look, I'm selling this house myself because I need every dime I can get. I can't afford to pay a commission. Besides, I sold my last house myself and I had no problem."

Your answer: "If you felt that you could actually get the most money, the quickest sale and the fewest problems, by listing with a professional real estate agent, would you do so?"

The prospect answers: "Sure. But I don't feel that way because I don't see how I can get more money after paying you a commission."

Now, turn to Chapter 9, "Listing Private Sellers", and see how neatly those ideas and techniques prove our belief that sellers net more by listing with a real estate firm.

"How would you like to have your cake and eat it, too?" That's the first question of our next technique. The title, to keep it short, is "Eat Your Cake" and it's used when a private seller says he may have a buyer.

Let's create a sample situation. We have called on a prospect who has a "For Sale By Owner" sign on the lawn. We qualified him, as outlined in Chapter 7, and found out that he has been transferred and is highly motivated. We have given him the private seller presentation, as outlined in Chapter 9. The prospect agreed that the odds are against him, so we then presented a listing presentation as outlined in Chapter 11.

Us: "Mr. Prospect, do you see how all of those ideas will help you get the most money and a quicker sale?"

Seller: "Yes, but I should have mentioned that I may have a

246

buyer. They are checking with their bank now."

Us: "In addition to that, is there any other reason you would hesitate to have me represent you to sell your home?"

Seller: "Not really, but I want to see how this buyer works out before I sign. Also, I've only had the ad in for a week, so even if this buyer doesn't work out, I'll probably try it for another week or so. Then if I haven't sold it, I'll probably list with you."

Us: "How would you like to have your cake and eat it, too?"

Seller: "What do you mean?"

Us: "You list with me tonight, and I'll give you a ten-day exclusion on this particular buyer. That will put you in the best possible negotiating position with your buyer. Here's why. As soon as we have selected a price, you will know exactly how much you have to get from the buyer in order to come out ahead. In addition, you can tell him that you have signed a listing with me and that you have a ten-day exclusion on him. Now the pressure is on him. If he really wants your house, and is willing to pay a fair price, and can afford to pay a fair price, and can do it quickly — you have a quick sale. If he cannot afford the house, or is not willing to pay a fair price, you already have me working for you to find a qualified buyer. Fair enough?"

Salespeople who have tried this technique in situations similar to our sample - the objection is given after a private seller and/or listing presentation is made - almost always report success. Can you guess why? Because 50% of the time, there is no buyer. The objection was just a cover for indecision. And in the other 50% of the cases, the sellers had very little confidence that the buyer would come through. If they had confidence in the ability of the buyer, we would not have had a chance to make a presentation at all. When they answered the door or telephone and discovered we were in real estate, they would

247

have said, "You are too late. We have sold the house."

We can also use this technique if we get the objection immediately on first contact.

Us: "Hi, I saw your sign. May I ask, are you cooperating with real estate firms?"

Seller: "You are too late. I think I have a buyer."

Us: "Have they signed an actual purchase agreement?"

Seller: "No, but they said they will buy it. They have gone to their bank to set things up."

Us: "How would you like to have your cake and eat it, too?"

Seller: "What do you mean?"

Us: "You list with me now and I will give you a ten-day exclusion on this particular buyer. That will put you in the best possible negotiating position . . ."

Let's analyze the psychology behind all this. The reason we can afford to offer the ten-day exclusion is that 90% of all direct buyers are not qualified to buy the homes they look at. So, we have a 9:1 chance that the sale won't go through. Even if it does go through, you have lost nothing except the time to write up a listing agreement. If you sign the seller up and he sells it to the buyer, you don't get a commission. If you don't sign him up and he sells it to the buyer, you don't get a commission. However, if you don't sign him up and he doesn't sell it to this buyer, but does eventually list with someone else, you also don't get a commission. By signing him up, you actually do put him in a better negotiating position, and you put yourself in the best position, too. Sign him up!

We can also use this basic idea when a private seller says he just put the ad in the paper a few days ago and wants to see how it works out. It's important to keep in mind that most private sellers know in advance that the odds are against them. They just feel they should at least try to save the commission. That's not at all unlike going to Las Vegas. We all know the odds are against us, but most of us feel we should at least try; so we budget what we can afford to lose and have a go at it. That's all most private sellers do. They budget the time they think they can afford to lose and have a go at it. If we can show them that the risk is greater than they thought, we get the listing.

Here's one last technique for this chapter. The title for this one is, "Convert To Price," and it is used when we get objections that just don't make sense, or types of objections that are apparently not valid. It goes like this:

"Mr. Seller, it has been my experience that when someone, like yourself, who understands the value of all the services I have to offer still hesitates to list with me, it's generally because of my price. He just is not sure that I am trying to get him the most money possible. Is that perhaps the case here?"

Most often the answer is yes. At this point, we then review all of the financial data and ask the sellers to pick the price. If it is reasonable, we take the listing. If it is unreasonable, we usually reject the listing—unless there are counterbalancing circumstances, such as a high urgency to sell and a belief that the sellers will reduce the price quickly or will accept a reasonable offer quickly.

249

A GOOD ANSWER FOR EVERY OBJECTION

SUMMARY

I know that you have heard that 80% of the business is done by 20% of the salespeople, but did you know that 60% of the business is done by just 4% of the salespeople? That's right.

> 4% of the salespeople write 60% of the business.
> 16% write 20% of the business.
> 80% write 20% of the business.

My experience is that 4% of the salespeople earn $40,000 or more. 16% earn between $10,000 and $40,000. And 80% starve. A few years ago, several experienced real estate people and I did some research concerning those statistics. We were trying to determine the common denominators for each group. Here's what we found.

Four percent of the salespeople had developed excellent sales procedures, and developed an extremely effective listing or sales presentation, and knew 50 or more techniques for closing and handling indecision and objections.

Sixteen percent of the salespeople had pretty good sales procedures, pretty good listing or sales presentations, and they knew about 10 ways to close and handle indecision and objections.

Eighty percent of the salespeople had a marginally effective or downright poor sales procedure, marginally effective listing or selling presentations, and they knew from 0 to 3 techniques for closing and handling indecision.

The conclusion is inescapable. The more you know and the better you know it, the more you earn.

Somewhere, I once read that the average prospect has to be "closed" five times, but the average salesperson only knows three techniques for closing or dealing with objections. It doesn't take a genius to figure out the problem. The average person is two techniques short for the average situation.

My friend Leo "walked on water" because he was in that exciting 4% that had developed good procedure, had developed a good presentation and had answers for almost every objection.

Someone once said that in selling, we get paid for talking. That's not true at all. We get paid for knowing what to say . . . and being able to say it when it counts.

The key to the top in selling effectiveness is to develop a system that prevents most objections from arising in the first place- but having all the answers if they come up anyway.

Now, here are the techniques covered in this chapter, arranged for easy study.

ISOLATE   **"In addition to** - **selecting the best price**
                               - **thinking about it**
                               - **your friend**
                               - **another appointment**
                               - **that**
      is there any other reason you would hesitate to
                               - **have me represent you?"**
                               - **let me get started?"**
                               - **give me the listing?"**

**DELAYED
LISTING
CLOSE**

"Do you feel confident about me now?"

"If you feel confident about me at nine o'clock tomorrow morning, do you think I might have the listing then?"

"I have a great idea. Let's fill out a listing agreement and select the listing price now. That way, you will have something <u>specific</u> to think about to-night. Fair enough?"

Measure the house, fill out listing, discuss and select price, ask for listing. If prospect still hesitates, proceed to part 2.

"What time do you leave for work in the morning?"

"I have a great idea. Why don't you let me take the listing with me tonight. I'll call you at seven-thirty and if you say 'Go,' I can get everything started right away. But if you say 'No,' I'll tear it up and throw it away. Fair enough?"

EQUAL TO OR BETTER THAN

"I appreciate that you want to talk to another salesperson, but may I ask - if I am equal to or better than the other salesperson, may I have the listing?"

"I have a great idea. Let's fill out the listing agreement and select a listing price now. That way you will have something specific to compare. Fair enough?"

Measure the house, fill out listing, discuss and select price, ask for listing. If prospect still hesitates, proceed to part 2.

"What time are you going to see the other salesperson?"

"I have an idea. Why don't you let me take the listing with me now. I'll call you at (allow the other salesperson one hour) and if you say 'Go,' I can get everything started right away, but if you say 'No,' I'll tear it up and throw it away. Fair enough?"

CCA CANCEL COMPETITIVE APPOINTMENTS

"Oh!! If you have other appointments, please let me cancel them for you. Here's why. If you keep the appointment, but do not give them the listing, they may be so disappointed they may not try to sell your home. But if I call them, I can give them first-hand information and give them a head start on finding a buyer. Fair enough?"

253

FRIEND 1   "If you felt that someone else could actually get you more money, a quicker sale and fewer problems, would you still be committed to listing with this other person?"

FRIEND 2   "Do you feel obligated because of the friendship, or because you truly think the other person can get you the most money, the quickest sale and the fewest problems?"

FRIEND 3   "You owe me nothing. You owe the other person nothing. But you owe yourself the very best."

SILENT PARTNER   One partner has just said, "We'll think it over and let you know." Isolate the objection with that partner, then turn to the other partner and say. . .

"If it was your own decision . . . if you had to make the decision by yourself . . . if (the other party) wanted you to make the decision by yourself . . . then based on the information I have given you, would you give me the listing?"

If "yes," then turn back to the first party and ask for the listing.

MISSING PARTNER

"If it was your own decision . . . if you had to make the decision by yourself . . . if (the other party) wanted you to make the decision by yourself . . . then based on the information I have given you. . . would you give me the listing?"

If "Yes" - "Let's fill out the listing, subject to their disapproval."

If "Maybe" - "If (spouse, parent, attorney, etc.) says OK, would you approve?"

If "Yes" - "Let's fill out the listing, subject to his disapproval."

READY WHEN YOU ARE

"May I represent you when you are ready?"

"I have a great idea. Let's fill out the listing agreement and get all the paperwork done. We can even discuss the price and have a general idea now and make any adjustments necessary when we actually put your home on the market. Fair enough?"

XYZ 4%

"If you went to work tomorrow and your boss asked you to take a 40% pay cut, what would you tell him?"

"If you made your living selling real estate, and there were many, many homes for sale at 7% and someone brought a listing in at 4%, would you try to sell it?"

"Are you serious about selling?"

"Do you want a quick sale?"

"Pay 8%! I'm serious! Do you realize how excited I can get the salespeople if you will pay them a bonus?"

"Look at it this way - suppose your boss offered you a good bonus if you worked extra hard for the week. Would you do it?"

"Do you want to list at 8% . . . or do you want me to do my very best at 7%?"

XYZ HAS A BUYER	"Great! Super! Excellent! We work together through our Multi-Listing Service. Give me the listing. I'll call the other salesperson right away. If their buyer buys, you get a quick sale! If their buyer does not buy, you get all of my services: Highlight Sheets, Highlight Cards, Check List, (etc., etc.)! You are in a win - win situation!"

YOU'RE TOO PUSHY

"Two weeks from now . . . a month from now . . . we have a young couple who <u>need</u> a home . . . <u>like</u> your home . . . <u>want</u> your home . . . and <u>qualify to buy</u> your home . . . scared to death to make a decision. At that point in time . . . what kind of salesperson do you want to have representing you . . . one who can help them decide . . . or someone who will collapse with them?"

YOU'RE TOO YOUNG

"If you felt that you could actually get the most money, the quickest sale and the fewest problems, by listing with a young, energetic, well-trained salesperson, would you do so?"

EAT YOUR CAKE

"How would you like to have your cake and eat it, too?"

"You list with me tonight, and I'll give you a ten-day exclusion on this particular buyer. That will put you in the best possible negotiating position with your buyer. Here's why. As soon as we have selected a price, you will know exactly how much you have to get from the buyer in order to come out ahead. In addition, you can tell him that you have signed a listing with me and that you have a ten-day exclusion on him. Now the pressure is on him. If he really wants your house, is willing to pay a fair price, can afford to pay a fair price and can do it quickly, you have a quick sale. If he cannot afford the house, or is not willing to pay a fair price you already have me working for you to find a qualified buyer. Fair enough?"

CONVERT TO PRICE

"It has been my experience that when someone like yourself who understands the value of all of the services I have to offer still hesitates to list with me, it's generally because of price. He just is not sure that I am trying to get him the most money possible. Is that perhaps the case here?"

258

CHAPTER 22

EFFECTIVE PROSPECTING
PART I

In my dentist's office there is a sign that reads, "You Only Have To Brush The Teeth You Want To Keep." You can't argue with that.

Ralph, a Realtor friend of mine saw the sign, smiled at the effectiveness of that short message and forgot about it. A few weeks later he held a sales meeting on the subject of prospecting. He was encouraging his salespeople to make 10 calls a day when someone asked whom they should call. Suddenly, he had an inspiration. Without a further word, he went to the back of the meeting room, picked up a copy of the local Cross-Index Directory, handed it to the salesperson and said, "You only have to call the ones you want to list:"

You can't argue with that.

My friend Leo, who had an answer for every objection, had another talent. He knew how to prospect. He knew how to "rifle in" on a specific prospect, and he knew how to "shotgun" to develop lots and lots of leads.

EFFECTIVE PROSPECTING
PART I

Early in his selling career, Leo worked for Royal Typewriter. He was a top salesman and belonged to the "MAD" club, which meant he was delivering a "machine a day". Only 2% of the entire national sales force was maintaining that level of sales.

In spite of being very busy delivering and installing a machine a day, Leo decided to see what would happen if he made 50 prospecting calls a day for thirty days. He decided that the only way he could maintain that level of contacts was to make the effort a "fact finding survey" and make no attempt to secure appointments or sell any leads. He would take care of those the following month.

His plan was to call on all the offices and businesses in his territory, without pre-judging their potential to buy, and only ask how many clerical employees they had, how many typewriters, make and year and the name of the boss.

One thing about Leo, when he made a committment, he stuck to it. True to his word to himself, he made 50 new contacts every working day for one month. The results were astounding. He delivered 83 machines that same month - and developed enough prospects that he hardly had to do any other new prospecting for a full year. His income, already substantial, increased more than 50%.

Would you consider the name, address and phone number of someone who planned to sell or buy a new home within the next year a good lead? Would you like to have 15 to 30 such leads in one week? You can obtain them by using a "Fact Finding Survey."

A good "Fact Finding Survey" has several good purposes and benefits.

1. It produces many good prospects for listing and buying.
2. It's the fastest way to get started in real estate brokerage.
3. It's the fastest way out of a sales slump.
4. You learn more about a specific area very fast.
5. You save gas, money and travel time.

Here's how to get started.

Select an area in which you wish to specialize. It should contain approximately 500 homes. You can enlarge or reduce the size of the area later, based on the rate of turn-over that you determine as a result of the survey. Using your local Cross-Index Directory, contact, on the telephone, each residence as follows:

"Mr. (Mrs.)_____, please"

Thank you. My name is_____ of _____. I'm doing a special survey. May I ask, do you plan to move sometime within the next two or three years?"

"May I ask, approximately when?"

"May I ask, will you be staying in this area?"

"Thank you. Have a nice day. Good-bye."

(If someone asks why you are doing the survey, say:)

"I plan to specialize in this neighborhood so I can be of more help to sellers and buyers. I need to have some idea of how many people plan to move and approximately when."

There are three specific points I'd like to make about that survey.

261

EFFECTIVE PROSPECTING
PART I

First, I recommend that you make 50 calls a day for five consecutive days. The survey is short, so it takes less than two hours to make 50 calls. The reason for that many calls a day for five days is simple: the purpose of a survey is to cover a lot of ground in a hurry and secure the name, address and phone number of people who plan to buy or sell within the next 12 months. Since you are calling from your local Cross-Index Directory, (also known as Criss + Cross, Cross Reference, City Index, Metropolitan Householder Guide) you will have the name, address and phone number of your prospect in front of you. Simply make out a prospect card on anyone who indicates he will be selling or buying within 12 months and begin following up after you complete your survey.

Additionally, I believe it is important to make 50 calls a day, every day, for five consecutive days because it sometimes takes more than a few calls to get into the swing of things. Over the years we have found that a lot of people need to make 10, 20 and even 30 calls before they begin to get results because it takes that many calls before they begin to sound smooth and confident.

A number of years ago, I was training a group of thirty people. We were meeting each Monday for a series of 8 weeks. On one Monday I gave the assignment to call 50 people a day for 5 consecutive days. The following week, I asked for results. The first person I called on apparently had decided to prove that the method would not work, so with great agitation, she reported that she had made 15 calls, that everyone had said it was none of her business if he was planning to move and would she get off the phone and stop bugging him, so she quit.

Personally, I find it hard to believe that 15 people in a row would respond that way, but I thanked her for her response and asked the next person for a report. Apparently, he had not made many or any calls, so he mumbled something about

LIST MORE - SELL MORE

having a similar experience. The next person had the same experience, and the next, and on and on.

Finally, Shirley, a hard-working mother of 4 with an invalid husband said that she was embarrassed to report her results- not because of poor results, but because the others probably wouldn't like to hear what she had to say. She had made all 250 calls. From the first 45 calls she had no leads, but from the remainder she secured 52 leads of people planning to buy or sell within the year. And she had listed, from those leads, nine homes, one farm and two other properties which were split into a total of eleven lots, for a total of 21 listings. Not too bad for a survey effort that took less than ten hours total!

If you live or work in a small town that does not have a Cross-Index type of directory, you may find it effective to use your local telephone directory for the survey. A glance at the street names can help you restrict your calls to a certain area. Or, since telephone exchanges often cover specific areas, you can restrict your efforts to certain areas by staying within one exchange. Your local phone company office may be able to give you an idea of the boundaries of each exchange.

The second point is that it is important *not* to attempt to make appointments while you are doing a survey. It makes a lie out of your reason for calling. When good leads are obtained, make up a lead card and contact them later.

In one of our courses, a salesperson asked me what I felt he should do if he were doing the "Fact Finding Survey" and one of the people he called said he had just decided to sell that very day. With tongue in cheek and smile on face, I said, "Thank them for the information, hang up, count to 15, call them back and tell them you are done with your survey and ask for an appointment." But one of our graduates, who was repeating the course said that when that happened to him, he just put the

263

prospect on "hold" and drove out there.

In that same group with Shirley, another saleswoman, Maxine, reported that she had made about 150 survey calls when a prospect said that he was most interested in finding another home and asked if she would come right out and talk to him. Maxine said she would be glad to, *after* she finished her survey, which she felt would take another hour and a half. The prospect was amazed. "You really are doing a survey," he said. "I'll be darned. An honest saleman." Because of his urgency and because of his respect for her professionalism, Maxine dropped all other efforts, found him a suitable house, presented an offer that was accepted, and secured the listing on his present home. A sales commission and a listing is not a bad result from about six hours of survey work.

The third point is that in survey work, the key to getting good responses is to make sure that your questions are non-threatening.

If we asked, "Do you plan to move within 90 days?" the question could be taken as too personal, too specific and therefore, threatening. Two to three years is not specific, therefore, not threatening.

If someone says "Yes" to the first question and we immediately ask, "When?," they could also feel threatened or pressured, because the question is too specific. Therefore, the question, "May I ask, approximately when?" is a better question.

In summary, the "Fact Finding Survey" works. It produces listing and buying leads, both long and short range. It's a fast way to get started in the real estate business, and it's a fast way to get out of a slump. You can serve your clients more professionally by becoming a specialist in a specific area and you can save time, gas and money. What more can you ask?

Another effective method of prospecting for listings is by
contacting private sellers, whom we usually refer to as "For-Sale-
By-Owners."

Before I cover the language, I'd like to make a most important
point. Private sellers, or "FISBOS" for short (I put an 'I' in the
acronym to make it look like a word) have decided to sell their
homes themselves because they believe they have a good chance
to save the commission, or because they have had a bad
experience with a real estate salesperson or firm. As a result,
they can be extremely challenging . . . or abusive. Therefore, I
do not believe that a new salesperson should call on FISBOS
until he has learned to fluently express the key reasons why the
odds are stacked against the private seller. Let me reinforce that
with an analogy.

If you had just begun taking flying lessons, your instructor
would be training you how to fly in good weather, in a simple,
single engine airplane and away from congested airspace. He or
she would *not* have you trying to make an approach into
Chicago's O'Hare airport during a thunderstorm at rush hour
with one engine out in a complex twin engine airplane. A
FISBO can whip up a "thunderstorm" in a hurry.

He can challenge your knowledge, your experience, your
credibility, and, as Joe Tusco said, your heredity. May I strongly
suggest, therefore, that you read or re-read Chapters 8 and 9
and memorize the appropriate language.

On the other hand, FISBOS are a highly visible source of
prospects. With the techniques in Chapter 9 well-mastered, you
may find them very easy to sell - "a piece of cake," as many of
our graduates have discovered. Just a week ago, Dan called to
say that he had listed 41 FISBOS out of 41 attempts in the last
12 months. A few years ago Bob made 60 presentations and

secured 59 listings. A lot of people love the challenge of FISBOS, just as most experienced pilots, myself included, love the challenge of flying into O'Hare at rush hour. It's really neat to know that you have the skill to stay even with 747's and DC 10's . . . in any weather.

In our system, there are four basic techniques for contacting a FISBO. Since each of our techniques has a title, the title for these are, "FISBO 1," "FISBO 2," "FISBO 3," and (naturally) FISBO 4." Additionally, we need a way to invite ourselves into a home, as you will see, so there is a technique titled, "FINE."

Since these are the techniques used by Leo in Chapter 8, let's review his initial contact.

> Leo rang the bell and stood fairly close to the front door. When he saw a face peer through the little window in the door, he took a step backward. When the door opened he took another small step backward and said, "Hi, I saw your sign. May I ask, are you cooperating with real estate?"
>
> "No, we are not," was the curt reply, "and I wish you real estate people would just stay away."
>
> "Well," responded Leo quickly, "may I ask you just one quick question? If . . . *if* I had a *qualified* buyer, *willing* to pay a price *acceptable* to you, would you accept such an offer through our company?"
>
> "No, I don't think so. We need all the money we can get."
>
> "I appreciate that," said Leo, "but if you felt that you could actually get *more* money, a *quicker* sale and *fewer* problems by doing business with real estate, would you do so?"
>
> "Yes, I guess we would. As long as we came out ahead."

"Fine," responded Leo. "It will take just a few minutes to see enough of your home so I can tell potential buyers about it. May I do that now?"

"Well, I suppose so. Come on in."

Leo began with the technique we call "FISBO 1", "Hi, I saw your sign. May I ask, are you cooperating with real estate?"

There are only five ways a person can answer that question: "Yes," "No," "Maybe," "What do you mean by cooperating?," and "Yes, but if I list, I have a friend who is in real estate."

If the seller answers "Yes, come on in," you need to say nothing more. You are in the house, which was your objective.

If the seller answers "Yes," but does not invite you in, then you need a way to invite yourself in. For that, we have the technique, "FINE," which is, "Fine, it will take just a few minutes to see enough of your home so I can tell potential buyers about it. May I do that now?" The answer is almost always "Yes."

If the seller answers "FISBO 1" with a "No," "Maybe," or "What do you mean?", then our response is, as Leo's was, "FISBO 2", "May I ask just one quick question. If . . . *if* I had a *qualified* buyer, *willing* to pay a price *acceptable* to you, would you accept such an offer through my company?" Our experience is that 80% of the time, people answer "Yes," and we then say, "Fine, it will take just a few minutes to see enough of your home, etc."

If, as happened to Leo, the answer to "FISBO 2" is "No," then we usually use "FISBO 4", which is, "May I ask, if you felt that you could actually get the *most* money, the *quickest* sale and the *fewest* problems, by doing business with real estate, would you do so?"

Generally, a logical person will answer "Yes," or "Yes, if I felt that way." That's what Leo's prospect said. And our next step is to repeat "FISBO 2," "So, if I had a *qualified* buyer, *willing* to pay a price *acceptable* to you, would you accept such an offer through our company?" The usual answer is now "Yes," and we follow up with "FINE."

Leo's third prospecting call in Chapter 8 went a little differently. Let's review it.

> Leo rang the bell and stood close to the door.

> "Hi," he said when the door opened. "I saw your sign. May I ask, are you cooperating with real estate?"

> "What do you mean by cooperating?" asked the owner.

> "Well, if I had a qualified buyer, willing to pay a price acceptable to you, would you accept such an offer through my company?"

> "Sure," responded the seller, "if you add your commission on to the price I'm asking, why not?"

> "Fine," responded Leo. "it will take just a few minutes to see enough of your home so I can tell potential buyers about it. May I do that now?"

There are two key points here. First, "FISBO 2" is the right answer any time the prospect's answer to "FISBO 1" is anything other than "Yes," or "Yes, but I have a friend . . ." The second point is that any time the prospect's answer to "FISBO 2" is "Yes," or "Yes, but you will have to add your commission on to my asking price," or "yes, but I won't sign anything," or "Yes, but . . . (anything)," the correct response by us is "Fine, it will take just a few minutes to see enough of your home so I can tell potential buyers about it. May I do that now?"

Why? Because until we qualify them, we don't know if we even want the listing. And the front porch is no place to engage in a discussion of price, or commissions, or exclusive listings or whatever. Our purpose, when we ring a door bell, is to get into the house so we can, in the proper environment, qualify the prospect - which means to determine why he is selling and his motivations - and decide if we want the listing. If we decide we want the listing, we can then point out the disadvantages of selling privately, as Leo did in Chapter 8 and as covered more fully in Chapter 9.

The other possible response to "FISBO 1" is, "Yes, but if I list, it will be with a friend who is in real estate." In this case our response would be "FRIEND 1," "May I ask, if you felt that someone else could actually get you *more* money, a *quicker* sale and *fewer* problems, would you still be *committed* to listing with your friend?" The most frequent response is "No," and we then follow up with "FISBO 2" and "FINE."

Keep in mind that a FISBO who says he has a friend in real estate is very seldom *committed* to that friend, if indeed there is a friend at all. Why? If he was really committed, he would have already listed with the friend.

Often, you can tell the level of commitment by how the prospect refers to the friend. Our experience is that if the seller says he has a friend, you have a 90% chance of getting the listing; if he mentions a company name, you have a 50% chance of getting the listing; and if he mentions a person's name, you have a 10% chance. Notice that you always have a chance.

OK, the sign on the lawn says, "For Sale By Owner - No Agents." What do we do? We cannot use "FISBO 1." If we did, the prospects would almost always say, "No, dummy, what do you think 'No Agents' means?" For these situations, we have a technique called "FISBO 3" and it sounds like this: "Hi, I saw your sign, and I saw the part that says 'No Agents.' May I ask

EFFECTIVE PROSPECTING
PART I

just one quick question . . . If I had a qualified buyer, *willing* to pay a price *acceptable* to you, would you accept such an offer through my company?"

Notice that "FISBO 3" is the same as "FISBO 2" except for the opening line, "I saw your sign and I saw the part that said 'No Agents.' " Our experience is that by acknowledging the "No Agents" part of the sign and then asking the key question - if we had a qualified buyer, willing to pay a price acceptable to him, would he accept such an offer - we do not irritate the prospect and usually get a "Yes" or "Yes, if you add your commission on" answer. We then proceed just as we did in a regular FISBO situation, as above.

It's interesting to note that most experienced salespeople who work with private sellers have found that those who add "No Agents" to the sign are actually the easiest ones to deal with. Pete S., a course graduate, once listed a private seller who had the "No Agents" part added on the sign. After he had the signed listing in his pocket, and was about to leave, he asked the seller why he had put "No Agents" on the sign. The sellers answer: "I knew the odds of finding a good buyer on my own were against me, and I figured I'd wind up listing with someone in real estate, but I felt that the "No Agents" part would keep the amateur away. I was right. In three weeks, you were the only salesperson who called me . . . and you are a pro."

Now, I'd like to make a few additional comments regarding what we have covered so far.

You may have noticed that in "FISBO 1" we say, "Are you cooperating with real estate?" Many salespeople have asked why we don't say "real estate firms" or something similar. The answer is that the word "firms" or "salespeople" is implied. Everyone understands exactly what we mean, even though, grammatically, it is incorrect. Also, we found that when the salesperson asked, "Are you cooperating with real estate firms?" the sellers occasionally responded with, "It depends. What firm are you with?" Notice that the seller has just taken control of the situation.

Another point is that we have found that in contacting FISBOS, it is best not to introduce yourself immediately. Who you are is of no consequence unless you are invited in the home. We found that by introducing ourselves or offering a card, we usually triggered a negative response, sometimes polite, sometimes not, but almost always negative. We found, conversely, that by starting right out with "FISBO 1" or "FISBO 3" the prospect knows we are in real estate and we are better off getting right down to business.

My next point is a fascinating one. Notice that when Leo first rang the door-bell, he stood fairly close to the door - then, when he saw someone peek through the little window, he took a step backward, away from the door - and when the door opened, he took another small step backward. Why? To reduce or eliminate any possibility of a threatening situation. Many, many experienced salespeople have discovered this important technique.

Consider what the prospect usually sees. The salesperson rings the doorbell, then steps away from the door. When the door opens, he moves *towards* the door. For many people, a stranger moving towards them is a threatening situation. Of course, the importance of this technique is in direct proportion to your sex and size. A wee 90 pound saleswoman would probably not be threatening on a dead run. But a 6'4", 240 pound man can be threatening just standing still. Rule of thumb, if you are tall, back up when the door opens.

My final point has to do with emphasis of certain words. In "FISBO 1," "FISBO 2", and "FISBO 3" we almost always emphasize the words "qualified," "willing," and "acceptable."

EFFECTIVE PROSPECTING
PART I

Private sellers often are individuals who have had a previous, unsatisfactory experience with real estate. Perhaps the last time they sold, they listed with real estate, and the salesperson brought no one out to see the house. Maybe the sellers were told that the few potential buyers that did see the house could not afford it. The word "qualified" tells them your potential buyer, if you had one, would be able to afford the house.

The word "willing" is important. I cannot force anyone to buy your home. They must be *willing*. And the word "acceptable," when emphasized, usually eliminates a discussion of a specific amount, or a discussion of whether our commission is included.

Expired listings are another highly visible source of leads. You know, of course, that timing is critical. It is unethical to "jump" listings by contacting someone who is listed with another firm or salesperson before the listing actually expires. However, once the listing has actually expired, you are free to call and, with the right techniques, it is usually quite easy to list the property because the sellers are usually very motivated.

In our experience, the best opening statement is, "I see your home is off the market. Do you still want to sell?" There are only four basic responses open to him. "Yes," "No," "Yes, but I'm going to try XYZ Realty," "Yes, but I'm going to try it myself," or (angrily) "Where were you during the last 90 days? You belong to the same Multi-Listing Service as XXX Realty. Why didn't you sell it while it was listed with them?"

If his answer to our opening question is "Yes," "No," or "I'm going to try it myself," we can respond with "FISBO 2." "If I had a qualified buyer, willing to pay a price acceptable to you, would you accept such an offer through my company." The usual answer is "Yes."

If his answer is that he is planning to list with XYZ Realty, our response is "FRIEND 1" - "If you felt that someone else could actually get you more money, a quicker sale and fewer problems, would you still be committed to listing with this other firm?" The usual answer is that he is not committed, and we follow up with "FISBO 2".

If his answer to the opening statement is how come we didn't sell it while it was listed with XXX Realty, our response is modification of "ONCE/TWICE." "Mr Seller, in order to sell a home once, we have to sell it twice. First we have to sell it to the salespeople and second, they sell it to their buyers. The reason I didn't show your home so far is because no one . . . sold your home . . . to me. May I show you how I will *sell* your home to the other top agents in our Multi-Listing Service?"

EFFECTIVE PROSPECTING
PART I

Now, here are the key techniques of this chapter arranged for easy study and memorization.

FACT FINDING SURVEY

"Mr. (Mrs.)_____, please"

Thank you. My name is__ of __. I'm doing a special survey. May I ask, do you plan to move sometime within the next two or three years?"

"May I ask, approximately when?"

"May I ask, will you be staying in this area?"

"Thank you. Have a nice day. Good-bye."

If someone asks why you are doing the survey, say:

"I plan to specialize in this neighborhood so I can be of more help to sellers and buyers. I need to have some idea of how many people plan to move and approximately when."

FISBO 1   "Hi, I saw your sign. May I ask, are you cooperating with real estate?"

FISBO 2   "May I ask just one quick question. If. . . if I had a qualified buyer, willing to pay a price acceptable to you, would you accept such an offer through my company?"

FISBO 3   "Hi, I saw your sign, and I saw the part that says 'No Agents.' May I ask just one quick question . . . If I had a qualified buyer, willing to pay a price acceptable to you, would you accept such an offer through my company?"

FISBO 4   "If you felt . . . that you could actually get more money, a quicker sale and fewer problems, by doing business with real estate, would you do so?"

EFFECTIVE PROSPECTING
PART I

EXPIRED 1   "I see your home is off the market. Do you still want to sell?"

EXPIRED 2   "Mr. Seller, in order to sell a home once, we have to sell it twice. First we have to sell it to the salespeople and second, they have to sell it to their buyers. The reason I didn't show your home so far is because no one . . . sold your house . . . to me. May I show you how I will 'sell' your home to the other top agents in our Multi-Listing Service?"

REMINDER: You only have to call the ones you want to list.

CHAPTER 23

EFFECTIVE PROSPECTING – PART II

Tom was a full time school teacher who worked real estate every day after school, plus one day each weekend and one month each summer; yet, for four years, he was the top salesperson in a company of 65 salespeople. That either doesn't say much for the other salespeople, or it says a great deal for Tom.

Bill and Bob worked as a team. Bill produced leads and Bob secured the listings. Once, in a company-wide sales meeting, when many salespeople were complaining about the difficulties of getting listings, Bill and Bob bet that they could out-list the rest of the company for 30 days. The other salespeople, 54 of them, had a hearty laugh. Bill and Bob produced 48 listings; 54 chagrined salespeople produced 43. That either doesn't say much for the 54 salespeople, or it says a great deal for Bill and Bob.

Robert, a mortgage broker with many years of general brokerage experience, claimed that the secret to success in sales, in just about any field, is to make ten calls a day, every day. He

EFFECTIVE PROSPECTING
PART II

claimed that any salesperson who would do that could earn at least two or three times as much as the average income of the top 20% of the sales force. He claimed further that he could start into a new line of work and by simply making ten calls a day be among the top 10% of the sales force within 90 days. Experienced veterans laughed and called his bluff. A bet was made and Robert secured a license to sell life insurance. He sent out ten letters every day. He followed up with ten phone calls two days after each batch of letters went out. The average life insurance salesman at the time was selling $500,000 of face value a year. Robert sold $787,000 in 87 days. That either doesn't say much for the average salesman, or it says a great deal for Robert.

The key to greatness lies not so much in education or brilliant thinking but rather in persistence. We would all like to find a short-cut to success. There is none. We'd all like to win the lottery and be set for life. The odds are against it. Tom was a part time salesman with a full time attitude. The key to his success was 10 calls every day. He prepared his list each night and made prospecting his first business effort each day. Bill and Bob were ordinary producers until they mastered the techniques in our system and, more importantly, developed a personal non-revocable goal of making 10 new calls a day. Bill made ten new prospecting calls every day, and Bob took the leads. Two people out-produced 54. Robert had his secretary send out ten letters a day. The letters simply said that Robert would be calling them in two days. He enjoyed the income of the top 10% of the life insurance industry in just 87 days.

Prospecting is the act of contacting great numbers of people in order to uncover the few that will result in business and income. There are times when just about every call can be to a motivated prospect: a private seller or an expired listing. But there is a limit to these leads. There are times when we can skim an area with a "Fact Finding Survey," and produce a bunch of leads in a very short time. But we cannot conduct a survey in

278

the same area every month. Finally there comes a time, if we wish to be among the top producers, that we have to buckle down and begin - and maintain - a consistent prospecting effort. Ten calls a day will carry just about anyone to the top of the field.

In 1969 I had the privilege of introducing to the real estate industry in the metropolitan Detroit area a newly organized way to contact neighbors to a listing. Jim, a sales manager from a large, east side firm, was in my first class. He became excited about the system and its potential. Returning to his office, he taught it to two young salesmen who had been unable to secure any listings or sales in sixty days. Jim demanded that they make 10 calls a day for thirty days. They listed 32 homes. Within 90 days 22 of the listings had sold, and they had secured an additional 19 listings or sales from the referrals. Not a bad comeback for two guys going down the tubes.

"Neighbors To A Listing" is a prospecting technique that involves a present listing you have right now. Whether it sells quickly, slowly or not at all, your listing is far more valuable than meets the eye because through it, you can generate many other listings and many other sales. How? Through the neighbors.

Never underestimate the interest that people have in their own neighborhood when a "For Sale" sign goes up.

"Will we like the new owners?"

"Will they like us?"

"Will they have 16 jillion kids to knock down my fence and tear up my garden?"

EFFECTIVE PROSPECTING
PART II

"Will they be miserable old people who scream if a kid steps on their precious grass?"

"Wouldn't it be nice if they were our age and we had something in common?"

"Wouldn't it be nice if they had a teenage girl who could babysit?"

"I wonder how much the Dudleys are asking. Our house should be about the same."

"The Dudleys are moving to a newer, nicer home. Why don't we?"

These are real thoughts and real concerns by real people who care about their neighborhood or who are influenced by the actions of others. Therefore, never underestimate the willingness of a neighbor to talk to you, help you or do business with you when you secure a listing nearby.

Using the procedure that follows, you can secure more listings, make more sales and enjoy more income.

Here's how to procede. Use your local Cross-Index Directory to obtain the names, addresses and phone numbers of 20 neighbors. As a general rule, when you locate the address of your listing in the directory, you can then list ten addresses above it and ten addresses below it for a total of 20 neighbors. Generally, this will give you five houses to the right, five to the left and ten across the street. This is considered to be the ideal *minimum* range of influence. (See Illustrations, page 291, 292.)

You can simply draw a bracket in the directory which encompasses the names and addresses you plan to call and then call directly from the directory. However, experience has proven that it is far better to transfer the names, addresses and phone numbers to a form similar to the one illustrated. These forms are available inexpensively from most of the Cross-Index publishers or from my company or you can make them up yourself.

Now, by telephone, contact each neighbor using the following dialogue.

"Hello, Mr./Mrs. (Name), please."

(They respond or identify themselves)

"Thank you. My name is_____of_____. We have just listed the Dudley home at 54 Crestview Drive. I'm calling to let you know it is for sale and also to let you know that I will be very pleased if I can locate new owners who will become real fine neighbors for you. Would you mind if I ask you a few questions that will help me do that?"

(The most frequent responses are, "how can I refuse?" or "Certainly. How can I help?")

Once you have secured their agreement, you are in a position to gain some very valuable data. In fact, we can ask for six different bits of information: Who do they know who might buy the listed home; who do they know who might buy a different listing; have they considered buying a home or property in the area as an investment; what do they like about the neighborhood; have they considered selling; and do they know of anyone to get the additional information.

To locate prospects for the listed home.

"Have any of your friends or relatives ever mentioned that they would like to locate in this neighborhood?"

281

EFFECTIVE PROSPECTING
PART II

"Do you know anyone who has outgrown his apartment or home?"

"Do you know anyone who is renting, but would rather own a home?"

To locate prospects for other listings:

"Can you think of anyone who might be looking for a home other than this one? I have some other good homes listed."

To find investors:

"Have you considered buying a home or property in this area as an investment?"

"Can you think of anyone who might like to buy this home as an investment?"

To obtain information that will help you sell the listing:

"Tell me, what do you like about this neighborhood?"
(A negative answer is a listing prospect!)

"How long have you lived here?"

"What kind of work do you do?"

"Do you have children? How many? What ages?"

To obtain additional listings, use information you have just obtained:

(Lots of children): "Have you considered buying a larger home as your family grows?"

(Children grown and gone): "Have you considered buying a smaller home now that your family has grown and gone?"

(Older couple or single): "Have you considered buying a condo or townhouse so you won't have to shovel snow/cut grass/etc.?"

(If no special conditions exist): "Do you plan to move within the next two or three years?"

To obtain special referrals:

"Do you know of anyone, either here or elsewhere, who might be thinking of selling his home in the near future?"

One of the great tragedies of life is that most people don't even try something that looks like a lot of work, and, as a result never experience the excitement of high production. This "Neighbors To A Listing" procedure is an example. For almost all of 1969, I conducted a special course exclusively devoted to this effective prospecting system. The sales people attending averaged just a bit more than a listing or sale per person in the three days by calling 10 neighbors a day for three consecutive days. In one firm, one salesman got 12 listings and 5 sales in 30 days by contacting 10 people a day, and the fellow at the next desk would not even try. "Too much work," he said.

Here are some questions I have been asked frequently:

Q. "Should I phone or make personal calls?"
A. I recommend the telephone because you can make many more contacts, you won't get trapped into lengthy non-business discussions, and you can more easily recall which people were not home the first time you called. However, personal calls

should be made whenever convenient and practical; especially to the homes immediately to the left and right of your listing.

Q. "Will people really answer all those questions?"
A. You bet! You are in for a delightful surprise. People are always helpful when it is in their best interest. Additionally, as you become more experienced and smoother in the presentation, you will notice a definite increase in people's willingness to answer questions and help you.

Q. "What if there is a restriction against soliciting?"
A. First, secure an exact copy of the local ordinance and read it carefully. My experience is that the ordinances are not nearly as restrictive as word-of-mouth has built them up to be. Local restrictions are usually against soliciting for a listing using scare tactics or implications of drastic changes in ethnic, racial or religious make-up, not against soliciting itself. Obey the law. If the ordinance actually prohibits soliciting in any form, you can still call every neighbor, asking for leads to buy the listing, leads to buy other listings, leads for investment opportunities and likes and dislikes about the neighborhood. Avoid asking, in any way, if they are thinking of selling, and you will be safe. Read the law and obey the law, *but do not assume, or let anyone else assume anything about the law that is not there.* Your professional and ethical approach will get you the results you want.

Q. "How many calls should I make a day?"
A. 10

Q. "What do I do if I only have one listing and I don't get more listings right away. How can I still make 10 calls a day?"
A. First, no one says you are limited to only 20 neighbors. Contact 30, 40, 50, though 20 is the ideal *minimim* range of influence. Second, you can contact the neighbors to listings of other people in your company and even listings by other conpanies, providing you cooperate with the other company. In those cases, contact the neighbors by saying, "The XYZ

284

Company has just listed the Dudley home at 54 Crestview Drive. We work with them through our Multi-Listing Service. I'm calling you to tell you that the home is for sale and that I would be very pleased if I could find new owners who would become real fine neighbors for you. Would you mind if I asked you a few questions that would help me do that?" In spite of a few sales people's immediate reaction, that is legal, ethical, moral - and fattening of the wallet.

Q. What time of day is best for calling?"
A. I recommend 9:30 to 11:00 a.m. as the best time generally, but local or personal situations may require a different time. Set aside an hour and a half every day for telephone prospecting and you will succeed.

Q. Do I have to memorize this techinque before using it? It looks like it could be read over the phone."
A. You are right. No, you don't have to memorize. But I do recommend that you read it out loud to someone else in your office, preferably over the phone where you cannot see them. Once it is reasonably smooth, get right on the phone with real prospects and begin building your business.

Several years ago I conducted a special series of six separate workshops for 72 real estate people varying in experience from brand new to 20 years in the business. I had read them the procedure to each other about ten times and then I assigned each person ten calls a day for the next three days. Three days later 52 people had at least one additional listing. Several had more than one - and one person had seven. Not too shabby for about ten hours of prospecting.

Zig Zigler says he thinks most people use the wrong words lots of times. He says most people refer to money as "cold, hard cash", but he thinks a hundred dollar bill is "soft 'n warm." Bill Haines, president of Haines Criss-Cross, thinks most salespeople psych themselves out of a good form of prospecting by calling it "cold canvassing." He calls it "Criss-Cross Canvassing" and says why waste time going slowly down a street pushing doorbells when you can sit in a nice, comfortable office and push buttons on the phone. If comfortable "Criss-Cross Canvassing" will produce "soft 'n warm" hundred dollar commissions, I'm all for it.

Here are six proven telephone canvassing techniques that also work on a door-to-door basis if you prefer.

METHOD ONE

"We have a family very interested in finding a home in this neighborhood right now. Are you thinking of moving in the near future?"

If the party that you are calling indicates that they plan to move sometime in the future, you should ask:

"If I could find the home you want, to fit your budget, would you make the move sooner?"

Also ask:

"Do you know of anyone else who is considering moving in the near future?"

METHOD TWO

"We have been doing a lot of advertising lately, and, as a result, I have a family that is most anxious to find a home in this area. Are you thinking of moving in the near future?"

METHOD THREE

"We have recently sold a home near here on _____. We showed that home to several families who really like this neighborhood. They are very anxious to find a home. Are you thinking of moving in the near future?"

"Do you know of anyone else in the neighborhood who is?"

METHOD FOUR

"The value of homes in this particular neighborhood is exceptionally high right now. That has made it practical for some families to move into the new or larger home they have always desired, yet stay within their budget. Would you consider such a profitable move if that would work for you?"

METHOD FIVE

"We have had several serious buyers inquiring about homes in this area recently. I have no specific buyer right now, but because of our advertising and our interstate referral service, we frequently have out-of-town buyers who need to make a fairly quick buying decision. May I ask . . . are you planning to move in the near future?"

"Do you know of anyone else who is?"

EFFECTIVE PROSPECTING
PART II

METHOD SIX
"Interest rates have just been reduced, making it possible for many people to qualify for mortgages who could not do so recently. We need to have some idea of how much property is seriously for sale. May I ask . . . do you plan to move in the near future?"

Whenever you use any of the preceding six techniques, the statement should be true. So, for example, if you are using "Method One," you should have a buyer who is interested in buying right now. If the statement in "Method Two" is true, use that. If it isn't, don't. If we want to be professional and feel professional, I don't believe we should be starting a relationship with a potential client with a lie. If none of these six methods is what you need at the moment, do a little research and testing and find a prospecting method that is more effective and truthful for you.

In many companies and in many industries, the prevailing attitude is that no sale is complete until you obtain one good referral. Here's a good, proven technique for asking satisfied clients for referrals. When you have just listed and sold a home, ask the sellers:

"Are you pleased with the job I did for you?"

"Do you know of anyone else who is about to sell or will be selling in the next year?"

(If yes): "Do you know them well enough to call them on the phone?"

(If yes): "Would you do me a favor? Would you please call them on the phone and tell them how pleased you are with the job I did for you and that I would be delighted to show them how my selling methods will work for them when they are ready?"

As we discussed in a previous chapter, it is very difficult for people to say no to a reasonable request made by someone for whom they have some respect. If you have made a professional listing and pricing presentation, if you have professionally prepared the home for showing and professionally merchandised the home, and if you have professionally assisted in a satisfactory sale, then you should have earned the respect of your clients. They should be eager to spread the word about your skills, abilities, and professional attitude. But most people don't volunteer, so we have to ask.

Have you ever heard the expressions, "What have you got to lose?" or "What's the worst thing that could happen?" Sandy D. uses that philosophy when contacting people who, according to the "grapevine," are about to sell their homes. In these cases, she does not call on the phone, but rushes right out to the prospect's home or place of business.

Sandy: "I heard you are selling. Is that correct?"

Prospect: "Yes, we just bought another home." (or have been transferred)

Sandy: "Great! I'd like to represent you to sell your home. May I?"

Sandy explains: "I operate on the basis of what's the worst thing that can possible happen if I ask. They could say 'No' because they have a friend in the business. Or they could say 'No' because they want to sell it themselves. Or they could say, 'Well,

289

maybe. How much do you think our house is worth?' Or they could say 'Yes, we have to list with someone.'

"If they say they have a friend in the business, I use 'Friend 1' and unless they are really commited to a real professional or a close relative, I usually get the listing. If they say they want to try it themselves, I go through the 'FISBO' presentation, and if they are at all logical and motivated, I usually get the listing. If they say 'Maybe' I almost always get the listing."

Peter, Sandy's brother, has a different view. He likes to hit objections head on. His approach begins the same as Sandy's but takes a different turn.

> Peter: "I heard you are moving. Is that correct?"
>
> Prospect: "Yes."
>
> Peter: "May I ask, are you committed to list with a particular person?"

Peter explains: "If they say yes, I use 'Friend 1', and, like Sandy says, unless they are really committed to a pro or a relative, I get the listing. If they say no, I say 'Great! I'd like to represent you to sell your home. May I?' Almost everyone says OK. It's easy as pie."

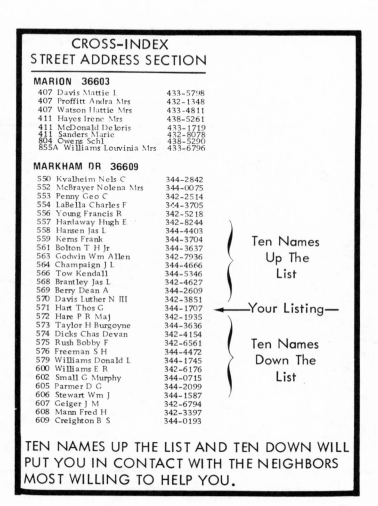

CROSS-INDEX
STREET ADDRESS SECTION

MARION 36603

407	Davis Mattie I.	433-5798
407	Proffitt Andra Mrs	432-1348
407	Watson Hattie Mrs	433-4811
411	Hayes Irene Mrs	438-5261
411	McDonald Deloris	433-1719
411	Sanders Marie	432-8078
804	Owens Schl	438-5290
855A	Williams Louvinia Mrs	433-6796

MARKHAM DR 36609

550	Kvalheim Nels C	344-2842
552	McBrayer Nolena Mrs	344-0075
553	Penny Geo C	342-2514
554	LaBella Charles F	344-3705
556	Young Francis R	342-5218
557	Hardaway Hugh E	342-8244
558	Hansen Jas L	344-4403
559	Kerns Frank	344-3704
561	Bolton T H Jr	344-3637
563	Godwin Wm Allen	342-7936
564	Champaign J L	344-4666
566	Tow Kendall	344-5346
568	Brantley Jas L	342-4627
569	Berry Dean A	344-2609
570	Davis Luther N III	342-3851
571	Hart Thos G	344-1707
572	Hare P R Maj	342-1935
573	Taylor H Burgoyne	344-3636
574	Dicks Chas Devan	342-4154
575	Rush Bobby F	342-6561
576	Freeman S H	344-4472
579	Williams Donald L	344-1745
600	Williams E R	342-6176
602	Small G Murphy	344-0715
605	Parmer D G	344-2099
606	Stewart Wm J	344-1587
607	Geiger J M	342-6794
608	Mann Fred H	342-3397
609	Creighton B S	344-0193

Ten Names
Up The
List

Your Listing

Ten Names
Down The
List

TEN NAMES UP THE LIST AND TEN DOWN WILL PUT YOU IN CONTACT WITH THE NEIGHBORS MOST WILLING TO HELP YOU.

Your local Cross-Index Directory
will provide you with the names,
addresses and phone numbers of
the immediate neighbors of
your lister.

EFFECTIVE PROSPECTING
PART II

REAL ESTATE LISTING FORM

Name	Address	Phone	Date Mailed	Date Phoned	Date Personal	Remarks
HUGH E. AARDAWAY	557 MARKHAM	342-8244				
JAMES L. HANSEN	558 MARKHAM	344-4403				
FRANK KERNS	559 MARKHAM	344-3704				
T. H. BOLTON JR	561 MARKHAM	344-3637				
WILLIAM ALLEN GODWIN	563 MARKHAM	342-7936				
J. L. CHAMPAIGN	564 MARKHAM	344-4666				
KENDALL TOW	566 MARKHAM	344-5346				
JAMES L. BRANTLEY	568 MARKHAM	342-4627				
DEAN A. BERRY	569 MARKHAM	344-2609				
LUTHER N. DAVIS III	570 MARKHAM	342-3851				
THOMAS G. HART	571 MARKHAM DR	344-1707				
MAJOR P. R. HARE	572 MARKHAM	342-1935				
H. BURGOYNE TAYLOR	573 MARKHAM	344-3636				
CHARLES DEVAN DICKS	574 MARKHAM	342-4154				
BOBBY F. RUSH	575 MARKHAM	342-6561				
S. H. FREEMAN	576 MARKHAM	344-4472				
DONALD L. WILLIAMS	579 MARKHAM	344-1745				
E. R. WILLIAMS	600 MARKHAM	342-6176				
G. MURPHY SMALL	602 MARKHAM	344-0715				
O. G. PARMER	605 MARKHAM	344-2099				
WILLIAM J. STEWART	606 MARKHAM	344-1587				

INSERT NAME AND ADDRESS OF YOUR LISTING BETWEEN HEAVY LINES IN MIDDLE OF PAGE. THEN USE YOUR LOCAL CROSS-INDEX DIRECTOR TO OBTAIN NAMES, ADDRESSES AND PHONE NUMBERS OF NEIGHBORS.

From the Cross-Index Directory, make your own list of the lister's neighbors. The minimum number should be ten neighbors to his right and ten to his left. Include people directly across the street from him, too.

292

CHAPTER 24

WHEN YOU'RE HOT,
YOU'RE HOT

Gregg Scott squinted into the glare of a bright morning sun as he turned his car into the Hyatt House parking lot, gunned the motor and raced to an opening along the fence. He slammed on the brakes and slid to a stop, jerking the car door open and spinning out of the seat in one quick motion. Irritation oozed from every pore. He slammed the car door and strode briskly towards the main entrance of the hotel.

"I hate sales meetings," he said out loud. "Flaming waste of time."He was doubly irritated because his manager had virtually threatened him with terrible and unknown penalties if he missed this particular meeting. His manager had even gone so far as to suggest stopping by Gregg's house to bring him to the meeting. "It's as though I am not old enough to be trusted to come on my own," Gregg muttered. Even the luxury of the fountains at the entrance and the cheery "Good Morning" of the doorman did not lessen his irritation. He did not like sales meetings and he didn't like being threatened.

He shoved his way through the main lobby and ballroom foyer. Finding the meeting room, he sharply pushed the door open

293

WHEN YOU'RE HOT,
YOUR HOT

and, ready to do battle, took three steps inside and stopped. Applause echoed through the entire ballroom as over 250 real estate people rose to their feet to acknowledge his entrance. Stunned, he looked for the reason and found it in a huge banner across the wall behind the dais and head table. "Gregg Scott - Realtor Associate of the Year," it proclaimed in huge letters.

Gregg's manager emerged from the crowd, grinning from ear to ear, shook Gregg's hand and escorted him to the dais. "Sorry about the threats," he said, "but it was the only way I knew to get you here. Congratulations!!"

An hour later, after the breakfast dishes had been cleared, the Board President rose to address the group. "Ladies and gentlemen," he said, "I could easily give you a half hour speech praising Gregg Scott. In fact, I have such a speech prepared. But I am highly interested, and I think you are too, in finding out how Gregg amassed his outstanding record this past year."

Then turning so he was addressing Gregg but still speaking in to the microphone, he continued, "Gregg, when your manager submitted your listing and sales record to me in consideration for this award, I was absolutely amazed. Your record shows that you listed five homes in one day on three occasions, five homes in five days on eight separate occasions, ten homes in ten days on three occasions, and that you listed twenty-five homes in twenty-five days on one occasion. The record also shows that you listed 103 homes for the year and that eighty-seven sold within the original listing period of ninety days.

"You have definitely set a record for this Board. You may well have set a record for the state, perhaps even the nation. This is a fantastic accomplishment and I know I would be most appreciative if you would share a few ideas with us this morning about how you accomplished this amazing feat."

The resounding applause was ample evidence that the assembled brokers, managers, and sales people were also interested in Gregg's secret. He rose slowly from his chair, shook hands with the Board President, turned and adjusted the microphone, placed his hands on each side of the lectern as he had seen other speakers do and gazed out across the expectant faces of his audience.

"Well," he said after a rather long silence, "I guess I owe it mostly to Flip Wilson."

He put up his hand to silence the laughter at his opening remark and said, "No . . . really . . . seriously . . . I believe I owe it to Flip Wilson. Let me tell you what happened and I think you will agree.

"Think back with me," he said, "to early June, 1974. At that point in time Flip Wilson was solidly established in the national limelight. His weekly TV programs had great ratings and many radio stations were carrying audio versions of his night club routines. At that same point in time I was definitely not established in a career in real estate. I had, in fact, been in real estate for ten months and had total earnings of just $1,400. That averaged out to $140 a month or about 70 cents an hour.

"One morning, I decided that if I did not get a listing that week and get enough additional listings by the end of the month to justify staying in real estate, I would leave and find another job.

"That same morning, I made a call on a tough prospect and got the listing. I was really pleased, in fact, enthused. The prospect had some tough questions, but I got the listing anyway. As I drove back to the office I had the car radio on and I heard Flip Wilson say, 'When you're hot, you're hot!'

"Just then I saw a For Sale by Owner sign I had been passing for the last two weeks and I thought, 'When you're hot, you're hot-

295

that applies to me!' I parked the car and rang the doorbell. To make a short story shorter, I got the listing in less then thirty minutes.

"I jumped in my car and headed back to the office, but once again the car radio was on and I heard the announcer quoting Flip Wilson, saying, 'When you're hot, you're hot!' I decided to make another call before going back to the office. A few blocks away was a prospect who had asked me three months ago to give him a price on his home as he was retired and thinking of buying something smaller. I drove over and in fifteen minutes I had his listing. I decided I would not go back to the office until someone said no. At 7:00 p.m. I returned to the office with five listings!

"That night I made up a little sign for the dashboard of my car that said, 'When you're hot you're hot!' At the end of June I had eighteen listings.

"On July 4th, I'll never forget the date or place, I was in my brother's row boat. I was alone and thinking more about the future and my life than of catching perch when I had an idea that has made me thousands and thousands of dollars.

"As I relaxed in the boat, it suddenly occurred to me that when I was successful I was enthusiastic, and when I was enthusiastic I actually told the prospects a lot less then I did at other times. I realized right then that enthusiasm is a fantastic substitute for a display of knowledge.

"I also made myself a promise. I promised myself that whenever I got a listing I would not go back to the office or home until I had made another listing presentation or secured two solid appointments for the next day.

"Mr. President, ladies and gentlemen, if there is a single secret to my success, it lies in the fact that I have never broken that promise.

"Very shortly after making that promise, I was leaving a home with a signed listing agreement in my hand, precisely at midnight. I was extremely enthused, for I had accomplished three transactions for the day. You see, my listing prospect was also the buyer of another of my listings. He would not list until I found him a home. Earlier that evening he had made an offer on another of my listings. It took three trips back and forth between buyer and seller to negotiate a sale, and then three full hours helping my buyer decide on a good listing price for his home. When I left his home I was enthused but exhausted.

"I jumped in my car and drove home. But in my driveway, I was confronted with my own promise. I had only one appointment for the next day. I rationalized - all rules have *some* exceptions. I'd make a call *first* thing in the morning. Still I could not bring myself to turn off the motor. Instead, I backed out of the driveway and drove to an all-night diner where for fifteen minutes I sat nursing a cup of coffee, trying to think of some place to go . . . some place I could make a call.

"After a while the fellow at the next table said, 'What do you do that keeps you out so late?' 'I sell real estate,' I said, 'and just finished with a client.' 'Real estate, eh?' he said. 'I'm planning to move. How much do you think my house is worth?'

"Mr. President, ladies and gentlemen, ten minutes later I had a *solid* appointment for the next morning."

Enthusiasm *is* a fantastic substitute for a display of knowledge. More sales are made through enthusiasm than have ever been made based only on logic. Excitement and enthusiasm are contagious. People respond positively when you are up;

297

WHEN YOU'RE HOT,
YOUR HOT

negatively when you are down. Success breeds success. When you are hot, you are hot. Capitalize on it!

CHAPTER 25

TAKE A
GIANT STEP

PROLOGUE

For 20 years, Sam Brown had earned between $20,000 and $30,000 listing and selling real estate. Then one day he discovered one of the great secrets of the super sales producers - completely memorized language techniques presented in a selected sequence to provide the necessary flexibility. He set a goal to acquire the best language for every sales situation and to memorize it to the point of instant, word-perfect recall. He achieved that goal and jumped his income from $25,000 to $60,000 in one year. He proved it was not luck by earning nearly $75,000 the following year. This year he set a goal of earning $90,000. But life is strange. The future is not always predictable. Events often come out differently then we plan. In Sam's case, events will come out better than he planned because, today, Sam Brown will be introduced to another great secret of the super achievers - super goal setting.

"Sam, I have a challenge for you. How would you like to list 100 homes in 100 days and make sure 90 percent sell within 90 days?"

299

"Do what?" replied Sam, looking up from a purchase offer he was typing.

Russ, Sam's sales manager, stood in the doorway of Sam's office, a big grin on his face. "List 100 homes in 100 days, and make sure 90 percent sell in 90 days," he said again.

"You're nuts," said Sam, and he resumed his typing.

"No, I'm not," said Russ. "Look, before Roger Bannister ran the four minute mile, everyone said it couldn't be done. And once he did it, many other runners did it."

"Yeah," said Sam, without looking up, "but before he did it, many other runners were close. I don't think anyone has ever listed 30 homes in 30 days and had 90 percent sell in 90 days, let alone 100 homes in 100 days. You're nuts."

"No I'm not," said Russ. "Look," he persisted, "how many hours does it take you to get a listing? Five or less, right?"

"Yes," conceded Sam, "counting all the time spent prospecting and driving, face-to-face time with the prospect and the time writing up a listing - about five hours."

"OK, it's 1 o'clock. If you started phoning or calling on new prospects right now, you could get at least one listing by 6 pm right?"

"Yes, most likely."

"And some days you get listings from referrals, and it only takes one hour, right?"

"Yes."

"And you already have listed five homes in one week on several occasions, haven't you?"

"Yes."

"And if you can do it for five consecutive days, why can't you do it for 50 consecutive days or for 100 consecutive days?"

"Why don't I just try it for 10 days?"

"No," said Russ. "Ten days - even 50 days - is not a big enough challenge. Ten days wouldn't get you excited and if you don't get excited enough, you won't stay interested."

"One hundred listings in 100 days," mused Sam. "That's a ridiculously big goal."

"How do you eat an elephant?" queried Russ, with a smile.

"I know," said Sam, smiling back, "one bite at a time. But there is no way I could possibly service that many listings! I could wind up with 50 or 60 active listings at one time. How do you propose I maintain proper contact with that many clients?"

"I've been thinking about that," said Russ. "Look, for the past year, you have proven your ability to get good listings. You're the top lister in this company and in the whole multi-list system. Your listings are almost always priced right and show well, and everyone knows a good listing is three-fourths sold, right? You keep saying that it takes you five hours to get a listing and 25 hours to get a sale, so my idea is that you concentrate on getting the listings, and we'll get someone else to sell them. I think I can get Skipper to lead a special effort to get your homes sold within 90 days. She already sells half your listings anyway. And I'll have my secretary call each of your listings once a week to give them your regular weekly progress report. She can also make all showing appointments."

301

"Well, I don't know," responded Sam, changing tack. "It's one thing to find enough prospects to get five or ten listings, but 100 listings? I would need 200 or more good leads. That's a lot of prospecting in three months."

"I've been thinking about that, too," said Russ. "Who said you have to do all your own prospecting? If you have floor time and a listing lead comes in, you take it. If you get a listing lead as a referral, you take it. You don't prospect for those. Why not train a new salesperson to make appointments for you? Then you get the listings and share the commission on those."

"Well, let's see," responded Sam, "100 days is about 14 weeks. I get a referral a week. That would give me 14 listings. If I train a new person to get three or four leads a week and I list two of them, that would give me 28 - plus 14 is 42. That leaves me 58 to get on my own. That's about four a week. No, it can't be done." And he turned back to the typewriter.

Russ stood quietly in the doorway watching Sam type hunt-and-peck style. He knew Sam hated typing but accepted it as a necessary part of the business. Suddenly he had an idea. He waited until Sam made an error and began making the correction on the five carbon copies before he spoke again.

"Sam, how much do you think your listings sell for, on the average?"

"Are you still here?" replied Sam, without looking up.

"Yeah, I'm still here. How much do you think your listings average?"

"I dunno - $80,000, maybe $85,000. Why?"

"Well, then you average about $1,500 in commissions for each listing that sells, and if it takes five hours of work to get a listing, your time is worth about $150 an hour when you work on listings, right?"

"So?"

"So, if you can hire a typist at $4 an hour to do what you're doing right now, you are paying yourself $4 an hour when you type and $150 an hour when you go and get listings. Even if only two-thirds of your listings sold, you'd still be worth $100 an hour selling. So why not let a secretary do your paperwork, and you go and get 100 listings in 100 days?"

Sam took a deep breath, looked disgustedly at the smeared erasure on the third carbon copy, turned to look at Russ and said, "Russ, you have just convinced me to hire a typist or pay you $4 an hour to get a company secretary to do my typing, but I still don't see how I could get 100 listings in 100 days. Anyway, what's in it for you? And why are you so fired up on having me do it?"

"Well," replied Russ slowly, "I have several things in mind. Naturally I get an override, so the better you do, the better I do. But more important than that, I'd just like to be the first manager ever to set a big goal like this and pull it off."

"But why such an unrealistic goal? One hundred listings in six months would be more reasonable."

"Well, for a long time I've been thinking about the purpose of life. You know, why are we here and what are we supposed to do with our minds besides just making a living. Then, about two weeks ago, I read something that was really challenging, 'Our duty as men is to proceed as if limits to our ability did not exist.' So I got to thinking about big goals and I came up with 100 listings in 100 days and selling 90 percent in 90 days. It's a big challenge for me to organize it, it will be a big challenge for you to list them, and it will be a bigger challenge to make sure

90 percent sell on time. Will you do it?"

"Well," said Sam slowly, "it would be a challenge, but you'd have to show me a darn good plan to get those listings sold, or I'd be ruined. Do you have any idea what would happen to my reputation if I had 50 angry clients all at once? You're going to have to come up with a mighty good plan."

"Yes," responded Russ, "I realize the danger. And right now I don't know how we'd make sure 90 percent will sell. But I'm convinced that if you say yes, we'll soon come up with an idea. As a matter of fact, I think Skipper already knows how to do it. She listed 26 homes last year, and 19 of them sold; plus, she sold about 20 of yours."

Several days later, Russ invited Sam and Skipper to lunch at the country club. Russ had arranged for a table next to the trophy display. As Sam sat down, he couldn't help seeing all the first-place trophies for swimming, golf, tennis. And right in the middle, almost hidden by two other trophies, was a large trophy with a plaque which read:

WORLD FIRST
100 Listing in 100 Days
90 Percent Sold in 90 Days
All Listings Secured By:
SAM BROWN

Sam chuckled, "Russ, you are about as subtle as a brick. You surely make it hard for people to say no, but I'm going to stick to my position. If you don't have a good plan to sell my listings, I'm not going to risk my reputation."

"I accept that," said Russ, "but you've had several days to think about it. If we had a plan to service and sell your listings, could you get the 100 listings in 100 days?"

"Sure," said Sam. "It won't be easy, but it's not impossible. I'll have to triple the area I cover. Maybe I'll have to get two new salespeople prospecting for me instead of one. Yes, I can do it. But. . ."

"I know," said Russ, "we need a sales plan. And I think Skipper knows how to do it."

"I do?" questioned Skipper. "What's going on?"

"Skipper," said Russ, "suppose Sam could list one house a day, every day for 100 consecutive days. And suppose it was your responsibility to see that every listing sold within the 90 day listing period. How would you go about it?"

As Skipper leaned back and relaxed in her chair, pondering the question, both Russ and Sam had the same thought: Whatever plan she would devise, it would be as gracious and dignified as she was. There would be no hint of high pressure. No prospect would ever feel rushed.

Suddenly Skipper burst out laughing. "You're right, Russ," she said. "I do know how to do it. I just never thought about it in such volume."

"How?" said both men simultaneously.

"Why, we'd just do exactly what I do to sell my own listings now. We would use my three-step plan for selling any house. For the first 30 days we would just do the conventional things: put a sign on the lawn, ads in the paper, turn the listing in to the multi-listing service and, of course, our own company inspection. If it hasn't sold in 30 days, we contact at least 20 neighbors to see if they know someone who might be interested, and we hold an open house every week.

305

"If the house hasn't sold in 60 days, we contact another 20 to 50 families in the area to see if they know someone who would like to buy the house. And we bake a large ham, buy some bread and hold an open house for the sales people who work for all the other firms in the area. I'd like to make sure that at least one person comes from each firm. And I'd like to make sure that we personally invite every person whose name shows up often on the sold sheets."

"My gosh," said Russ, "if we didn't sell most of the houses in less than 60 days, we'd be serving lunch all over town."

"That's OK," said Skipper. "Remember: to sell a house once, we need to sell it twice. First, we sell it to the salespeople, and then they sell it to their buyers.

"One more thing," she continued. "Anytime a buyer asks what is wrong with a house, he is telling you he thinks it is worth more than the asking price. So we raise the price, and the house almost always sells in one week."

"You're kidding!" said Sam. "When a house doesn't sell, you lower the price, not raise it."

"It depends," replied Skipper. "Sometimes a house is underpriced in the first place."

"Well, Skipper," said Russ, "will you head the sales team?"

"Will I get a trophy?" she asked, in jest.

"It's right behind Sam's," said Russ, reaching up and moving Sam's trophy aside. And it read:

WORLD FIRST
100 Listings in 100 Days
90 Percent Sold in 90 Days
All Sales Made in Whole or in Part By:
SKIPPER MORRISSEY

On December 8, just as the church clock down the street struck 10 p.m., Russ sat down in his office musing over the events of the last six months.

Sam had never fallen more than three or four days behind schedule and was often more than 10 days ahead. The two young agents who made appointments for Sam were more than happy with the program. Both were off to a good financial start, and more importantly, both had become experts at prospecting. Combining their leads with his own prospecting. Sam hit the 100th listing on the 97th day.

Skipper's program to sell the homes worked like a charm. For the most part she stayed right in the office, taking all inquiries on Sam's listings. Expertly, she would qualify potential buyers as to seriousness and urgency, then convince them to come to the office for a pre-buying interview. There she qualified their needs and financial status before turning them over to a member of her sales team who would take them out for showings.

Her three-step plan for selling homes proved to be a stroke of genius. Only seven homes failed to sell during the original 90-day period. And for the first time in his career, Russ felt a sense of control with a step-by-step program to make sure each listing sold.

Skipper's three-step plan had some very interesting benefits. First, it gave their own company the best chance to sell the home for the first 30 days, but when a home didn't sell then the salespeople were far more willing to put forth the effort required to call 20 neighbors and hold open house. Because everyone knew the plan, no one felt hassled when Russ continually requested status reports. "And," he smiled to himself, "it cost me only 27 hams."

For his own part, Russ had been extremely active, coordinating activities, moving the paperwork along after the sale and attending closings when Sam or Skipper were busy. And best of all, the office as a whole had nearly 200 listings and 150 sales. No other salesperson had lost any personal business due to Sam's special effort. Yes, it had been worth the effort. He had set a giant goal and taken a giant step. Best of all, he could motivate people to become champions!

EPILOGUE

Most people will never develop their full potential, or even a great part of it, simply because it never occurs to them to try. But, ironically, if one develops one's basic talent and abilities, ultimately it is just as easy to accomplish great things as it is to accomplish little things - it is just as easy to earn $100,000 as it is to earn $10,000. All you have to do is set a giant goal - and take a giant step.

CONCLUSION

As I write this conclusion our plane has just lifted off from Midway Airport in Chicago. In a moment we will be heading east, across Lake Michigan, to Detroit and home. It is 5 p.m., December 23.

As the plane banks gently to get on course, the brilliance of Chicago on a winter's night, hidden at first by the huge wing, suddenly comes into full view. Street lights mark the orderly rows of buildings, apartments and homes for as far as the eye can see. Christmas lights on ten thousand stores and homes add to the color and excitement.

We pass low over the south end of the famous "loop" and must look up to see the tops of the taller buildings. We are close enough to some of the buildings to see into the brightly lit offices and see people talking on the phone, raising glasses in holiday cheer and putting on hats and coats to conclude another business day.

Looking down, we can still see people on the sidewalks in the hustle and bustle of last minute shopping and it occurs to me that some of them must be real estate people. I wonder what they see.

Do they see a city of despair or a city of hope? Do they see this vast area of 200 square miles, of over 7 million people and more than 2 million homes, condominiums and apartments as a challenge to survive or an opportunity to achieve? I wish they could be up here with me tonight.

As our plane rushes across the black expanse of Lake Michigan, picking up altitude and speed, the lights of South Bend, Michigan City, St. Joseph, and even Muskegon come into view. More people. More opportunities.

Now we pass quickly through a thin layer of winter clouds and climb above an endless panorama of rolling hills of white, highlighted by a brilliant full moon. What a wondrous world this is.

Four years have passed since I wrote the "Introduction" to this book. Much has changed; yet much remains the same. Great changes in interest rates and the economy have brought great changes to the real estate industry; yet, God still has not created any failures. Still, as always, we can only fail ourselves. Still, as always, we were born to win. Still, as always, there are no limits to what we can achieve except the limits we impose upon ourselves. Still, as always, we can control our destiny on earth by the use of our minds.

The purpose of this book is to open the doors of opportunity for those who are serious about developing more of their true potential through a professional career in real estate brokerage.

The ideas and methods described in the preceding chapters have worked for thousands of people, and they will work for you . . . as soon as you learn them. The techniques are timeless, seasonless, constants in an everchanging world. Once mastered, they will give you the confidence to persevere . . . and to bring to reality the loftiest dreams and goals of your life.

Life is a challenge. A great, interesting, exciting challenge. I offer you now a personal challenge. You hold two pictures of yourself in your mind. You see yourself as you are, and you see yourself as you would like to be. I challenge you to become the person you would like to be. I challenge you to become the master of your mind . . . and your destiny. I challenge you most of all to become the person God had in mind when He placed you here on earth.

There
Are Eight
Good Reasons...

Why You
Will Benefit
By Having Us
Represent You
To Sell
Your Home...

You Want
The Most
Money

Quickly

And With The
Fewest
Problems

1

We Can
Make Your
Home More
Attractive
To Potential
Buyers

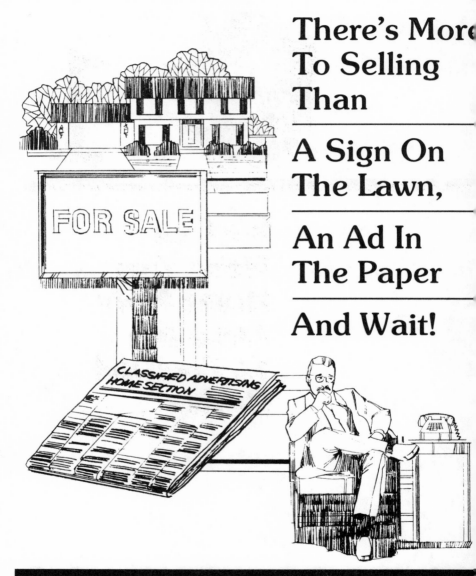

There's More To Selling Than

A Sign On The Lawn,

An Ad In The Paper

And Wait!

On The Average . . . Buyers Inspect 12 Homes Before Deciding.

That Means 11 Other Homes Are Competing Against Yours.

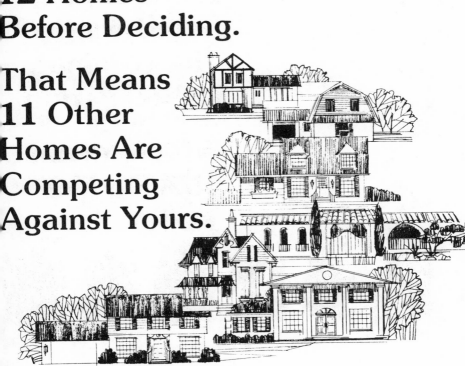

In Average Years Only **60%** Of All Listed Homes Sell During The Original Listing Period.

Which Means.. **40%** Do Not Sell!

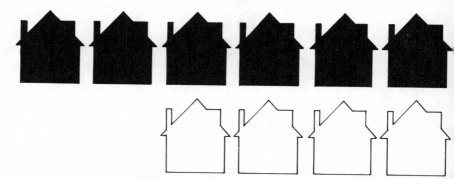

For A Quicker Sale, Make Sure Your Home Is Exciting!

We don't get a second chance to make a good first impression. Most buyers look for homes that are well cared for and bright. In general, clean and spiffy.

CHECK LIST FOR FASTER SALES

Lawns and yard — remove clutter, cut grass, edge walks, trim hedges, weed gardens.
Front of house — paint, fix or wash railings, steps, storms, screens and/or front door.
Other exterior — side or back door, gutters, wash windows.
Garage — straighten up, paint, fix or wash doors and windows.
Plumbing — repair dripping faucets, leaky toilets.
Heating/cooling — clean exterior of unit.
Lights — replace all burned out bulbs, faulty switches.
Halls and stairs — remove any clutter to give wide appearance.
Hardware — oil hinges, tighten door knobs, faucets.
General condition — dust, wash, paint, fix defects, as required.
Consider feeling of spaciousness — store unneeded items to "enlarge" room size.

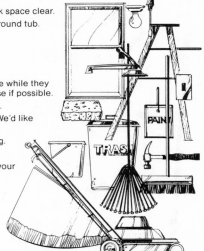

THESE ITEMS ARE SUPER CRITICAL

- Kitchen — stove, refrigerator, sink should be spotless, all work space clear.
  Bathrooms — neat, spotless and fresh. Repair broken putty around tub.
- Closets — untidy or over-crowded closets suggest inadequate storage space.

HOW TO HELP OUR SALES AGENTS

- Children, pets and adults can keep buyers from feeling at ease while they look through a home. For showings, please be out of the house if possible.
- Tell us which rooms benefit from sunshine or cooling breezes.
- Tell us what you like about the house, the yard, the location. We'd like husband's and wife's feelings separately.
- Turn on all lights, or let us turn them on, for the entire showing.
- Open drapes in the daytime, close them at night.
- Strong cooking or smoking odors can ruin a sale. Make sure your home is fresh for showings.
- Small signs highlighting the special features of your home will make sure buyers see all the benefits. We'd appreciate your ideas.

Highlights of this Home ✦✦®

WELCOME TO 5070 RANGELINE ROAD

•FANTASTIC•

LIVING ROOM 21X14
- WITH HUGE BRICK FIRE PLACE

DINING ROOM 17X12
- WITH BOXBEAM CATHEDRAL CEILING

SUN ROOM 14X10
- CARPETED PLUS EIGHT FOOT SLIDING DOORS

KITCHEN 21X12
- U-SHAPE WITH BEAUTIFUL BUILT IN CABINETS

THREE BED ROOMS
- 10X11 BUILT IN CLOSET (4') HARDWOOD FLOOR
- 14X11 BUILT IN CLOSET (5') HARDWOOD FLOOR   } PLUS ALL CLOSETS ARE LIGHTED
- 14X13 BUILT IN CLOSET (13') HARDWOOD FLOOR

BATH ROOMS
- 12X7 HUGE DRESSING MIRROR WITH FULL CERAMIC TUB AND SHOWER AREA
- 6X4 JUST INSIDE REAR ENTRY FOR EASY ACCESSIBILITY

GARAGE
- 2½ CAR IN BASEMENT AREA WITH DOOR OPENER

UTILITY ROOM
- IN BASEMENT AREA APPROXIMATELY 26X26 IN SIZE

PLUS!!!

- 1 1/8 ac. of ground
- New draperies through out
- Anderson casement windows
- TV antenna on tower
- Well insulated
- Extra thick padding under carpet
- Covington School District
- Paroch School Piqua
- Outside lights in corners of house
- Gas force air furnace
- Level billing in 1975--47.00

There's More To Selling A Home Than A Sign On the Lawn, An Ad In The Paper, And Waiting For Buyers To Come.

The conventional marketing effort is a sign on the lawn, an ad in the paper, a tour of the listing company's salespeople, and turning the listing in to the local Multi-Listing Service. Occasionally "Open House" is held.

Our Three-Step Extra Effort Marketing Plan

1st Level of Effort:

1. Use a 21 point Check List to make sure the home is very showable and will compete well against other homes for sale.

2. Use HIGHLIGHT CARDS to make sure that all good buyers find all the good features in the home.

3. Use HIGHLIGHT SHEETS to make sure that buyers remember all the good features they saw.

4. Use a COMPARATIVE MARKET ANALYSIS so seller can select the best price to put the home on the market.

5. Sign on lawn.

6. Ads in paper.

7. Turn in to Multiple-Listing Service.

8. Inspection tour and evaluation by our company salespeople.

If the home does not sell in 30 days, we proceed to . . .

2nd Level of Effort:

1. Contact 20 neighbors to the listing using the unique "Portfolio of Homes and Neighborhoods" method.

2. Review the CHECK LIST and COMPARATIVE MARKET ANALYSIS to make sure home is as showable and priced right as possible.

3. Start holding OPEN HOUSE on a regular schedule.

4. Invite neighbors to open house and/or ask them who they know who might like to buy the house.

If home does not sell in the next 30 days (total of 60 days) we proceed to . . .

3rd Level of Effort:

1. Review the COMPARATIVE MARKET ANALYSIS and CHECK LIST. Update the CMA if required by change in market conditions.

2. Continue to hold OPEN HOUSE.

3. Contact additional 50 to 100 families in neighborhood to invite them to open house and/or ask who they know who might like to buy the house.

4. Hold a special OPEN HOUSE for the top agents in our MLS. Coffee and donuts or baked ham and cheese, as required, to increase attendance. Mail extra copies of HIGHLIGHT SHEETS with the invitation.

2

We Can Help You Determine The Right Price.

Get The Market Value!

COMPARATIVE MARKET ANALYSIS
FOR

ADDRESS	RECOMMENDED PRICE	BEDROOMS	LOT SIZE	EXTRAS

1. SIMILAR HOMES RECENTLY SOLD. These tell us what people are willing to pay . . . for this kind of home . . . in this area . . . at this time.

	ADDRESS	PRICE	BEDROOMS	LOT SIZE	EXTRAS
1					
2					
3					
4					

2. SIMILAR HOMES FOR SALE NOW. These tell us what we are competing against. Buyers will compare your home against these homes.

	ADDRESS	PRICE	BEDROOMS	LOT SIZE	EXTRAS
1					
2					
3					
4					

3. EXPIRED LISTINGS — SIMILAR HOMES UNSOLD FOR 90 DAYS OR MORE. These illustrate the problems of over pricing.

	ADDRESS	PRICE	BEDROOMS	LOT SIZE	EXTRAS
1					
2					
3					
4					

PROBLEMS OF OVER-PRICING
1. Hard to get sales people excited.
2. Hard to get good buyers to look.
3. Hard to get people to make an offer.
4. Hard to get financing.

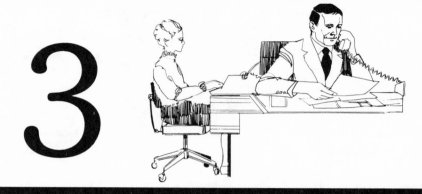

3

Four Ways We Can Expose Your Home To A Great Number Of Potential Buyers

1 Through our own sales people. We co-operate with others.

2 Creating additional prospects through advertising.

3 Continuous calls from qualified buyers.

4 Specialized work developing additional buyers.

90% of all homes are sold through a Real Estate Firm.

4

We Can Sort Out Prospects

1 Some are in a hurry to move.

2 Some are serious, but not in a hurry.

3 Some are bargain hunters.

4 Some will never buy.

We can save you from having a lot of unqualified "strangers" wandering through your home.

Right Now — Today Serious Buyers Go To Real Estate Because **85.8%** Of The Homes For Sale Are Listed By Real Estate.

Only **14.2%** Are By Owner.

ACTUAL STATISTICS! Real Estate VS. For Sale By Owner

	Total Homes For Sale	For Sale By Real Estate		For Sale By Owner	
		Number	Percentage	Number	Percentage
Albany, N.Y.	250	175	70.0	75	30.0
Albuquerque, N.M.	610	545	89.3	65	10.7
Atlanta, Ga.	3423	2968	86.7	455	13.3
Baltimore, Md.	214	192	89.7	22	10.3
Birmingham, Ala.	242	214	88.4	28	11.6
Boston (Globe)	1310	984	75.1	326	24.9
Buffalo, N.Y.	565	546	96.6	19	3.4
Charlotte, N.C.	300	265	88.3	35	11.7
Chicago	527	480	91.1	47	8.9
Cincinnati, Ohio	1544	1474	95.5	70	4.5
Cleveland	1176	990	84.2	186	15.8
Columbia, N.C.	278	243	87.4	35	12.6
Columbus, Ohio	1874	1814	96.8	60	3.2
Dallas	721	612	84.9	109	15.1
Davenport, Iowa	222	203	91.4	19	8.6
Denver	634	548	86.4	86	13.6
Detroit	934	770	82.4	164	17.6
Fort Worth	388	282	72.7	106	27.3
Grand Rapids, Mich.	314	241	76.8	73	23.2
Harrisburg, Pa.	148	138	93.2	10	6.8
Hartford, Conn.	94	74	78.7	20	21.3
Honolulu	1234	1162	94.2	72	5.8
Houston	1181	1067	90.3	114	9.7
Indianapolis	584	437	74.8	147	25.2
Jackson, Mich.	118	105	89.0	13	11.0
Kalamazoo	420	371	88.3	49	11.7
Kansas City	252	199	79.0	53	21.0
Lansing, Mich.	400	336	84.0	64	16.0
Las Vegas	489	408	83.4	81	16.6
Lincoln, Neb.	131	99	75.6	32	24.4
Little Rock	84	71	84.5	13	15.5
Los Angeles	1068	788	73.8	280	26.2
Madison, Wis.	285	252	88.4	33	11.6
Miami	1532	1308	85.4	224	14.6
Minneapolis	333	280	84.1	53	15.9
Moline, Ill.	244	221	90.6	23	9.4
Nashville	451	418	92.7	33	7.3
New Orleans	2376	2274	95.7	102	4.3
Oklahoma City	366	292	79.8	74	20.2
Orlando, Fla.	268	235	87.7	33	12.3
Patterson, N.J.	193	168	87.0	25	13.0
Philadelphia	1157	1061	91.8	96	8.2
Pittsburgh	232	204	87.9	28	12.1
Phoenix	1290	1108	85.9	182	14.1
Portland, Oreg.	1432	1303	91.0	129	9.0
Portland, Me.	60	55	91.7	5	8.3
Richmond, Va.	275	246	89.5	29	10.5
Riverside, Calif.	274	228	83.2	46	16.8
St. Louis	426	351	82.4	75	17.6
St. Paul, Minn.	270	206	76.3	64	23.7
San Bernardino	488	380	77.9	108	22.1
San Diego	476	409	85.9	67	14.1
San Francisco	332	316	95.2	16	44.8
San Jose	814	596	73.2	218	26.8
San Rafael	230	208	90.4	22	9.6
Sante Fe, N.M.	116	101	87.1	15	12.9
Seattle, Wash.	910	748	82.2	162	17.8
South Bend	246	224	91.1	22	8.9
Tampa, Fla.	376	277	73.7	99	26.3
Toledo, Ohio	626	615	98.2	11	1.8
Union City, N.J.	98	88	89.8	10	10.2
Virginia Beach	474	386	81.4	88	18.6
Washington, D.C.	1864	1620	86.9	244	13.1
Canada					
Edmonton	295	256	86.8	39	13.2
Edmonton	497	424	85.4	73	14.6
Edmonton	326	280	85.9	46	14.1
Calgary	662	568	85.8	94	14.2
Toronto	734	590	81.6	144	18.4
Regina	289	270	93.4	19	6.6
Winnipeg	520	467	89.8	53	10.2
Ottawa	613	555	90.5	58	9.5

The preceding research was done by Jerry Bresser from the spring of 1973 to the fall of 1974. Subsequent research in 1975, 1976, 1977 and 1978 indicates little, if any, significant statistical difference.

You Will Probably Lose 3%

On the average, an owner loses 3% to 5% when he sells his own home.

1. The Owner Accepts Less.

- Direct buyers are usually bargain hunters looking for desperate sellers.
- A ten year study in Philadelphia showed owners selling direct grossed 9-1/2% less than real estate firms.
- Generally, serious buyers are willing to pay a fair price for the convenience and security of dealing through a licensed real estate firm.

2. The Owner Pays For All Advertising.

- Even a $10.00 a week ad becomes big money as weeks and months roll by.

3. It Usually Takes Owners Longer to Get a Sale.

- Result: Extra Taxes   Extra Utilities
          Extra Interest   Extra Insurance

4. The Owner Often Pays Higher Attorney Fees . . . And You Pay His Fee Even If The Sale Does Not Go Through.

- When sold through real estate — an attorney <u>checks</u> our work.
- When sold by owner — an attorney <u>does</u> the work. You get billed accordingly.

90%
Are Not Qualified!

You Qualify For
$70,000

$80,000

$85,000

I'll Give You
$70,000

FOR
SALE
BY OWNER

$90,000

©Jerry Bresser 1978

5

We Can Help
Prospects
Decide On
Taking <u>Action</u>
On Your Home.

**We can follow up
on buyers —**

**you can't,
without appearing
anxious . . .**

6

We Can
Negotiate Better...

**as a third party,
we are in a
much better position
to maintain
the asking price.**

**We can demand
a sizable deposit.**

7

We Can Help Buyers Find Mortgage Money When Necessary . . .

we might save a sale, when the buyer needs a little help.

8

We Can Eliminate A Lot Of Red Tape.

We know
the efficient ways
to process
the mortgage, and
we can save you
a lot of work
and running around.

To Get More — Ask For Less!

Normal Situation

Average Asking	$60,000	Average time to first offer
Seller Asks	60,000	9 - 10 weeks.
		Not much time
		to negotiate.
Average Offers	54,000	
Sellers Counter At	57,500	
Buyers Counter At	55,000	
Sellers Counter At	56,500	
Average Selling Price	56,500	

Slightly Less/Slightly More Pricing Concept

Average Asking	$60,000	
Sellers Ask	59,000	**Extra Activity**
		Extra Enthusiasm
		Extra Showings
Good Chance for Full Price Offer	59,000	
OR		Average time to first offer
First Offer	54,000	5 - 6 weeks. Faster Action.
Sellers Counter At	58,000	More time to negotiate.
Buyers Accept	58,000	
Average Selling	58,000	

Using Slightly Less/Slightly More Pricing Concept — Average Gain — $1,000 to $1,500 . . . and 30 Days Faster!

©Jerry Bresser 1978